FOOTLOOSE
IN AMERICA

For Tracy Smith

I hope you enjoy
the Journey!

from a poet who
performs on the
fringe

Bill

Ada OK 2019

FOOTLOOSE IN AMERICA

DIXIE TO NEW ENGLAND

Bud Kenny

AUTHOR'S NOTE

All of the events and persons in this story are real. However,
I did change some names.
It just seemed like the right thing to do.
-bud-

For Patricia and Della.
This would not have been the adventure that it was without them.
-bud-

*"People in love don't look at each other,
they look in the same direction."*
-dancer Ginger Rogers-

TABLE OF CONTENTS

PREFACE

"YOU SURE AIN'T DOING VERY good!"

His wrinkled face spit the words at me from across the road. With a cigarette in his hand, he leaned out the window of an old blue pickup idling in the west bound lane.

I asked, "What do you mean?"

He wore the kind of sunglasses they give cataract patients. His voice was mean and raspy. "You passed my house a couple of days ago, and you only got this far?"

With Della-the-mule pulling our pack cart, Patricia and I were walking east toward the Mississippi River. In his beat-up Ford, he was going the other way.

I said, "So?"

"The paper said you was walking to New England." He started stubbing out the cigarette on the outside of his door. "Hell, you'll never get there going this slow."

"I'm not in a hurry."

"You're the only one who ain't." He tossed the butt into the road. "Everybody's in a hurry these days. You've got to be if you're goin' to get anywhere."

"I've been in a hurry before, but I didn't like where it was taking me. So I thought I'd slow down and see where that got me."

Suddenly, on the road behind him, we both heard the roar of an engine approaching. He glanced in his rear view mirror, grabbed the gearshift and turned his old face toward me. I thought he was going to say something, but he just shook his head and sped away.

CHAPTER 1

NEW ROAD LEGS

⟊⟋

BEHIND ME I HEARD A thud. It sounded like a tire on the pack cart had
rolled over something. Suddenly, there was screaming–painful screaming.
Della bolted, the cart lunged forward and the scream turned into a gut-
wrenching howl punctuated by yelps. It was our dog Spot, and he was
under the cart. *Did it run over him?*

I jerked Della's lead rope and yanked on the brake cord. "Whoa!"

It didn't make any difference. All she wanted to do was run away from
that screaming. Only the brake was keeping her from doing so. Behind her,
the cart's tires were skidding through roadside gravel. I jumped directly in
front of Della, grabbed both sides of her bridle and growled, "Whoa, dammit! Whoa!"

She did. But all eighteen hundred pounds of her was shivering as Spot
continued to cry out from under the cart. When I let go of the bridle, Della
turned her long face around to see the commotion. Her huge ears were
rigid toward the screaming. I dropped the rope to see if she would stand
ground-tied. She did. I whirled around and ran back to the cart.

Patricia, who'd been walking several yards behind us, was running toward me yelling, "What happened? Where's Spot?"

I said nothing, dropped onto my belly, scooted under the back of the
cart and across the gravel to him. A chain attached to Spot's collar was
tangled around the back axle, and his head was pinned to it. His right rear
leg was covered with blood. When I tried to get the chain off his collar, the
screaming got worse. I couldn't reach the snap.

"Let me see if I can do it," my wife said as she crawled under the cart beside me.

I rolled out of her way, got up and ran back to Della. She was shuffling her feet and jerking in her harness like she wanted to take off. And if I hadn't set the brake on the cart, she would have. I grabbed the lead rope and stroked her nose. "It's okay, Big Sis."

Patricia yelled, "Bud, see if you can get him loose from that side!"

When I slid under the cart, my body was directly in front of the back wheel. If Della were to take off, it would roll over me. But, I didn't have time to dwell on that. My wife was frantic. "Lift him from that side! He's going to break his neck if we don't get him loose!"

When I put my hands under his back, Spot shrieked. Della jumped and the tires skidded. I dropped him and rolled out of the way as Patricia shouted, "I've got him!"

I jumped to my feet and scurried around to the back of the cart, where I found my wife cradling Spot in her arms. Both were out of harm's way. So I ran and grabbed Della's lead rope then tied her to a nearby sign post. When I went back to where all this happened, I found Patricia on the ground holding our white and brown spotted hound. I asked, "Is he hurt bad?"

"I don't know."

Spot was whimpering in her embrace, as she said, "It looks like his back leg got run over. What happened?"

For the first half of that day, Patricia had walked with Spot on a leash. But all morning he pulled so hard on it that by noon her right shoulder was sore. Fifteen years ago she injured it in an elevator that broke loose and fell seventeen floors. Spot's pulling had aggravated her torn rotator cuff. So we opted to let him ride the rest of the day in the cart.

On the floor of the cab, we had a rug for him to lay on. To keep him from jumping out, we fastened two light weight chains to his collar. One attached to each side of the cart. Somehow, a link on the left chain had come undone. When he jumped out the right side of the cab, that one got tangled around the back axle and pulled him under the cart. That's probably when the wheel rolled over his leg.

"Do you think it's broken?" I asked.

My wife ran her hand over his bloody right rear leg, as she said, "Even if it is, what can we do about it? It's not like we can jump in the car and run him to the vet."

She had a point. We were sitting alongside Arkansas Highway 5 north of the Garland and Saline County Line. The nearest veterinarian was fifteen miles back in Hot Springs. Patricia added, "Even if we could, try to find one open at this hour on a Saturday. Trust me, it ain't happening."

For the past ten years my wife had owned and operated a dog grooming business in Hot Springs. She knew what she was talking about. I asked, "So what do we do?"

We pulled the first aid kit out of the cart, cleaned his leg and coated the abrasions with antiseptic. Although he cried as we treated his wounds, Spot didn't have much of a reaction when I moved the leg around.

Patricia said, "If it was broken, I don't think you could do that."

She decided to spend the rest of the day riding in the cart with Spot so she could keep an eye on him. I was laying our injured hound in the cab when my wife said, "Can you believe this? It's only our second day on the road, and already we've run over our dog."

"Pretty impressive, eh?"

⊰⊱

The next day was June 24, 2001. It was the hottest, most humid one so far that year. Everything we did made us sweat. That morning, as I tied the laces on my hiking boots, perspiration dripped off the end of my nose down onto my fingers. When Patricia handed me the nylon tent bag to pack on top of the cart, my hands were so damp it slipped out of them and landed on the ground. While I harnessed Della and hitched her to the cart, I was constantly wiping my eyes with the back of my hands. Hands that

3

were wet with sweat. Eyes that were already stinging from my salty special juices.

For more than twenty-five years I had fantasized about doing this—leaving it all behind to travel this country and others on foot. Whenever I visualized this dream, it was always my wife and me walking along a country road with our mule and dog on a beautiful day. I realized some days would be hot and others cold. And there would be times we'd be walking in the rain or snow.

I knew from experience, it wasn't always going to be a walk in the park. In the 1970s, with a pack pony and dog, I spent three and a half years traveling 8,000 miles of America's highways and byways on foot. From eastern Pennsylvania, I walked to Pacific City, Oregon, down the coast across the Golden Gate Bridge then east to my mother's home in Hot Springs, Arkansas. I was struck by lightning in South Dakota, got my feet frost bit on the Continental Divide in Montana and was literally blown down to the ground by a wicked westerly in the Columbia Gorge.

But never did I have such a miserable sweat as Patricia and I experienced our third day on the road. By noon we had perspired so much it looked like both of us took a shower with our clothes on.

We were walking north on Arkansas Highway 9, which traversed the eastern slopes of the Ouachita Mountains. Unlike the Rockies, the Ouachitas weren't soaring highlands with imposing stone peaks or rugged promontory precipices. They're older mountains that time has worn down into rounded large humps, green with pine, oak and other deciduous trees. The range runs east and west. So the highway went over the ridges with lots of ups and downs that, in a car, would have felt like a roller coaster. None of the hills were monumental, but to us sweaty, middle aged tenderfoots, each subsequent climb was a greater challenge than the last one. While the day sweltered on, we became acutely aware of how out of shape we really were. Sure, we may have practiced hiking the mountains and steep country lanes around our house, but now we were on the road really doing it. And today the slopes were one after another.

Late in the afternoon, we came to a hill that I thought we'd never get to the top of. Those hot humid miles had wilted our cadence with Della. The cheerful cajoling of "Come up Della! That's my girl!" had been sizzled and scalded to, "Dammit, we're almost to the top of this stinking hill–quit poking along!"

At the summit, we could see where the highway crossed Alum Fork River on a long bridge. On the left side of the road was a wide gravel area where fishermen would leave their vehicles while down on the river. It looked like a good place to park the cart and pitch our tent. Below it was a large grassy area for mule grazing. Our camp would be up on the public right-of-way, but the grass was on private property. So I hiked to the nearest house and got permission to tie Della out in that field for the night.

The post we tied her to was about fifty yards from where we pitched the tent. After we gave her some grain and water, Della began to peacefully graze. But as the sun settled onto the horizon she got restless. First, she pawed the ground and tossed her head about like she was angry. Then Della commenced to pace around the post she was tied to. Within minutes, the rope was so tightly wrapped around the post she couldn't move. I was unwinding it when I said to Patricia, "For a mule who was so tired on that last hill, she's certainly full of energy now."

"I think she wants to be up there with us."

"What?"

My wife said, "Without Jim, we're all she's got."

Della had been in our lives for less than six months. Originally, we planned to start this journey a year earlier with a mule named "Buck." For fifteen of the twenty-five years that I had dreamed of this journey, Buck was going to be the traveling mule. But three weeks before our scheduled departure, we discovered he had cancer. Buck is now buried on a hillside behind our home in Hot Springs.

It was several months before I could bring myself to go looking for another mule. Eventually, in Breaux Bridge, Louisiana, we found a pair of big Belgian mules named Jim and Della. They were sorrel colored with flaxen manes and tails, and Della was the prettiest mule I had ever seen. She was also very much the alpha-female and dominated Jim. We nicknamed her "Big Sis."

She had been Jim's teammate for most of her six and half years, and we had to buy them both to get her. We sold Jim to my little sister. I knew she'd give him a good home.

Patricia said, "We're Della's herd now. She's lonely down here by herself."

"But there's no grass up there by us."

"Maybe if we moved her closer she'll settle down."

Halfway between that post and our camp I tied her to a small tree in the middle of a patch of tall grass. Then we stood and watched her graze for about ten minutes. Finally my wife said, "She seems to be happy. Let's go back to camp. I need to finish making up our bed."

Just as I stepped over the guardrail onto the highway shoulder, I heard a ruckus behind me. I turned around in time to see Della come to the end of her rope in the middle of a leap. It pulled her front legs out from under her and sent her crashing down on her side.

She rolled over and up onto her feet with the rope wrapped around her torso. Then she tossed her head around and started bucking until she came to the end of the rope. Again, it jerked her to the ground. This time when she rolled, the rope got tangled in some small bushes and wrapped around both of her back legs. Della tried to stand but couldn't. She had hog-tied herself. So she began to thrash around on the ground trying to get free from the rope.

I jumped over the guardrail and yelled, "She's going to break a leg!"

Both of us ran down the hill screaming, "Della, no!"

When I got to her, she was still flailing about trying to get her legs free. I didn't want to get kicked, so I stopped a few yards from her and squatted down. Then in as soothing a voice as I could muster, I said, "Settle down, big girl. I'll get you loose."

Patricia's was shaking when she ran up behind me. "Do something!"

I reached up, took my wife's hand and pulled her down beside me. "Looming is only going to make her more scared. First thing we've got to do is calm her down."

"Gotchya." Then Patricia softly said, "It's all right Della. We'll help you."

In a couple of minutes Della was lying still, and I was able to untangle the rope. After she got up on her feet, we checked her for injuries. Other than a few scratches from the bushes, and a small rope burn on her left rear leg, she was fine.

"It may be further away, but I think it's safer by the post," I said. "No bushes there."

Patricia nodded. "You're probably right. I'll sit with her for awhile."

She stayed with Della until it was too dark to see. Several times during the night I got up, and with a flashlight, hiked down to check on her. Every time I showed up, she would nicker and rub her head against my shoulder.

Della never got tangled like that again.

⫘

It took us a week to reach a town that had more than one store and was listed on the map as having a population. According to the sign on the highway, 1,458 people lived in Perryville. It had several stores, a court house and a Laundromat.

During that week Spot completely recuperated from being run over, and Della had gotten used to being tied out at night away from us. The only thing that hadn't improved was the weather. The heat and humidity was getting worse. Over the past seven days, perspiration had become our constant companion, and we had lots of dirty, sweat-soaked clothes. So in Perryville, the Laundromat was our first stop. I tied Della to a telephone pole out front, and toted our dirty duds inside. While Patricia did the laundry, I set one of our camp chairs next to Della and went to work on my journal.

I had only written three sentences, when a woman in her mid-twenties got out of a mini-van and introduced herself as a reporter for the *Petit Jean Country Headlight*. "The phone has been ringing off the wall about you folks."

"Really?"

She pulled a digital camera out of her purse. "It's a small town. You know how small towns are. Everybody's got to know everybody else's business."

While I explained what we were doing, she jotted notes on her pad. At one point she looked up at me and asked, "What'd you do before starting this trip?"

"The past four years I ran a coffee house in Hot Springs called 'The Poet's Loft.' Before that I owned the Mule Line Trolley and gave tours of the city and national park. I've been a disc jockey, a time share salesman and I wrote for a weekly newspaper."

The reporter turned a page on her note pad as she asked, "What about your wife?"

"Patricia owned a dog-grooming business in Hot Springs for nine years. Before that she managed a trust company in Dallas, and before that she was a cop and legal secretary in northern Illinois."

She nodded and grinned as she scribbled in silence for a few moments. Then she looked up and said, "You guys have had an interesting life. So what do your children think about you doing this trip?"

"I haven't any. Neither does my wife."

"Huh?" Confusion riddled the woman's face.

"We're newlyweds."

Although Patricia and I had been together for a couple of years, we didn't get married until New Year's Eve 2000 on the stage at the Poet's Loft. Both of us were fifty-one, and when we took those vows we promised to make this journey the grandest of all honeymoons. We hit the road six months later.

When I told the reporter that, I left out a few facts: Patricia was my seventh bride, and the second one to strike out on this adventure with me.

Like Patricia, the previous half dozen all wanted to do it, but either they changed their minds or tried to change mine—except wife number six. Sue and I got married and hit the road in May 1996 with a pair of mules and a gypsy wagon that I had built. We returned home three days later–initially because the wagon broke down. We stayed there because our relationship was broken too.

Sue was beautiful. An artist with black hair that draped halfway down her slender back. She was fifteen years younger than me, and when she smiled her whole being glowed. Sue really radiated when she talked about the journey. "A vagabond artist. I like the sound of it."

On the surface, Sue was perfect. But there were a couple of problems that I just couldn't get past. One of them was her smile. After we got back home I never saw it again, privately. When we were around other people the smile came easily–she was always positive and upbeat. But at home, Sue's glass was always half empty, destined to be dry. Then when we discovered the problem with the wagon was in my design, it triggered geysers of criticism. And not just of me. It got so that to her, no one seemed do anything right. She would talk kindly to people in person, but verbally slash them to ribbons behind their backs. It felt like I was drowning in a sea of negativity.

And then there was our love life, which was non-existent. When we first got together the sex was okay. Not great, but I figured it would get better with time. Instead, it got to where she seemed to just be indulging me. Then she quit doing that.

I know the marriage vows are, "For better or worse," but if worse is all I'm going to get, then it's time for me to get going. Sue and I were married less than six months.

I vowed then, "Never again! It's going to be just me and the mule."

Then along came Patricia. She was a little older than me. (I was fifty-one at the time.) She had a hardy laugh, a sharp tongue and an opinion on everything. Her know-it-all attitude really grated on me. She was not at all the kind of woman I had dreamed of making this journey with. But doing things with Patricia was more fun than anybody I had ever known. Hiking, dining, swimming, camping it was all better with her. And as a lover, Patricia was what this man had always dreamed of.

This was scary. A person can't have so many failed relationships without thinking, *Something is wrong with me.* I finally concluded that my obsession to see the world on foot was my problem. That question, "Do you want to go with me?" had broken a lot of hearts. Mine the most–because I was both the repeat offender and victim. The past two decades of emotional scars now were calluses. And I had learned that it was best not to shed them, because the flesh underneath is going to be real tender. But *now* I was having the time of my life with someone I really loved being with. That question–"Do you want to go?"– could ruin it.

But eventually I did ask, and Patricia said, "Yes, but you don't have to marry me. We've got a great thing going here–let's keep it that way."

When she said that I felt like I'd been let off the hook. No commitment meant no responsibility. If everything worked out, great! If not, she could go her way and I'll just get on the down the road with the mule. But as I watched Patricia throw herself into making it happen, that bulwark began to crumble.

She shut down her business, auctioned her home and sold most of her worldly possessions. Her car, golf clubs, big screen TV, antiques, jewelry and stuff she'd been saving for decades–it all went for pennies on the dollar so she could live with me in a tent on the road with a mule.

Someone who was willing to do all that to make my dream come true deserved a commitment from me. The question was, "Can I keep it?

⊰⊱

When we walked into Perryville, the sky was overcast. Although it was just as hot and humid as the days before, it was a treat to walk under a gray sky. While we packed our clean clothes, a steady westerly started wafting the scent of rain our way.

Patricia sighed, "Does that smell heavenly, or what?"

Just as we turned east on Highway 60 toward Toad Suck, suddenly the breeze began to pelt us with fat drops. My wife sang out, "Bring it on, baby. Let it rain!"

It lasted a couple of minutes. The two of us had just gotten our rain coats on, when it quit. Patricia was unzipping hers when she said, "Come on, is that it?"

Six miles later, when we walked into the hamlet of Houston, Arkansas, both of us were sopping wet. Not from rain—from sweat. The clouds went away, the sun came out and turned that little bit of rain into steam. Patricia was wringing out the bottom of her T-shirt when she said, "It's like a damn sauna out here."

We were pitching our tent near the Houston water tank, and the sun was slowly sliding toward the horizon when my wife said, "I can't wait till it gets dark."

But dusk brought an onslaught of mosquitoes, the likes of which I'd never seen before. When I waved my hand to shoo them away, it felt like I was stirring them instead. Patricia and I looked like we were doing a strange dance as we stomped our feet, slapped our legs, smacked our arms and swatted the air about our heads.

I don't remember what we had for dinner that night, but I do know we didn't eat outside. Even in the tent, dinner was not without an occasional swat at a rogue who found her way inside.

Nightfall brought no relief from the heat. The air inside the tent was so stifling that sweat flowed out our pores like water from a spigot. Pillows and sheets were soon drenched, and there was that occasional whine of a mosquito in the tent.

Around five in the morning, a flash of white light and a boom of thunder bolted us all awake. The first huge rain drops hit the tent so hard they sounded like rocks. Suddenly, the wind kicked up and bellowed the nylon walls in toward us. Then the sky let loose with a deluge. It was like someone was dumping a barrel of water on the tent. The overhead poles bowed down toward us, turning the top into a bowl full of rain, which became a sieve with us underneath it.

We scurried to pull our rain coats over the bedding, but it was too late. Everything was already soaked. Soon, so much water was gushing through the seams in the bottom of the tent, that our air-bed began to float with us and Spot on it.

The storm raged on for five hours. Shortly after it stopped I crawled out of the tent and found us camped in the middle of a huge puddle. Every step we made sloshed. The grass we camped on was growing in red clay, so the water was red too. When we pulled our soggy bedding out of the tent, we were careful not to drop anything. The stain of Arkansas red clay can be permanent.

I strung a clothes line from the cart to a tree, and as we hung sheets on it, Patricia said, "At least Della got a good shower out of the deal."

My wife and I are convinced this mule understands everything we say. Those words were barely out of her mouth, when Della laid down and rolled in the muddiest spot she could find. When she stood up, all of her was caked in red clay.

⌁

In the south, nearly every hometown café has a "good-ole-boys' table." Usually a large one toward the back of the dining room, close to the coffee pot. A gathering place where locals congregate to discuss the goings on of the world. Conversations are punctuated by stirring spoons that clink against the insides of coffee cups. At these tables, local gossip always has priority.

In Heber Springs, Arkansas, we sat a couple of tables away from the good-ole-boys at the Smoke House Restaurant. It was Thursday around two in the afternoon. A few days earlier a man took our picture and gave us a twenty dollar bill. "Buy yourselves a nice dinner." So we staked out Della behind Miss Magnolia's Wedding Cottage, then hiked to the restaurant to spend the man's money.

After we ordered, Patricia went to the ladies room while I sipped iced tea and tried to eavesdrop on the good-ole-boys. At first, I thought they were talking about someone's hay harvest. The old guy at the head of the table said, "Looked like pretty nice hay to me."

A man half way down the table asked, "How much were they hauling?"

"Two bales."

I had to agree with the one who said, "That ain't much of a load."

"I don't see how they could've got anymore on that thing."

A younger man at the other end said, "That's for sure. I seen them yesterday down on Highway 5 between here and Rosebud. Got themselves a damn good-looking mule!"

They were talking about us! It had been nearly four weeks since we left Hot Springs. So far, we had walked a hundred and fifty-five miles and our story had been in five newspapers—including the *Dallas Morning News*. And now we were the main topic at the good-ole-boys' table, in Heber Springs, Arkansas. How I wished I were closer. If my ears could rotate like Della's, they would have been aimed at that table. This was exciting!

"I seen them down that way too. Then I seen them coming into town a couple of hours ago. Where do you suppose they spent the night?"

"I hear they camped in Deputy Moss's yard."

We met Joyce Moss under a shade tree, in the parking lot, at a flea market. She was a short, feisty little blond who looked to be in her mid thirties. Three kids were in the back seat of the mini-van, and her mother-in-law was in the front. When Joyce pulled up, she leaned out the window and asked, "What're you doing?"

The car hadn't quite come to a complete stop when she asked that question. And the motor was still idling when I answered, "Traveling."

Joyce turned the key and the engine stopped, as she said, "With the mule?"

A pretty teenaged face, with too much makeup, popped out the window behind Joyce and asked, "Where you going?"

After we answered their questions, Joyce invited us to camp in her yard. "I've got horses and llamas, and plenty of grazing for your mule."

The girl behind Joyce pulled her long dish-water-blond hair back from her face as she said, "And you can go for a swim in our pool."

It was another hot afternoon and their invitation was music to our ears. When we got to the house around five, Deputy Sheriff Marty Moss was in the driveway, leaning against his cruiser, obviously waiting for us. He struck an imposing figure in his brown and tan uniform with a cream-colored western hat. As we approached the driveway I figured he'd come home to nix his wife's invitation. But when we got closer I could see there was a smile on his handsome face. I greeted him with, "Never know what the wife is going to drag in, eh?"

He shook his head and chuckled. "It's never a dull moment with Joyce."

The Moss's had only been married a few months, and each of them brought three children into their new family. Joyce got the house in a divorce. It was a sprawling, red stucco, Spanish-style villa. The kind of home you would expect to find in Southern California. She also had the llamas and horses when Marty married her.

Joyce used to keep chickens in a small fenced yard, but she got rid of them a couple of years ago. The grass in the chicken yard was waist high—a feast for a mule. I had just turned her loose and latched the gate, when Della met Super Man.

The llamas all came out of the barn and spotted Della at the same time. They skidded to a stop and stared. The llama in the lead was Super Man, and his eyes looked like they were about to blast out of their sockets.

Super Man was a big, handsome, sorrel llama—about the same color as Della. The front of his long neck had white fur that went from his chin down to his puffed-up chest. In the middle of his black head was a white blaze. He stared at Della while his small pointed ears twitched back and forth. *Who is this stranger in my yard?*

Della made the first move. A length of grass hung out the side of her mouth as she slowly walked toward the fence between them. The other three llamas cowered back a few steps, but Super Man stood fast and hissed at the Big Sis.

Joyce gasped, "Lord, please don't let him spit on her."

Her teenaged daughter squealed, "Oh man, it is so gross!"

Joyce pointed to several dark stains on the side of the barn, as she explained that spitting is a llama's first line of defense. What they spit comes directly from their gut. "It really stinks—and it hurts."

Della stood and watched Superman slowly strut up to the fence. Each step appeared calculated, as if he was stalking her. When he got to the fence, Super Man stopped and sniffed the air, while Della commenced to chomp on the grass in her mouth. Again he hissed at her.

Joyce shrieked, "Oh no, he's going to do it!"

But he didn't. Instead, Della nonchalantly stepped up to the fence while Super Man stood his ground. Then they both started sniffing the air around each other. Suddenly, Super Man whirled around and ran down the hill followed by the other llamas.

So far, Della had paid no attention to any of the livestock we had encountered. But when Super Man ran away, she whinnied to him. Immediately, he whirled around and trotted back up the hill where he strutted back and forth in front of her. Della followed him on her side of the fence and when he stopped to flirt, she flirted back. They sniffed the air around each others head—she would squeal when he got a bit too close. But when he looked as if he was going to leave, she would whinny, "Where you going big boy?"

To which he would turn around and start sniffing toward her—her always squealing when he got too close—her always whinnying when it looked like he might turn away. After a few minutes of this, Super Man had enough, and off he ran to join the other llamas at the bottom of the hill. Again, Della called to him, and he ran back up the hill.

That flirtation must have gone on all night. Because in the morning, when I hooked Della to the cart, she was tired. Normally as I harness her and we hitch her up, she's constantly fidgeting around, anxious to get going. But that morning she stood still with her head drooping. Della was worn out from her one night stand with Super Man.

❧

"Boy did that feel good!"

My wife had just returned from the ladies room in the Smoke House Restaurant and was about to sit down when I held a finger to my lips. "Shush!"

"What do you mean, shush?"

I motioned for her to sit and pointed to the good ole' boys table as I whispered, "Be quiet and listen."

The waitress had just freshened everybody's coffee. So the cups were really clinking from stirring spoons when one of the older men said, "Me and the wife saw them this morning on the mountain. They was pulled off to the side of the road. Looked like they was broke down."

Nearly 6,000 people live in Heber Springs, which is situated among the Ozark foothills. Downtown is in the Little Red River Valley. The main road into it is a steep winding descent. So Patricia rode in the cart and operated the brake. When we started down the hill, the cart began to push Della. So I yelled, "Brake!" (My signal for Patricia to apply more brake.) The cart continued to push Della, and she was almost at a trot.

"Brake! Brake!"

Patricia yelled something, but I couldn't understand her because of the traffic. I was jogging when I shouted over my shoulder, "Patricia, give me more brake!"

This time I understood when she screamed, "It's not working!"

We were gaining speed. Della was no longer holding the cart back. She was just trying to stay ahead of it, and I could barely keep up with her. The highway was cut into the side of the mountain, so there was no place to pull off.

"Pump the brake!"

"I am pumping, dammit! It's not working!"

Then my wife yelled, "On the right! Look!"

We were approaching a driveway that led to a wide level spot with a pile of gravel at the back of it. It was dotted with deep pot holes, so it would be a rough exit. But it would put an end to this dangerous descent. I turned Della to the right and yelled, "Hold on baby!"

Della hopped over the holes, but the cart tires bounced in and out of them. Then the right front wheel dropped into a small gully in front of the gravel pile. The cart clanged and banged to a halt.

I took a deep breath and looked up at Della's face. Her nostrils flared while her ears turned back and forth. When I looked back at the cart, my wife was shaking her head. I called back to her, "Some adventure! Eh baby?"

"Some adventure? I just had the be-Jesus scared out of me, and all you can say is, 'Some adventure baby?'" She was climbing out of the cab as she said, "I'll show you some adventure!" Stumbling around the pot holes toward me Patricia said, "I damn near wet my pants back there. I'm not leaving this spot until you fix those brakes."

⌘

Halfway down the good-ole'-boys' table was a short round man in farmer's overalls and a black cap with a confederate flag and "Forget, Hell!" on the front of it. He took a sip from his cup, then said, "I hear-tell they're walking to the East Coast. I think New York."

In unison, half a dozen of them said, "New York?"

The man at the head of the table said, "They're crazy! Hell, in New York they'll steal everything they've got!"

We had just begun to eat our dinner when three older men came in and sat down at a table next to us. The oldest was tall and skinny with every silver hair in place. Before his butt even hit the seat, he put his right hand on my shoulder and asked, "You folks live around here, or you just visiting?"

No introduction, no hello or anything. He just grabbed my shoulder, smiled like a politician up for re-election and posed his question—it made me bristle. "Just visiting."

"Just visiting, eh? Where you from?"

"Hot Springs."

"Hot Springs, eh? You going to be in Heber long?"

This was beginning to feel like a police interrogation. "A couple of days."

"A couple of days, eh? You visiting family or you out at the lake?"

"We're just passing through."

"Just passing through, eh? Where you staying?"

This was getting tedious. It interfered with my eavesdropping, and I didn't like his hand my shoulder. I turned toward him hoping to shake his grip, but he held on.

I said, "We're camped behind Miss Magnolia's Cottage."

"Miss Magnolia's Cottage?" He let go of my shoulder. "I've lived in Heber all my life, and I ain't never heard of any Miss Magnolia's."

Joyce Moss had opened her wedding cottage a year earlier. It was in a quaint stone house across the street from the city's park that had Heber's springs in it. Miss Magnolia's Cottage sat on three acres surrounded by lawn and trees. She invited us to camp there as long as we wanted.

Speaking so I couldn't be heard at the good-ole-boys' table, I described where Miss Magnolia's was and told him about our journey. Then I gave him a flyer that explained what we were doing. After reading a few sentences he folded it, stuck it in his starched shirt pocket and turned to his companions. "You boys go on and eat. I've got to check this out."

We had just finished our meal and were about to get up from the table, when the man returned. "I went by and saw your mule. She's sure a pretty thing. Hope you don't think I'm nosy or anything like that. I just had to see it for myself."

When we walked toward the cash register he got up and went to the good-ole'-boys' table with our flyer in his hand. While the manager rang up our bill, I complimented him on our meal. Then nodded toward the good-ole'-boys. "That's a busy table over there."

The manager grimaced and shook his head. "You want to take them with you?"

At the door I turned to see the man with our flyer holding court at the table. His thumb was in our direction and all faces were turned toward us.

Miss Magnolia's was on a corner lot with streets on two sides and an alley beside it. After dinner, we went back and set up camp. We were rolling out the tent, when Patricia said, "Sure a lot of traffic on these back streets."

Most were pick-up trucks, and as they crept by I began to recognize some of the faces from the good-ole'-boys' table. Throughout the afternoon traffic increased. A few times it was almost bumper to bumper, and many of the same vehicles went by numerous times. Some of the truck beds were filled with kids, and all eyes were on us.

Patricia said, "Now I know how a fish in an aquarium must feel."

"Della and the cart."

CHAPTER 2

KEEP THE FAITH
AND LET GO

⊹⊱⊰⊹

THE PLAN WAS WHENEVER DELLA pulled the cart, I'd be at her side on foot. It really wasn't a cart because it had four wheels. But I called it a "cart" anyway. It had eleven doors. Some of them opened up, others swung out and there were doors that folded down as work tables. Behind each one was a compartment. One held the computer and printer. Others had plastic drawers with food, clothing, and first-aid supplies. And we had a junk drawer. Who can live without one?

On the front was a compartment with a door that opened up like a luggage trunk. That was Della's part of the cart—we called it "the nose." It held feed, grooming and shoeing tools, extra mule shoes and the top of it could hold two bales of hay.

But the most interesting door was on the back. It folded down. When it was up it held our bicycles on metal pipes that extended from it. When the door was down, the pipes were legs for our dinner table or stage.

I've always been fascinated with traveling entertainers. Not musicians or actors who rush from one gig to another in jets or buses. It's the wandering minstrels, small big top circuses and old traveling medicine shows that intrigued me. What a way to make a living! Amble into town, pitch a tent or drop the stage and entertain the locals.

That's how I planned to finance this odyssey—as a vagabond poet. Like the old traveling medicine men, I'd put on a show. But instead of pushing potions and pills, we'd pass the hat and peddle my self-published poetry books–books that we printed on the cart.

Electricity for the stage lights, sound system, computer and printer was produced by a solar panel on the top of the cart and two generators that were turned by the rotation of the back wheels. The power was stored in two golf cart batteries.

So the cart was our closet, kitchen, pantry, office, feed room, workshop, dining room, publishing company, theater and power plant. How's that for mule power?

Several people said our cart looked like a red Model T Ford. My artist friend Benini dubbed it, "Model P"–P for poetry.

⚜

Two weeks after hitting the road, we produced our first show in Conway, Arkansas. It was in a vacant lot next to a coffee house on Front Street. "Something Brewing" was on the first floor of an old two-story white clapboard house. The front yard was covered with wooden decks that had tables and chairs on them. We parked the cart in the lot with our stage facing the decks.

I'm a performance poet. Meaning, I don't just read the poems, I perform them– often acting out the parts of the characters in the verse. Like my poem, "Old Drunk Paul– A Tribute to Perfection" where I become stumbling-stuttering drunk. The show opens with "The Great American Way." I hop on stage in the character of a TV car salesman and yell, "Boy have I got a deal for you!" In this piece I renounce the common conventions of American society. Things like owning an automobile, belonging to a church and holding a steady job. But in the end, the poem pokes fun at me when I ask, ". . . if you're headed that way, could I catch a ride to Walmart?"

We only had two days to promote the Conway show. I put a handmade sign up in front of the lot, we hung posters in the coffee house and pinned some on bulletin boards around the campus of nearby Hendrix College. We had no press coverage, and yet, more than thirty-five people showed up. They were generous when we passed the hat, and I sold several copies of my book *Songs Of Politics and Other Social Diseases*.

For me, the most memorable part of the evening was a conversation I had with a man after the show. He was dressed in faded denim overalls and wore a tattered red cap with the words "Woo-Pig-Sooie!" across the front. His right cheek bulged from the wad of tobacco behind it as he shook my hand and said, "The only reason I'm here is 'cause the wife dragged me. I'd planned on going cat-fishing tonight, but she insisted." He stopped and spit on the ground to his left. "And to tell you the truth, I'm glad I came. Ain't never seen anything like this. I had a damn good time."

He extended his hand, and as I shook it I asked, "Was it better than cat-fishing?"

"You're pushing your luck, son."

⊣⪧⪦⊢

The morning we walked out of Conway on Highway 64 East, it was hotter than any day so far. Above the pavement, the air wavered like a desert scene in a movie. The four lanes of cars and trucks charging past us created a wind that felt like it came from a blast furnace. And the forecast was for even hotter days ahead. So we decided to find a shady place to camp for a few days.

Several people suggested Lester Flatt Campground. They said it was in a pretty mountain valley with lots of shade and a spring-fed lake. Going to Lester Flatt meant an eight mile detour, but everybody said it would be worth it.

That morning, as we walked down Highway 107 toward Lester Flatt, it was so humid I felt like we were wading there. I usually wore a bandana headband under my straw hat to keep perspiration out my eyes. But that day it didn't make any difference. I was constantly wiping sweat out of them. Each time we stopped to drink water, I had to wring a small stream from my headband. It was like the water was flowing directly from my mouth to my pores.

Around two in the afternoon we got to the dirt road that led into Lester Flatt Campground. It had taken us nearly five hours to walk eight miles. Worn out from trudging through the mugginess, we were more than ready to put down for the day. Especially if it was in shade next to a spring-fed lake.

But it was still a mile back into the campground and most of it was uphill. In that mile we stopped to rest and drink water more than any other mile in my life. Finally, at the top of the hill, we found ourselves gazing down at a shimmering pool of blue cradled in the lush green Ozark foothills. It was oblong and prettier than I had fantasized it would be. Just the sight of it refreshed me. Before long we'd be soaking in cool spring water.

But on the road down to the campground we came to a hand-painted wooden sign nailed to a tree that read, "Absolutely no horses."

"It doesn't say anything about mules," Patricia said, as she handed me the water jug. "Maybe when we tell them what we're doing, and that we walked out of our way to camp here, they'll let us stay."

Before I took a drink, I said, "That sign is mighty emphatic."

"We've come this far, I say we go down and ask."

"And if we can't use the campground maybe we could set up in the woods."

The park was only on the east end of the lake. The rest of it was undeveloped woodland. Camping in the woods might be a solution to the "Absolutely no horses" rule at Lester Flatt. So we walked down into the valley.

Lester Flat had a sand beach, several RV sites, a large pavilion and a small store. When we stopped in front of the store, a man in his late sixties, wearing Bermuda shorts and flip-flops, walked out. His right arm below the elbow was missing. With that stub he pointed up the way we came and said, "We don't allow horses here. There's a sign up on the hill."

"We saw it," I said. "But we walked out of our way to get here because everyone said we'd be welcome. Are you the owner?"

He shook his bald head. "No. The lady who owns this place isn't here. She works in Cabot. I camp here and keep an eye on the place for her. And one of her rules is no horses."

It felt like I was whining when I said, "If I'd known that before, we wouldn't have come here. It's awfully hot. I sure would hate to go back out on the road in this heat. Do you suppose we could camp tonight in the woods somewhere around the lake? We'll leave first thing in the morning when it's cooler."

He thought about it a moment, then said, "I don't know if she'd go for that or not. She owns all the property around the lake. Let me call and see what she says."

A few minutes later he came out of the store with a frown on his face. "She said no. Not in the campground or anywhere else."

Now it felt like I was begging. "Did you tell her we walked out of our way because everyone said we'd be welcome here?"

Up to this point I had the feeling the one-armed man wanted to help us. But now he had a job to do. "She said those people don't own this place, she does. And they had no right to tell you to come down here. She wants you to leave now!"

Flabbergasted I said, "I can't believe as hot as it is she's going to make us leave!"

"That's not her problem. Her words were, 'If I let one outfit traveling with a mule and a cart come in then I'll have to let them all in.' "

"Right! And how many mules and carts does she have come by here?"

❧❦

According to our map, there was a dirt road that would take us through a forested area to State Highway 5. Rose Bud was our first mail stop, and it was on that highway. I figured if we took the dirt road we'd find a shady place in the woods to camp. And at one time Ballard Road probably *was* a shady lane—but not when we walked on it. Property on both sides was private, fenced and posted. The forest had been cut back from the road to make way for pasture and lawns. It's a valley road that skirts the base of the Ozark foothills. Long steep driveways led to hillside homes among the pines, cedars and oaks. It was fence after fence with signs written in various verbiage, all of which boiled down to one meaning—"Keep Out!"

Most of the folks who lived in that valley worked in or around Little Rock. So as our shadows grew longer, the traffic got heavier and the road dustier. The afternoon heated up and commuter dust turned our sweat into rivulets of mud.

Near the junction of Red Bird Lane, we stopped under an ancient pine whose shadow graced Ballard Road. We were there less than a minute, when two pick-ups sped past us. They were jacked-up and riding-high with wide knobbed tires that kicked up such a thick cloud of dust that Patricia and I couldn't see each other. We both were coughing when she screamed, "I'm sick of this!"

I was too, but I didn't want to feed her despair. So I said, "Something good is going to come out of this. I can feel it."

Patricia snapped, "Oh yeah, like what? A Holiday Inn?"

In the two years that we'd been together, that was the first time Patricia ever snapped at me. I had seen her angry before, but she was never nasty like that. I didn't know what to say.

She wiped her face with a sweat soaked bandana as she grumbled, "I knew we should have stayed on the pavement. It might have been longer, but at least we wouldn't have to eat all this god-damn dust."

Earlier, after looking at the map, we had mutually agreed to take this road. I toyed with the idea of reminding her of that, but thought better of it. The moment was too volatile. I simply said, "Well, we've gone too far to turn back."

With a smart-ass expression she quipped, "Ya think?"

Suddenly, behind us was the roar of an engine approaching. We both turned to see a sedan racing toward us with a plume of dust behind it. Patricia clinched both fists and growled, "You'd better slow down, Shit-head!"

And it did. Not enough to have no dust at all, but it wasn't a choker. When the man and his Mercedes slowly cruised past us, Patricia put on her best fake smile and waved as she muttered, "Thanks a lot, Ass-hole."

The next two miles took an hour and a half to walk–every foot of it was sweat and hot dust. I had grit in my mouth, behind my knees and inside my elbows. Every once in awhile, I had to take my sunglasses off to pick a batch of crud from the corners of my eyes. You can imagine what it was like inside my nose.

We paused at nearly every speck of shade we came to. If it was a wide spot off the road, we stopped to consider it for a campsite–especially if there was water nearby. Like a house with a spigot, or a pond to dip a bucket into, but every one of those places had something wrong with it–usually a sign that told us to keep out.

Ballard Road crossed a creek with a few scummy puddles, then made a sharp left turn and went up a steep slope. At the top of the hill, on the right hand side of the road, sat an abandoned brick house. Some of the windows were broken and the yard was knee high in weeds. Along the front of the property was a line of pine trees that made shade where we needed it, and there were no signs telling us to keep out. So we walked up the overgrown driveway, and stomped through the crackling dry weeds to get to a shady spot where we could tie Della.

We had two big blue plastic water jugs with us. Each held seven gallons, and all the water we had left was about two-thirds of a jug. I filled Spot's drinking bowl, poured Patricia and me each a tall tumbler and dumped the rest into Della's bucket. After I took our folding chairs off the back of the cart, my wife and I sat down to a tall drink of tepid water. It sure felt good to be off my feet. According to the pedometer, I'd walked over sixteen miles that day. And I felt every hot one of them.

With a damp rag across the nape of her neck, Patricia leaned forward in her chair and took a sip of water. Then she smacked her lips, turned to me with a Cheshire-cat grin and said, "Yes sir, after a hard hot day on the road, there ain't nothing I love more than a big tall glass of piss water. Nope, it don't get no better than that!" She paused, then asked, "So, is this the great treat up ahead?"

Okay, it wasn't great. The only shade was from tall thin pines, which is better than nothing. But it's not as refreshing as a big spreading oak, or maple, or just about any other deciduous tree. And the graze for Della wasn't good either. Mostly thistles and some tall parched grass. But we had plenty of hay for her.

I said, "Well, it's better than nothing."

Patricia grunted. "Not much."

Catty-corner across the road was a mobile home with porches, decks and wheel chair ramps around it. Earlier, when we walked up the hill toward the abandoned house, I spotted a garden hose in the backyard of that place. So I stood up, grabbed the jugs and said, "I'll see if I can't find us some fresh water." Then I headed toward the mobile home.

On the way there, all I thought about was how ugly Patricia had been earlier. The heat, sweat and dust were bad enough, but now I had to deal with an attitude, too? While I walked up the wheel chair ramp toward the front door, I was thinking, *Should have stuck with just having a mule!*

The small bent old woman who came to the door said I could use the faucet behind her house. She was standing on the back step watching me fill the jugs, when I asked, "Do you suppose it'd be all right if we camp tonight in the yard across the road?"

Her voice was weak and it shook when she said, "Well, I can't give you permission 'cause I don't own it. But those people haven't been down here in a couple years. I don't imagine anybody's going to say you can't."

Back at camp, we had just unhitched Della from the cart when a four-wheeler with a man wearing a straw hat pulled out of the driveway from the house next door to the old woman. He drove across the road, stopped behind our cart, turned off the machine and said, "You aren't going to camp here, are you?"

I'm six foot two, and he was a couple of inches taller than me. He was in his late fifties, and the left side of his face drooped as if he'd had a stroke. The way the question tumbled out the left corner of his mouth, I couldn't tell if he was for or against us being there. So I was cautious when I said, "We've had a tough day, and need to get off the road for the night. I asked the lady—"

"I know. That's my mother." His speech wasn't halted or stammered like most folks who've had a stroke. Still some of his words were slurred because of the way his jaw tugged down on his mouth. "Like she said, nobody's going to care if you camp here, but you don't want to."

"We don't?"

When he climbed off the ATV and walked toward us, his back was straight, and he didn't limp like someone who'd had a stroke. "The chiggers and ticks will eat you alive."

Patricia and I both had lived in Arkansas long enough to recognize a tick and chigger haven, and this was definitely one. For that matter, every patch of tall grass or weeds in those parts had the connotation of itch to it. We used insect repellent more than most folks use deodorant.

"You'd be better off in my yard. I've got lots of good grass for your mule."

His modular home was almost a hundred yards from the road. The lawn was lush with a few shade trees here and there. This man had obviously spent a lot of time taking care of his yard, and Della could do it a lot of damage. Most folks figured she'd just trim the grass and leave a bit of natural fertilizer behind. But her steel shoes could dig up big hunks of sod, and Della loved to roll and roll and roll. She'd roll so much that by the end of the day a dust-bowl would be where once was lawn.

"I know about livestock." The man's voice was as deep as he was tall. "I used to own a stockyard. Trust me, she won't hurt anything, and you can use our shower."

In less than fifteen minutes we were hoofing it across the road to Bill McKinney's place. After Della was unharnessed, I hosed her and Spot down. The dirt flowed off both of them in brown ripples. But after I tethered her, the first thing Della did was drop down and roll in the only patch of dirt in that part of the yard. When she rolled, Della moaned like some people do at the peak of their private pleasures with perfect partners. For Della, a good roll was always better than sex.

We pitched our tent in Bill's front yard, then went into his air-conditioned home to take showers. Anything wet poured over my body would have felt luxurious. When I hosed off Della and Spot, I nearly turned the nozzle on me. But I knew a real shower was coming up, and Bill's was heavenly. It had a massive head that created a rain effect that really did wash away the day.

Bill also invited us to dinner. He grilled huge pork chops, while his wife, Barbara, laid the table with homegrown tomatoes and the best dirty rice ever. And for dessert, she made a pineapple upside down cake. What a refreshing meal!

After dinner, in the glow of the McKinney's porch light, Patricia and I walked to our tent. Halfway there, my bride slipped her arm around my waist and said, "Well, you were right."

"About what?"

"About having faith that there was a treat up ahead. This has really been lovely! What nice people. What a wonderful meal."

"What a great shower!"

Then my wife whispered, "So what's for dessert?"

When I looked down at her, Patricia's dimly lit face had a feisty grin between her rounded cheeks. She turned and wrapped her other arm around my waist. Then, snuggling her voluptuous breast against me, she said, "After all, it's still my honeymoon, right?"

Now I remember why I wanted more than just a mule on the road.

⊣⊟⊢

Bill McKinney didn't have a stroke. He was a victim of agent orange from the Vietnam war. The contortions to his face were the result of the many surgeries to rid him of cancer caused by the defoliant. After his last operation at the Veteran's Hospital, Bill could not close his left eye. Doctors at the VA told him there was nothing they could do about it.

"I've gone through a lot of tough things in my life. But none of it was as bad as trying to sleep with one eye open. It was hell!"

Bill fought in Vietnam twice. The second time as part of special forces. He was married when he went in, and had a couple of kids by the time he got out. "When I came home, I was no picnic to live with. Then, just as I was about to get my head straightened out, the tumors started popping up. When they told me it was cancer, I slipped into a whole new kind of hell. Every time they cut on me, it got worse. Finally, my wife had enough. She took the kids and moved out. How could you blame her? I was nuts, and getting worse every day." Pointing to his face he said, "And who wants to be married to this puss?"

If the right side of Bill's face was any indication, he had been a handsome man with sharp features that complimented his tall straight physique. Although life had taken its toll on him, everything about Bill had a prodigious feel to it. The way he shook my hand, how he carried himself and the way the right side of his face lit up when he smiled—it all resonated strength.

Bill told us about the cancer during breakfast the next morning at his favorite café. The moment we walked in, it was obvious he was popular. Nearly everyone in the place greeted him. He brought his own cup. It had a lid with a spout so he could drink coffee without spilling it. At one point, he set the cup on the table and said, "When I was down and out, a lot of these folks came over and helped me. Barbara waited tables here then. Eventually she moved in to take care of me."

Bill paused for a moment as the right side of his mouth curled into a grin. "You know, she's young enough to be my daughter. When we got married, lots of tongues were wagging. But I didn't care. She was there for me when I really needed someone. It wasn't easy for her. I couldn't sleep—I was up and down all night. We tried a patch over the eye, I took sleeping pills and none of it worked. It was wearing me out."

A waitress came to our table and poured us more coffee. Bill snapped the lid back on his cup and said, "I've never been much of a church-goer, but Barbara is. Don't get me wrong, she's no bible-thumper, or anything like that. But she does a lot of praying. She kept telling me she had faith that it was all going to work out."

He took a drink from his cup, wiped his mouth with a napkin, then laughed. "In those days, I didn't have faith in much of nothing. But she said she had enough for both of us and kept praying for me. I guess it worked."

After a year of not being able to close his eye, they found a plastic surgeon who said he could fix it. But it would be an expensive procedure that entailed putting gold leaf in Bill's eyelid. The Veteran's Administration said they wouldn't pay because it was cosmetic surgery.

"When they told me that, I lost it. Good thing they told me over the phone. I could have killed them." Bill laughed. "I told them, 'You think I want to close my eye so I'll look pretty?'" Bill sighed, "I just wanted to sleep and dream like everybody else."

When the surgeon heard the VA's decision, he told Bill if he would pay for the materials, he'd do the operation for free. Now Bill can sleep and dream.

⁂

A couple of days later, as we walked alongside a road near Romance, Arkansas, five dogs ran from behind a farm house, stopped in the yard and watched us for a few moments. The gaggle included a Rottweiler, an Irish Setter and three smaller mutts. Suddenly, as if on cue, the five charged across the lawn in our direction. The intensity of their approach, and the timbre of their barking was ferocious. This was no social call. They were on the attack!

Patricia yelled. "They're coming for Spot!"

She had been walking with him on the leash a few yards behind the cart. Now they were running to catch up, but the pack surrounded them before they got to us. Everyone's hackles were up as they growled and gnashed their teeth.

Patricia screamed. "No! Get out of here!"

Just as she bent down to scoop up a handful of gravel, the Irish Setter charged. But before he got to Spot, my wife peppered his face with stones. He yelped and ran back to the rest of the pack.

I locked the brake on the cart and grabbed a rock from the ditch. Patricia had just picked up more ammunition when the Rottweiler lunged toward her. My rock ricocheted off the ground and up into his jaw as Patricia's gravel rained down on his face. We both yelled. "Get out of here!"

The massive black and tan dog turned, bared his teeth and growled as he stalked toward me. I grabbed our ax off the cart and ran at him swinging it. "Come on, you bastard!"

Patricia went on the offensive throwing several fists full of gravel at him and the rest of the pack. In unison they all–including the Rottweiler–turned tail and ran back into their yard.

Later that night, in the tent, my wife said, "That was real scary. They weren't after us or Della. They wanted Spot."

Spot's head was on Patricia's lap and she was petting it. "I love Spotty, but I'm afraid he's going to get killed."

"Or get one of us killed trying to save him."

In the past three weeks, Spot had been run over by the cart, darted out in front of numerous cars, and every chance he got, he'd take off to explore. Now the local dogs wanted to gang-up on him.

Patricia said, "That pack really frightened me today."

"What do you want to do about it?"

Patricia was slow but sure in her reply. "I think we ought to call Suzanne and ask her to come get him. You know how she loves Spot."

Everybody loved Spot. Over a year ago when he wandered into our yard as a stray pup, it was obvious from day one that he was a special hound. Within a week he learned to heel, sit and stay on voice command. "Come" was a different story. He learned it just as fast as the other commands, but he wasn't always obliging. Every time we called him, he would pause a few moments to think it over. It was as if he was trying to remember if there was something else he needed to do. Those times when he chose to go the other way, it wasn't like he was trying to get away from us. Spot just had something else he wanted to do. Aside from that, he was a smart loveable hound who loved to chase thrown sticks.

We had several friends tell us that if we ever decided to get rid of Spot, they wanted him. But our friend Suzanne, and her husband Dr. Paul Tucker, had the best situation. A secluded wooded estate adjacent to a national park. He would have room to roam and a swimming pool.

I could hear tears in my wife's voice. "I love Spotty, and I'll miss him. But I don't want to see him killed on the highway."

Four days later Suzanne and her nephew drove her motor home to Rosebud, Arkansas, to pick up Spot. They left with him about an hour before sundown. We had rendezvoused on the outskirts of town at a place that was being developed for new homes.

After Suzanne drove off with Spot, Patricia and I silently went about our usual evening tasks setting up camp. I took the gear down from the top of the cart, and we pitched the tent together. Then Patricia went in and pumped up the air bed, while I tended to Della. After we finished those chores, I set up our camp chairs, and we relaxed with a couple of the cold beers that Suzanne had brought us.

Conversation was minimal. Mainly about the gossip Suzanne brought from Hot Springs. But we didn't talk about what was on the forefront of both our minds. Spot's absence loomed over our camp like a cloud on the verge of deluge.

Shortly after sunset, Patricia said, "I'm pooped. Think I'll turn in." Then she kissed me on the forehead and climbed into the tent.

She usually went to bed before me, but Spot always retired before any of us. He would whine at the tent door until we let him in. Then he'd curl up on his blanket at the foot of our bed. When Patricia crawled in, she'd always chatter at Spot while she changed into her nighty. I always knew when she was under the covers, because the last thing I heard was "Good night Spotty. Your mama loves you."

This night, on the edge of Rosebud, the only sound from the tent was the rustle of clothes being changed. Then a soft, "I love you honey. Good night"

I couldn't stand it. She was hurting. Immediately I unzipped the door and laid down beside her. Patricia cuddled against me, as I said, "Baby, I think—"

She put her index finger to my lips and whispered, "It's alright. We did the right thing. He has a great life ahead of him and so do we."

A few minutes later she softly called out, "Good night Della, I love you. Good night Spotty. We will always love you."

⁂

The next morning, we biked to the Jim Dandy Convenience Store and Restaurant for breakfast. We had just finished ordering our meal when a petite woman, who looked to be in her mid seventies, walked up to our table.

"Are you the people traveling with the mule?"

Her name was Ruth, and she worked in the Jim Dandy kitchen. She wore casual blue slacks and a pink flowery blouse. Although she was delicate, there was nothing frail about this white-haired lady. Her voice was strong as she asked the usual questions of where we were going and why.

Then she said, "My husband always wanted to sail around the world. He talked about it on our first date."

A blush lit up her wrinkled face, and her eyes began to twinkle. "That's what attracted me to him. He had this wonderful sense of adventure that the other boys didn't have. Everybody made fun of his wanting to sail around the world. They said it was crazy talk, but I thought it was romantic–I never told anyone. They'd have made fun of me, too."

She paused for a moment and clinched her hands together in front of her. Then, as if embarrassed, said, "I'm sorry. I got carried away. I'm sure you're not interested in this."

When she turned to leave, Patricia reached over and grabbed her arm. "No, please don't go. We *are* interested."

"You are?"

Still holding onto her, Patricia scooted over so there was room for Ruth in the booth. "Please, sit and tell us about it."

She hesitated, then slid in next to my wife. "You really want to hear this?"

In unison we said, "Yes."

Ruth paused a moment, then said, "Well, when he proposed to me he asked if I would sail around the world with him. I think he was surprised when I immediately said yes. I had heard him talk about it so much, I already had it in my mind that I was going with him. Anyway, we decided that after we got married we would both work for a few years, save our money, buy a boat and do it before we had children."

Ruth folded her hands on the table in front of her and let out a sigh. "Then the war broke out and he had to go. When he was over there, in nearly every letter, he'd write something about the trip. He figured we'd do it a couple of years after he got back. But after he came home I got pregnant–twice. So then we decided we'd do it after the kids were grown. And then it was going to be when we retired."

She shook her head. "But the plant where he worked shut down before he could retire. When they gave him his severance check, he said 'Now's the time to do it!' But I had a good job. If I'd quit then, I would have lost my retirement and everything else I'd built up. Still, he insisted it was time to go."

While she was talking, Ruth had been looking down at her folded hands on the table. But then she stopped and looked up across the table at me with a sadness that accentuated every crease in her face. "I hated him going off without me. But I couldn't stand in the way of his dream. So we bought a twenty-seven foot sailboat and off he went."

Ruth paused and looked up at the ceiling. She was obviously fighting tears. Patricia put her hand on top of Ruth's, then tenderly asked, "Did he make it around the world?"

Her head began to nod, then she slowly turned toward Patricia with a big smile and a voice full of pride. "Oh yes! It took over two years, but he made it. A couple of times I joined him for a week or so."

Right then Ruth crossed her arms like she was hugging herself. She had the same twinkle in her eyes that she had when she talked about them being sweethearts. "But the best part was when I got to sail with him for two months. It was at the end of the trip. Just the two of us, alone on the ocean. Those were the best two months of my life!"

Someone yelled, "Ruth, they need you in the kitchen!"

She slid out of the booth, then turned and touched both of us on our arms. Tears were rolling down her cheeks when she said, "Oh, you two, I'm so proud of you. Stick with it! Do it *now* while you can. My husband died of cancer two years after he got home. I thank God he got to do it. It was the best part of both our lives."

Della—the heart and motor

CHAPTER 3

DELLA IN THE DELTA

FROM THE OZARK PLATEAU, ARKANSAS Highway 157 twisted down into the bottom lands of the White River. It was so steep that Patricia had to ride in the cart and operate the brake as the upland forests gave way to rice and soybean fields. Flat lands flooded by pumps drawing massive amounts of water up to the surface from the aquifer. In some fields, water flowed across the top of the ground guided by furrows that farmers had fashioned out of dirt. Water gushed from the open portals of metal pumps that looked like the nose of a missile poking up from the ground. In other fields, long pipes–some more than a quarter of a mile long–spanned out horizontally above the crops. Supported by metal legs on wheels, the pipes pivoted from a pump in the middle of the field. On top of the pipes were sprinklers that spewed and spit water across the plants. In the bottoms, in the summer, there's always the sound of pumps.

Another prevailing sound in the bottoms was the whine of mosquitos. They attacked Patricia first because she was sitting still in the cart. Then, when I stopped walking, if even for a moment, they'd swarm me. The sun was about to slip toward dusk, and we'd been told many times, in the bottoms mosquitos rule the night.

Oil Trough was the first town we came to–population 200. A couple of times on our way there we'd been warned that it was a town of rogues. "Don't stop in Oil Trough. They'll rob you blind."

It was next to the White River and called "Oil Trough" because in the 1800s bears were rendered there for their oil. Back then, the town had a bar that featured bear wrestling on Saturday night. In 2001, when we were there, Oil Trough had a couple of farm businesses, a café, a grocery store, an elementary school and about half a dozen churches—but no bears. And because it was a dry county, no bars either.

When we walked into Oil Trough the sun was low and those warnings about this town of rogues were ringing in our heads. It didn't sound like a good place to spend the night. But we hadn't come across a suitable spot to camp before we got there.

The Oil Trough Store was an old wooden building with four steps that led to the front porch. It had a steep pitched roof and the whole thing leaned toward the river. In the one-hundred years since it opened, the store had two presidents pass through its door. But neither Bill Clinton nor Jimmy Carter were in office when they were there.

The moment we pulled into the store's gravel parking lot, we were surrounded by people. A reporter for the Batesville newspaper had interviewed us the night before. They deliver *The Batesville Daily Guard* to Oil Trough in the middle of the afternoon. So a lot of the local folks had just read about us before we arrived. Many brought copies of the story for us to autograph. Some brought produce from their gardens. We ended up with so many tomatoes in Oil Trough, we had to give some away farther up the road. And because the story mentioned that our trip was financed by the sales of my poetry books, we sold a few in the parking lot. The atmosphere in front of the Oil Trough Store was so festive, it felt like we'd brought the circus to town. I performed a couple of poems for the group.

That night we slept in the fellowship hall of the Methodist church. They told us to make ourselves at home. "Help yourselves to anything in the refrigerator."

While I fed Della in the church yard, a man told me a great mule story: One of the guys he worked with had a garden mule that he used in the fall to haul firewood in a wagon. This mule was a good worker, but when it decided it was time to quit, that was it. The mule wouldn't move again until it was unhitched.

One autumn day, this man and some of his friends were cutting firewood, and on the last load of the day when owner told the mule to "Get up!" it refused. The man coaxed, cursed and then beat the mule to get it to move. But it wouldn't budge. One of the other woodcutters said, "When the old army mules balked, they'd start a fire on the ground under its belly to get it moving."

So the owner of the mule did that and it worked. The mule pulled the wagon about three feet. Then he stopped, with the wagon directly over the fire. The mule didn't move until they unhitched it from the flaming wagon.

⊰⧉⊱

Next morning, while we ate breakfast at the Oil Trough Café, some of the customers and the waitress treated us to lots of great stories about the town. And one of the customers insisted on paying for our meal. When we walked out, Patricia said, "So they'll rob you blind in Oil Trough, eh?"

From Oil Trough, we took Highway 14 east along the White River. On our right were endless plains of rice and soybeans that, in some places, stretched beyond the horizon. Occasionally we would see farm buildings or a house, but they were few and far between. About six miles east of Oil Trough, in front of one of those rare roadside homes, I heard a thud and the cart skidded to a stop. Della backed up a step, then lunged into the harness. But the cart only moved a little, with the sound of skidding from the rear. When I walked to the back of the cart, I found that the right rear wheel had struck an old telephone pole that was lying in tall grass next to the road. The impact broke a weld that held the wheel in place. So now it was cocked and skidded sideways instead of rolling. Della couldn't pull the cart with the wheel like that, and we were blocking the east bound lane of the highway.

Patricia asked, "What are we going to do?"

"Well, first we've got to get out of the road."

The wheel was still attached, and I was able to kick it back into place so it could roll. On the front porch of the house a woman was talking on a phone, and she said we could pull into her yard. So Patricia led Della, while I walked beside the cart constantly kicking the wheel into position so it could roll.

After we got off the road, the woman on the porch held up her phone and said, "Do you need to call someone?"

What we needed was a welder. In Oil Trough, several people gave us their phone numbers and told us to call if we had any trouble. So Patricia called the Oil Trough Store, and within thirty minutes six pickups were parked around us, and Stan Haigwood was under the cart welding the wheel back into place. During this whole affair, people came and went exchanging handshakes and backslaps. There was plenty of, "How you doing?" and "I ain't seen you in ages!" and "Did you hear about such and such?" Our little disaster had turned into the Saturday social event of Independence County.

Stan was in his late twenties, and built like someone who might ride bucking broncos in a rodeo. When he crawled out from under the cart, he pulled off his welding mask and wiped sweat off his forehead. "This is only a temporary fix. Our shop is two miles down the highway. When you get there, we'll jack it up and fix it right."

"What's this going to cost me?"

"Nothing. If you find someone in need, just pass on the favor."

Stan was the youngest of three brothers who farmed 7,200 acres of rice, soybeans, and corn. It takes lots of big equipment to run an operation like that. You also need a big shop to repair and store those machines. A 747 jet could have parked in theirs.

It took Stan three hours to fix the cart. Not only did he reinforce the problem wheel, he strengthened the other wheel welds and beefed up the suspension. When he finished, it was close to sundown, and the forecast was for a stormy night with a tornado watch. So they invited us to camp in their shop office, while a neighbor let us stake Della in a sheltered part of her yard.

That portion of Arkansas was known as "Tornado Alley." In those parts, nearly every home had a storm cellar. With new construction, they usually pour the concrete for the cellar at the same time they pour the foundation for the house. It seemed like most of the stories we heard around there had something to do with a tornado of a particular year.

Like the tornado of 1962 that tore up Oil Trough. A local woman got sucked up into the vortex and was conscious as it whirled her around with the rest of the debris. While in the cloud, she collided with a bull that was wrapped in barbed wire. After the storm, both the woman and the bull were found in a farmer's field. The bull died, but the woman lived to tell the story.

In 1995 a twister completely destroyed the Haigwood farm. Barns, silos and the three houses on the property—everything was demolished. Stan's wife, and five family members, took shelter in the middle hallway of their brick home. Not only did the tornado blow away all but one corner of the house, it literally sucked the carpet out from under the people kneeling on it. No one was seriously hurt.

With the help of family, friends and neighbors, the Haigwood's completely rebuilt their farm. Three years later they were voted Arkansas's "Farm Family of The Year."

After repairs to the cart were finished, everyone went home. So Patricia and I were alone at the shop when the wind began to pick up from the southwest. Sunset was shaded by a sullen sky with ashen colored clouds that boiled up into huge dark thunder heads. Within minutes, the wind turned into a gale that rattled the metal building and wailed through power lines. Ugly clouds churned toward us with gray and silver festoons that twisted up and down. The air was wild with the scent of storm.

In the shop doorway, as I watched all this turbulence, I couldn't help but wonder about those who had narrowly survived all those past tornados. What must they be thinking and praying at that moment?

Suddenly, jagged lightning bolts ripped in all directions as thunder cracked, boomed and reverberated throughout the heavens. Then the wind began to howl as if it was in pain.

In the 1970s, when I walked across America with my pack pony and dog, I was struck by lightning. It's not something I want to go through again. So we closed the shop door as fat rain drops pelted the sheet metal. Quickly it turned into a downpour that vibrated the entire building. The steel roof sounded like it had a thousand buffalo stampeding across it.

Eventually the storm settled into a steady pitter-patter. The prayers of the farmers were being answered. Soon, we all fell asleep to the sounds of a sweet summer shower.

⌐⊟⊟¬

Today in the bottoms—across the Delta—farming is king. But it hasn't always been that way. The Delta used to be a vast forest growing in a swamp that stretched west from the Mississippi River to the Ozark Mountains. It was more than a hundred miles wide, with trees so big around that it took a family of four to hug one. In some places the oak, cypress and other hardwoods were so dense their canopy kept sunlight from reaching the ground.

The first white men to harvest the Delta were loggers who waded through snake infested mire with cross-cut saws and axes. Back then, because it was so shaded, mosquitoes ruled both night and day. To fend them off, the timber companies usually had a barge with a man who tended a fire to keep the sawyers and logging mules engulfed in smoke. As for the water moccasins, the loggers and mules were on their own.

By the 1890s, most of the timber had been cut down and hauled away. Left behind was perpetually soggy ground, but under that water was soil that had been enriched by centuries of decay. So they dug trenches and built dikes that drained the swamp to make way for farms. Today there are drainage canals all across the Delta. And every highway is bordered by deep ditches that always seem to have water in them.

The Delta is so flat, that some highways go for miles before they curve. It was on one of those straightaways that two motorcycles stopped in the other lane about sixty yards ahead of us. Traffic was so light, that whenever

44

we saw a speck on the horizon, we would guess out loud what was approaching. Patricia was the first to figure out that this speck was motorcycles. Now as they idled in the southbound lane, she asked, "What do you suppose they're up to?"

"Probably want to visit with us."

Those words were barely out of my mouth when the engines revved and both bikes charged in our direction. One was a crotch-rocket that was reared up on its back wheel in our lane headed straight for us. With the deep ditch to our right and the other bike charging down the southbound lane, we had nowhere to go.

Patricia screamed. "Oh my God!"

The crotch-rocket roared to within twenty feet of us, then its front wheel came back down onto the pavement. Both tires squealed as the bike leaned to its right and swerved. The noise drowned the driver's sinister laugh, but as the bike screamed by I could see it on his face. Smoke from skidding tires and exhaust engulfed us as both bikes sped away.

My wife yelled, "Ass-hole!"

I was outraged, too. "Shit-heads!"

Of the three of us, Della was the least shaken. A few minutes later the bikes screamed by from the rear and cut in front of us as close as they could. Again, Della could not have cared less, but Patricia and I were really shook up.

She said, "I wish I'd had a handful of rocks."

"Where's a cop when you really need one?"

My wife vowed, "If they come back I'm really going to let them have it!"

We never saw them again. Patricia didn't get to "Let them have it!" And Della just kept plodding along.

Not many things bothered Della. Not traffic, sirens, horns or speeding trains. But fake yard geese–the plastic kind you see on front lawns–they really got to her. When she saw one, Della would snort, pick up her pace and try to veer out into the road to get away from them. Real geese didn't bother her. Just the fake ones.

But what upset her the most was road-kill. Deer were the worst. Most of the time Della knew we were coming to one long before we spotted it. She'd pick up the pace, her ears would be aimed straight ahead and she'd start to shake. If the carcass was close to the road, the Big Sis would pause and just stare at it for a few moments—as if paying tribute. Then with quick steps, she'd give it a wide birth and drag us away. One time, we came to a dead fawn that was so young it had spots. I thought we'd never get Della past it.

And we kept discovering new things that she liked. Little kids fascinated her. When they came up to her, Della would bend her head down so they could pet her face. A face that often was bigger than the child petting it. And she adored babes in arms. When a mother holding one was near, Della would stretch her neck so she could smell the baby.

But her favorite thing was vanilla ice cream cones from Dairy Queen. Della's big flapping mule lips and long slurping tongue would send geysers of white cream spewing out all sides of her mouth. If you were the one holding the cone, you did so at arms length. We soon learned to have water and a rag handy to clean ourselves and Della. A few times we took her through the drive-up window. By the time we got to southern Indiana, Della had come to recognize the Dairy Queen sign, and she was always ready to stop.

Then west of Jonesboro, Arkansas, Della saw her first marching band and has been a fan ever since. We had pitched our tent in a small roadside picnic area across the highway from Westside School. It was late in the afternoon of August 2nd, and I was gathering wood for our dinner fire, when the band members began to amble onto the football field. Patricia had just set up our cook stove when the first trumpet played a few scales. Della's head bolted up from grazing and she whirled around to face the school yard. Then a flutist shrilled through a set of notes. The Big Sis strutted in that direction until she came to the end of her rope. Then there was a toot or two on the tuba, thumps on a base drum and other assorted sounds in un-orchestrated warm-up. Della was all ears, and they were pointed that way. A large clump of grass hung out the side of her mouth, but she wasn't chewing.

Then someone blew a whistle and all of the sounds stopped. Still staring that way, Della started to chew. But a couple of minutes later a whistle blew four times, followed by the crash of cymbals, a roll of the drums, then the band began to play and march across the field. Majorettes were out in front twirling batons and flags, as the afternoon sun reflected off the tubas twisting back and forth in unison at the rear of the band. Della was mesmerized. For the half hour they were on the field, she never took her eyes off them. She just stood there with that same clump of grass dangling from her mouth. After the band quit, she just stood and watched as they wandered off the field. She didn't start chewing until the last band member had disappeared. Then she simply went back to grazing. But every once in a while, Della would stop and stare in that direction. It was as if she were wishing they would come back.

⇥⇤

Before the swamps were drained, all the towns in the Delta were built on high ground. In the Arkansas Delta, the highest spot was Crowley's Ridge. A narrow range of hills that runs 150 miles south from the Missouri border down to Helena, Arkansas—the home of the Delta Blues.

One of the oldest and largest towns in the Arkansas Delta is Jonesboro. In 1859, it was settled high and dry on Crowley's Ridge. Like the other older towns, it was originally a logging camp. But today, farming drives the economy of this city of 55,000. At a distance, the Jonesboro skyline looked like a metropolis—complete with skyscrapers. But they turned out to be huge grain elevators. The tallest belonged to Riceland Foods.

Although they cut down all the trees in the flat lands, they didn't up on Crowley's Ridge. So after a week of sweltering across the unshaded Delta, it sure felt great to be among trees again. It was just as hot in the hills as it was down in the bottoms, but at least the hills had spots to rest in the shade.

Jonesboro was our first big town. That Friday afternoon it was hot and sticky as we walked along Highland Drive toward the county fairgrounds. Rush hour was in full swing, so we were walking in heavy stop-and-go traffic. The exhaust and the heat that reflected up from the pavement was stifling. Still, it was a grand experience as horns happily honked, and people with smiles waved and gave us thumbs up. Several times I heard "Good Luck!" yelled at us from open car windows. It felt like we were in a parade.

With the rest of the traffic, we were at a standstill on Highland Drive near Caraway Road, when the passenger window of the car to my left rolled down. A woman with long blond hair, who could have been on the cover of *Cosmopolitan,* was in that seat with a pretty pink smile across her face. I didn't notice the man behind the steering wheel until he said, "Hey, we saw you on the news the other night."

Channel 8 interviewed us down in the Delta a couple of days before we got to Jonesboro. I replied, "How did we look?"

"Great! This is a wonderful thing you're doing!"

Then he pulled something out of his shirt pocket and handed it to the woman. "Here take that. It's just a little something to help you get down the road."

She handed me a twenty dollar bill as the man said, "Buy the donkey a sandwich."

I was thanking them when the traffic began to move. Their car was pulling away when the woman winked and said, "You look good in person, too. Good luck."

⊰⊱

We spent a week in Jonesboro at the home of my friend Bob Wallace. I met Bob through his daughter Ginna. She was on a team with me that represented Hot Springs at the 1999 National Poetry Slam in Chicago. Ginna was a minor then, and because some of the venues were bars, she had to have a parent or a guardian with her. So her father came along. And after that week in Chicago, I felt I'd found a new friend.

While in Jonesboro we put on a show at Uncommon Blends. It was a coffee house on Main Street that had opened only two weeks earlier–this was their first event. More than thirty people showed up, and half a dozen participated in the open mic session. Ginna was one of them. She kept a weekly reading going there for more than a year after that.

North of Jonesboro, we spent three days camped at Crowley's Ridge State Park. The forecast was for temperatures near a hundred and five. Our shady campsite was near a spring fed lake, which was a great retreat from the heat. But there was no escaping the bugs. At night the mosquitoes were as bad as down on the Delta, and during the day the horseflies were horrendous. They didn't bother Patricia and me very much, but poor Della. Some of those flies were almost as big as hummingbirds. Patricia called them "B-52s." And bug spray didn't faze them. Even when we sprayed it on their bodies, they'd just fly off, make a circle, come back and land on Della. Then the blood would start to ooze.

The horseflies were worse just before sunset. That's when they'd swarm her, and the only way we could help was to kill them with our hands. Let the bastards land and smash them before they could bite. Patricia and I took turns smacking Della's flies. And when your turn was up, the first thing you'd do was go to the hydrant and wash the blood off hands and forearms. We soon learned it was best to hit them with the center of our palms. That kept the blood from spraying up between our fingers and into our face.

Della quickly got used to the nightly fly-smacking. She would stand completely still and not even flinch as we flailed away. She actually seemed to enjoy it. For Patricia and me, it turned into a contest to see who could kill the most in one smack. Patricia was the champion. She got three with one blow.

One evening, while I was smashing flies on Della, I couldn't help but wonder about the horses out in the pastures around there. The ones who didn't have someone to smack their flies. They must dread summer sunsets.

❦

When I was a kid on vacation and riding in the back seat of our family car, every time we crossed a state line it felt like such a big deal. It seemed to me that we should have stopped at each one and commemorated the occasion. But I knew that idea wouldn't fly. So I simply celebrated those state lines in my own mind.

The St. Francis River separates Arkansas from the Missouri Boot Heel. I was standing at the Arkansas end of the bridge when I started to feel that same old state line excitement. Patricia was excited too. "Honey, I can't believe it. We're finally leaving Arkansas."

These may be the <u>United</u> States of America, but they are all very different. The contrasts are often obvious the moment you cross the state line. When we crossed the river into Missouri, we found the Delta to be just as flat as it was in Arkansas. But the dirt was redder, and the highway shoulders were much wider than in Arkansas, which made walking a lot easier. But the roadsides in both states had one thing in common—litter. Both had plenty.

August in the Show-Me-State was as hot as it had been in Arkansas. The day we walked up Highway 25 through Malden the temperature was near 100 and so was the humidity. North of Malden, the surface of the highway had been ground off to prepare for re-paving. The road was rough and rutted, and in some places, only half of our lane had been ground off. So we had to walk with one foot on a surface that was two inches higher than the other. We stumbled along that way for nearly ten miles as traffic flew past us churning up grit that landed on our sweaty bodies. And because there was no wind to blow it away, the exhaust hung above the road in a suffocating haze.

We walked nearly twenty miles that day before finding a place to camp. It was a wide spot where a county dirt road intersected Missouri Highway 25. On that spot were huge mounds of pavement that had been ground off the highway—mounds that would eventually be melted to make a smooth new road surface. This place didn't have much grass for Della and barely enough room for our camp. But it was late, and down in the Delta we needed to be in the tent before the sun touched the horizon. Because—as you know—after dark mosquitoes rule.

"You left the pee jar in the cart?" Patricia was outraged. "Now what?"

"I'll just have to go out and get it."

My wife was exasperated. "As soon as you unzip that door, half of the mosquitoes in the Delta will fill this tent. They can't wait to get in here!"

"So what do you want me to do?"

"I have an idea."

Then she started rummaging through the stuff next to her side of the bed. Suddenly with a flourish she pulled out a can of Raid and said, "I'll count to three, you hold your breath, unzip the door, go out and zip it back up. Don't breathe until you get away from the tent."

"What are you going to do?"

"I'm going to cover you with this." She shook the spray can at me. "When you come back we'll do the same thing. Out there, you're on your own, buddy-boy!"

"Oh great."

Patricia snickered, "Hey, you're the one who forgot the pee jar."

Across the highway, about 150 feet from our tent, were two sets of railroad tracks with a crossing for a county road. Every locomotive blew its whistle several times as it approached. That night, at least once an hour, a train would barrel down the tracks.

"I'll never forget *this* campsite." My wife smacked a mosquito on her face. "Got ch'ya, you little bugger!"

⊰⊱

Patricia said, "I'm not sure we should do this."

From where we stood on top of the levee at Tootsie's Landing, the Hickman Ferry looked like a toy in the churning brown Mississippi River. It was the only ferry still crossing the river, and we had just walked forty-two miles out of our way, down the Missouri Bootheel, to ride it.

"It's so small," my wife said. "What if Della freaks out and jumps off?"

The ferry was a small barge with a steel parking deck that had a tug-boat attached to the downstream side. It had a low railing on the sides and chains across both ends. If Della freaked out and bolted, she could easily go overboard. I shared Patricia's trepidation.

She said, "I'll stay up here with Della, you go down and check it out."

Right then, a man in an orange life jacket stepped out of the tugboat onto the deck of the ferry and motioned for us to come down. That's all I needed. "Let's go."

Patricia yelled, "Wait a minute!"

"For what?"

Her voice wavered. "Well, I just think we need to check this out first."

"If we don't cross here what are we going to do?"

Patricia looked down at the ferry, then turned back to me. "It looks scary."

"It's just part of the adventure. Let's go! Get in and work the brake."

My wife grumbled as she climbed into the cab of the cart. "It's just part of the adventure. You and your 'It's just part of the adventure.'"

The ramp down the levee to the river was concrete with ridges that ran perpendicular to the hill to give vehicles traction. With the tungsten-carbide cleats on Della's shoes, and the concrete ridges, she had good footing. But there was loose sand on the surface that made the cart's tires skid when Patricia applied the brake. So Della's butt was hunkered down in the harness as she struggled to hold the load back. But our big girl had traction, so it all went well.

That is, until she stepped onto the ferry's steel ramp. Then all traction was gone. The deck sounded like a stage full of tap dancers as her hooves scrambled for purchase on the smooth steel. I was scared that at any moment she would fall down. But within seconds she got her footing and we were standing solid in the middle of the ferry. Della was shaking, and so was I. From inside the cart, Patricia clapped and cheered. "What a good girl! That's my girlie pie!"

The deck hand was raising the ferry ramp as I locked the brake and blocked the cart wheels. I asked, "Are we the only ones going across?"

"Yep. We've been expecting you. The captain said he'll take it slow so we don't scare your mule."

The diesel engine on the tug revved up, black smoke swirled above the river and the barge slowly began to move. Della took a couple of nervous steps to the left as she turned her head to look at the tug. The stern of the boat swung away from the barge churning up a wake of frothy brown water. While the tug turned around to face Kentucky, I could feel Della tense up—her legs were quivering.

I stroked her neck. "It's all right, Big Sis."

After the stern of the tug was secured to the side of the barge, we slowly sailed away from Missouri. That's when Della began to relax. Soon she was looking up and down the river sightseeing. On her face I saw the same fascination she had for the marching band. But instead of music and twirling majorettes, it was boats in the roiling brown current that enthralled her. Several tugs pushing barges came close because our captain got on the radio and said, "Wait till you see what I've got on board." Then reading from our flyer, he told them about us.

At one point—mid-river—the ferry slowed so a parade of them could pass in front of us. Every one of them blew their horns with all hands on deck waving and shouting. We couldn't understand them, but it was obvious Della was a hit with the river folk.

For that half hour on the Hickman Ferry, Della was Queen of the Mississippi.

CHAPTER 4

THE STATE OF AMERICA IN KENTUCKY

⟨❧⟩

IN KENTUCKY, THINGS WERE DIFFERENT. Instead of the plainness of the Delta, there were rolling hills with oaks, elms and hickories–some of which shaded the road. And as we trekked through Kentucky's farm land, we started seeing a crop that we hadn't seen before–tobacco. Big green broad-leaf plants that were being cut down at ground level with machetes, then hauled to a barn and hung to dry Whether the barns were wood or metal, they all had their doors open so fresh air could circulate through the hanging plants. When the wind was right, we could smell a tobacco barn long before we got to it. It's a fragrance like no other. Although I'm not a smoker, I've always found the aroma of non-burning tobacco pleasing. Especially when it's in clean country air.

Back in the Delta, we didn't see many people out in the fields, because crops like corn, soybeans, rice and cotton were planted, cultivated and harvested by machine. In places like Grubbs, Arkansas, and Morehouse, Missouri, people blamed the mechanization of farming for the demise of their little towns. A visitor to our camp in Grubbs said, "One man on a tractor can do the work of dozens of people with hoes."

But tobacco was a hands-on crop. It still had to be planted and harvested by people. And the one's we saw wielding those machetes were mostly Mexican. Short, brown-skinned men, with jet black hair, who lugged the floppy crops on their shoulders across the fields to trailers. While we walked through rural Kentucky several small green school buses, packed with Mexicans, passed us. On the driver's door was usually the name of a corporate farm. And most of those buses had brown arms stuck out their windows waving.

"That's what happened to the jobs here. The Mexicans got 'em."

James Robert invited us to camp in the vacant lot across the street from his house in Crayne, Kentucky. He was born in 1926, and lived in the same house he grew up in. When John Robert asked us to stay in his lot, it was more like he insisted. He was a pasty little man who spoke in short nervous sentences. "The Trail Of Tears wagon train camped here in 1988. You heard of it? It was the 150th anniversary. They followed the Indian's route. They camped here. You should too. It's part of history."

Crayne had a few buildings that looked like they must have had a business in them at some time. But it had been quite a while and most were boarded up. It had a couple dozen homes, some were in good repair but others were not. And there were ruins. Concrete foundations with tall weeds and saplings growing in and around them.

"It used to be different," James Robert said. "We had three stores, a hotel and a train station. But they closed the mine."

Up until the mid 1980's, Crayne had a fluorspar mine. Fluorspar was a fluorite crystal used in making steel. "Still plenty of it in the ground around here. But they found some in Mexico. So the company closed the mine here." James Robert shook his head. "Mexicans work cheaper than folks in Crayne."

The train quit coming to town in 1990. Then, the hotel shut down and eventually so did the other businesses. James Robert said, "I kept thinking they'd start running the train again. Then the town would come back." He sighed. "But they pulled up the tracks. That was two years ago. Now we're done for."

Most of the ruins in Crayne were the result of a tornado that ravaged it in 2000–a year after they pulled up the tracks.

Lots of folks paid us a visit in James Robert's lot, and nearly all of them had a story about the storm. But it was the twins, Bonnie and Connie, who really put that storm and the fate of the town in perspective.

I figured the twins to be in their late forties. They, too, had lived in Crayne all their lives, and both had worked at the same factory for thirty years. TYCO made electronic relays, and the plant was just three miles away. When the tornado hit they were at work. It was Bonnie who said, "Nearly half the families in Crayne had someone working there. We all had our faces pressed to the windows watching that storm."

Not only did the women look alike, their voices were the same. They both dripped with that honey-sweet y'all sort of accent. The kind you'd expect from a woman born and bred in Kentucky. It was Connie who said. "It was terrible. We couldn't see what was going on. All we knew was that it was coming right through here, and there was nothing we could do about it. We were stuck in that plant just watching and praying."

Bonnie said, "I swear the worst part was the drive home. Remember that?"

"Oh lord! How could I ever forget it?" Connie turned to us and said, "Y'all just can't imagine what it was like. Usually, it takes five minutes to drive home. That night it took more than four hours. So many trees and power lines were down on the highway, we couldn't go anywhere. We had to wait for them to clear the way. It took forever."

Bonnie said, "She drove me nuts. Kept trying to get out of my car and walk home."

"I'd got here faster."

"If you didn't get electrocuted." Bonnie shook her head. "When she tried to do it, the police told her to get back in the car and stay there. They had live wires down on the road and it was raining."

Connie said, "When we finally got here the whole town was dark. Just car lights and flashlights, and debris everywhere. It took forever to find my husband and kids. I never did find my house." She clapped her hands together above her head. "But praise the Lord, nobody in our family got hurt."

A few days after the tornado, TYCO announced it was going to shut down the plant and move to Mexico. "And if we wanted our severance check, we had to teach the Mexicans how to do the job." Connie sighed. "What a week that was."

When Patricia and I met the twins, they were both taking computer courses. Bonnie said, "Maybe it will help us find a job that won't get sent to some other country."

⦾

Another thing that was different about Kentucky was its highways. Most had no shoulder, and the pavement was usually less than three feet from a deep ditch. The edge of the asphalt was notched so that drivers who fell asleep would be awakened by the thumping of their tires. It was a bad situation for us. We couldn't walk on the edge of the pavement because the notches tripped human and mule feet. And when the cart wheels rolled over them it sounded like a stick being dragged across a picket fence. It jostled the cart so much I was afraid it would vibrate to pieces. With no room between the pavement and the ditch, we had to walk in the lane of traffic.

Such was the situation on the west side of Paducah when ominous clouds began to roll in. It was a Thursday, in the middle of the afternoon. That morning on the radio, they said we could have severe thunderstorms later in the day. And as fast as those thunder heads were moving, it looked like their forecast was correct. Near the intersection for the road to the Paducah airport was a wide gravel spot where we pulled off the highway. I mounted our orange rotating beacon on the back of the cart, while Patricia pulled our rain gear out. She was handing me my yellow raincoat, when simultaneous lightning and thunder exploded overhead. A heartbeat later, the sky let loose with a deluge. It was so fast and furious, that both of us were drenched before we got our slickers on. I was shoving my arms into the sleeves when I said to Patricia, "Get in the cab!"

"Why?"

The rain was so intense, I had to yell. "No sense in both of us being out in this!"

It was such a fierce rain that it hurt our faces. But Della ignored it. The traffic, thunder and lightning, none of it phased her. She just tucked her ears back and plodded through the storm. I squished along beside her in my flooded boots, saturated socks and frayed nerves. The rain intensified, and so did the traffic. Rush hour was on, and we were in the way.

When we came to a place where we could pull off the road, we did. Usually it was someone's driveway where we would stand and let the traffic behind us get by. But those places were few and far between. Each time we pulled over, it would be several minutes before we could get back out on the road.

While we stood in one of those driveways, a car stopped and the driver motioned for me to get out into the lane. Through the storm, I motioned for him to continue on. But he kept waving for me to pull out. Finally, as I saw him roll down his window, I yelled, "Go on sir. It's OK."

He stuck his head out into the storm and yelled back. "No it's not! I live here!"

A couple of driveways later, we had just gotten back into the lane, when I heard a big truck pull up behind us. As the motor babbled down into low gear, I looked to my right at the ditch. It was overflowing and sending rapids across the pavement. I couldn't see the edge of the road—or the brink of the ditch. It was all covered with water.

Suddenly, from behind us, an air horn blared. Della bolted, but she quickly settled back into her normal pace. I turned around and found an eighteen wheel dump truck one car behind us. The driver blew his horn again and wildly waved behind the windshield for us to get off the road. His mouth was moving, but through the storm I couldn't hear him. But it was obvious what he wanted. It was impossible.

So sloshing backwards, I yelled, "What am I supposed to do?"

Out the window of the truck emerged a black hand with all of its fingers—except the middle one—clenched into a fist. And it was pointed skyward and shook as he screamed something. I couldn't hear, but I got the gist. So I shook my head, turned around and continued on. From then on, it seemed like every thirty seconds the truck horn would blast. But Della and I ignored it.

Finally we came to a driveway, and got off the road. The moment we started into it, the truck's engine revved spewing black smoke out its stack. I heard gears grind. Then after two rapid blasts from its horn, the truck roared around the car behind us. When it pulled up next to me, the passenger window was down. Again, he gave me the finger as he roared. "You stupid honky! Get your ass off the fucking road!"

About half a mile from there, Highway 62 turned into a four-lane with a wide shoulder. The rain had eased into intermittent sprinkles. We were out of the traffic lane, and the storm was going away. Patricia wanted to get out and walk.

While we three strolled further into Paducah, the rain stopped, clouds parted and people seemed to get friendlier. Every couple of minutes our arms were in the air returning waves, and a few times we heard shouts of "Welcome to Paducah!" And we saw several hands with their thumbs up. What a difference a digit makes!

⧙⧘

That night, a priest at Saint Thomas Moore Catholic Church gave us permission to camp in a field near the church. Next morning, when I poked my head out of the tent, there wasn't a cloud in the sky. The air was crystal clear from the rinsing it got the day before. I fed Della, got the stove out and started a pot of coffee. In the middle of breakfast, Father Ken Mikulcik walked into our camp and announced he had come to bless Della. Earlier that morning, when we went down to the church to use the bathroom, Patricia—who is Catholic—asked the priest if he would bless the Big Sis. She didn't tell me about it. So I was surprised when Father Ken showed up with his book and holy water.

While he performed the ritual, a few clouds began to sail over us. Later, while I took down the tent, a car pulled into the church parking lot and a man with a camera got out. He was a reporter with the *Paducah Sun*. During his interview the clouds got thicker, and a breeze picked up. The sky was completely gray when the reporter closed his notebook and said, "They're calling for thunderstorms this afternoon. What do you do when it rains?"

In unison, Patricia and I said, "Get wet."

Unlike the rain the day before, this one started gradually. Initially it was just occasional drops, but by the time we reached downtown, it was a steady downpour. I didn't walk on Jackson Street, I waded in it.

Paducah was founded in 1821 at the confluence of the Tennessee and Ohio Rivers. It quickly became an important river town. Fortunes were made trading tobacco, fruit, timber and coal. The ornateness of the buildings downtown–near the Ohio River–stand as testimony to the wealth that was generated there. Paducah is a treasure-trove of 19th and early 20th century architecture. But that Friday afternoon, as we sloshed toward the river front, I was not able to appreciate it. The rain was too heavy and the traffic too intense to do more than wade on by.

It was mid-afternoon when we pulled into a parking lot across the street from the Visitors Bureau. Behind their big front windows, I saw half a dozen ladies watching us. Regardless the age or configuration of the face, they all had one thing in common–the look of confoundment. Had I been one of them, I too would have wondered, "What are those fools doing out in this storm?"

When I went in, they were the epitome of Kentucky's state slogan "It's that friendly." They brought me hot coffee and a sandwich. And when I apologized for the water flowing off my raincoat onto their floor, a sweet southern drawl said, "Oh honey, don't you worry a thing about that. A little bit of water won't hurt nothing."

We stopped at the Visitors Bureau because they were in charge of an arts program called, "After Dinner Downtown." Every Saturday night, throughout the summer and early fall, the city of Paducah blocked off part of the historic district so artists, musicians and other entertainers could set up in the street. It sounded like the perfect place for us to drop the stage and put on a poetry show.

It took nearly an hour to get the coordinator on the phone. After Tom told me we could be part of it, I asked if there was someplace close where we could camp. He said, "I've already got that taken care of. You and your wife have a room for two nights at the Executive Inn."

A hotel room? This was too good to be true. "What about my mule?"

Tom ran horse-drawn carriages in downtown Paducah. He kept them in a warehouse a few blocks from the Visitors Bureau. Next to Tom's building was a large vacant lot with a high chain-link fence around it. When we met him there he tossed me the keys to the lock on the gate and said, "Park your cart, turn your mule loose and lock it up. Ain't nobody going to mess with her or your stuff in there."

Then Tom loaded us, our plastic bag of wet clothes and our bicycles into his truck and drove us to the Executive Inn. After I unlocked the door to our room, Patricia went in ahead of me and dropped her backpack on the carpet. I was lugging our wet clothes in as she slowly turned around and surveyed the room with its two queen-size beds. While I pulled my backpack off, my wife turned toward me with a huge grin. Although we both looked like drowned rats, Patricia was glowing when she put her hands on her hips and said, "Can you believe this? We have a hotel room!"

Her voice squealed, "For two nights! Just think about that, Bud!"

She scurried into the bathroom and turned on the light. "It has a shower and a tub. I can take a bath and soak as long as I want."

Patricia was like a little kid on Christmas morning. Who could blame her? Prior to her dog grooming business, Patricia had managed a trust company in Dallas. Before that, she'd been a legal secretary, and a police officer. During those years she'd owned homes and condos with real bathrooms, and some with swanky hot tubs. But for the past three sweaty months the only thing akin to a bath that she could count on, was our coffee-can-shower. If no one invited us in for a shower, or there was no stream or pond, then we took a coffee can with nail holes in the bottom, dipped it in a bucket, and held it over our heads. The two of us could get clean–including Patricia's shoulder length hair–with five gallons of water.

She stepped over to the hotel toilet, jiggled the handle and giggled. "Just listen." Then my wife flushed it, patted the tank lid and cooed. "Isn't that something?"

Patricia scooted past me, out into the hotel room and grabbed the remote off the TV. When she clicked it on, the theme from "The Jeffersons" was playing. My wife sang along. "Moving on up to the east side. To that deluxe apartment in the sky . . . ." She turned to me with a giant grin on her face. "We get to watch TV."

She tossed the remote onto one of the beds, scooted to the picture window and pulled the drapes back. Then, with outstretched arms, she declared, "Thank you Paducah!"

⊰⊟⊱

In the historic district, near the river, there were old warehouses and market places with elaborate cornices and slate roofs. Some of the store fronts looked like they could have been part of the set for "Hello Dolly."

It was in that part of town where the After Dinner Downtown program took place. We parked the cart and dropped our stage at the corner of First Street and Broadway–next to the twenty-foot high concrete flood wall. That poetry show was different than any I had ever done. Other entertainers and artists were set up along the street like a carnival. So we were just one of the sideshows. On the other side of the flood wall from us, down near the Ohio River, was a stage for bands. So we had to compete for the attention of a roaming audience and struggle to be heard above amplified rock-and-roll. But it worked. We made a few bucks in the hat, sold some books and had a good time.

The next morning, when I pulled back the hotel drapes, not a cloud was in the sky. We had spent part of Saturday drying out our clothes in the hotel laundry. The plan was for me to load them onto my bicycle and pedal to where Della and the cart where. After I fed her and packed the cart, I would return to the hotel for breakfast. Then we'd hitch up Della and head east.

When I got to the lot, Della was on the opposite side of it lying on the ground. I called to her, but she didn't get up. She just laid there looking at me. This was not good. I trotted across the lot and knelt beside her. "What's wrong, Big Sis?"

She leaned her big head against my chest and groaned as her long soft ears twitched about my face. Her breathing was shallow and gurgling. This was not good.

I gripped her halter. "Come on, Sis. You've got to get up."

When I tried to pull her up, she just laid there and groaned. I began to panic. *What if Della ate something that poisoned her.* At one time, farm supplies had been stored on that lot, but that was more than a decade ago. Before we turned her loose, I looked the place over to make sure there was nothing that could harm her. *Maybe I missed something.*

My mind whirled with "What if's" as I wandered around looking for clues to what was wrong. I found nothing. So I went back and grabbed her halter. "Let's go, Della."

She still wouldn't stand. I dropped to my knees and wrapped my arms around her neck. When I laid my cheek against her flaxen mane, a monstrous feeling of dread enveloped every fiber of me. It had been just a little over a year since we'd lost Buck– the mule who was originally going to be our partner. That scar was still raw in my heart. I closed my eyes and the tears flowed. "No! This can't be happening again."

Back in the hotel room, when I told Patricia about Della, horror ravaged my wife. "I've got to go to her!"

We forgot about breakfast, packed the rest of our things, checked out of the hotel and pedaled to Della. To my relief, she was on her feet. When we walked across the lot to her, Della took a couple of steps toward us. She was lame. Her right front ankle was swollen. I didn't see it before because she had it tucked under her when she was down.

I was elated. Not because she was hurt. But because this was something I knew how to treat. I just needed a medication called "Bute," ice and time for her to heal.

Patricia and I rolled the cart to the center of the lot so we could set up camp. That's when we discovered why Della was lame. It was a hole, about three feet deep, that had weeds laying over the top of it. From tracks around the hole, it was evident Della had stepped into it and turned her ankle. We were lucky she didn't break her leg.

After we set up camp, I biked to a fire station a couple of blocks from the lot. I figured they could direct me to the closest place to buy ice. After I told the captain about our predicament, he said, "We've got a whole machine full of ice. Help yourself, and if you need more come back."

Bute is an anti-inflammatory. It's like a big aspirin for horses. We had a few tablets with us, but not enough. I needed to find a veterinarian to sell me some more.

When we first came to Paducah and put Della in the lot, we met the man who owned a feed and garden store half a block away. Dan Phelps told us if we needed anything for Della to let him know. So, Monday morning I went to Dan and told him what happened. He put me in touch with a veterinarian. Then he told us we could use his restrooms while we were camped in the lot. "If there's anything else I can do, let me know."

"I need a couple of bales of hay."

Dan didn't sell hay. "But I should be able to get you some by tomorrow."

Shortly after we set up camp in the lot, an eighteen-wheeler backed up to the meat packing plant across the street. It was loaded with hogs. The squeals and grunts of swine overwhelmed the neighborhood as men prodded them through the loading gate. Above the pig sounds were shouts and curses of those who prodded, counted and weighed them. With a constant percussion of pops, snaps and slaps they were herded into the plant.

Trucks came and went all hours of the day and night. Sometimes the swine sounds lasted longer than others. It depended on the size of the truck. The big rigs, with double decker trailers, delivered the longest sessions. But often the small time operators brought more intense chaos. The ones who got their pigs to climb on top of one another for the ride to slaughter. Swine on top of swine in stake-side trucks or make shift trailers.

It was all unnerving. But the worst was when the final pig was ushered into the killing parlor. You could always tell it was the last one because the noise had died down to just an occasional grunt. Then there'd be frantic squeals that crescendoed to a sharp pop. Then silence.

It was either late Monday night, or early Tuesday morning, when the diesel motor of one of the big haulers woke me. It parked adjacent to our camp and the headlights went off. Then I heard the driver's door slam, followed by footsteps in the direction of the plant.

The hogs were fairly quiet. Only an occasional grunt now and then. While I laid in the tent and waited for the turmoil, I started to think about them. The pigs. Do they have any idea that this is the end of their life? When they're prodded out of the trailer down that narrow passage, are they frantic for understanding? At the end of the passageway, where the screams are louder, does it suddenly make sense when they see the piggies ahead of them drop in the parlor?

Through the dark, I heard the truck door open, then slam shut. With a soft blast of air, the brake disengaged and I could hear the gears shift. While the truck backed toward the plant, I began to wonder about the driver. The pilot who brought those hogs to their doom. Did he ever have a sense of remorse? Does he ever wish it wasn't this way? Or did he just see it as his job. It's just what he does for his pay. In the tent, in the calm before the chaos, this vagabond's brain couldn't help but wonder about those things.

⚎

Patricia climbed out of the tent Tuesday morning and said, "What a night!" When the pigs weren't keeping me awake, I had nightmares about them. It was horrible!"

After breakfast, I strapped a water jug onto the back of my bike. Then the two of us went over to Dan's store to use his bathroom and see if he had found hay for Della. When we got to the parking lot, I spotted Dan and one of his employees inside the warehouse. So I climbed up onto the loading dock while Patricia continued toward the bathroom.

"Good morning, Dan. Did you find any hay?"

He whirled around with a scowl on his face. "No! And I can't bother with it now!"

I was shocked. He had been so hospitable and eager to help before. What had I done —or not done—to upset him? "Is something wrong?"

He snapped back, "Is something wrong?"

The employee put a hand on Dan's shoulder. "Bud probably doesn't know."

I asked, "Know what?"

Dan's expression melted into one of despair. "I'm sorry. It's been one hell of a morning. Two passenger jets crashed into the World Trade Center in New York this morning. And another one hit the Pentagon."

His employee added, "They think it's terrorists. And may not be over, yet."

I couldn't believe what I was hearing. Suddenly everything seemed sur-real. They led me to the employee break-room where a TV was on. When I saw the smoking trade towers on the screen, and listened to the commenta-tors, I came to grips with the fact that this was real. And I wasn't the only one trying to understand.

A couple of minutes later Dan escorted Patricia into the room. He obviously had been explaining to her what happened. She stopped next to me, in front of the TV, just as the first tower collapsed. While I watched it crumble, it reminded me of footage I had seen of vacant buildings being imploded. But this one was not vacant.

We watched TV for an hour, then we headed back to camp. I needed to give Della her medicine and ice down her ankle. Patricia and I were silent while we walked back to the lot. I was filling a plastic bag with ice when my wife asked, "Where's the big flag?"

When we started this journey, we had a small American flag displayed on the back of the cart. We also had a bigger flag for special occasions, like the Fourth of July. I took one of the bamboo poles that I used for the stage lights and stood it up with the big flag attached. It just seemed like the thing to do. We spent the rest of the day in the shade, under the flag, listening to the radio.

That evening, we bicycled into the heart of town to find a place with a TV. We wanted to watch President Bush address the nation. Paducah's streets were nearly devoid of traffic. The sidewalks had nobody on them, and most of the shops were closed. The restaurant/bar we chose had only a couple of customers. Everything had come to a stand still. America had been put on pause.

But there was one thing that didn't stop. The delivery and slaughter of hogs. That night while I listened to them being prodded into the slaughter house, I began to think of the people on those jet liners—the ones that hit the towers in New York. Did the hijackers tell them what they were about to do? Or did they sit in their seats bewildered and afraid? Did they know they were about to die? Or were they clueless, until the planes turned and aimed at the buildings.

And what about the hijackers? In the last moments of their mission did they have second thoughts? Or were they so filled with hatred, so consumed with their mission, so sure they were doing Allah's work that nothing else mattered?

While I laid in the tent and listened to the slaughter house, my heart was astir with anguish and anger. And like every other American, I was worried.

From across the street, I heard the squeals of the last piggy in the parlor. Then, through the dark, came that final pop. In the silence that followed,

I wondered how this day would affect us as a nation. *How will this affect us on the road?*

⊰⊱

By Friday, Della was fit to travel. So that morning we walked out of Paducah headed east on US 62. Around noon, we stopped for lunch in the parking lot of a small Baptist church on the east side of town. Patricia handed me one of our plastic plates with a turkey sandwich on it. "Have you noticed the difference?"

"What?"

"Since this terrorist thing, being on the road is a lot different."

The difference I had noticed were the flags. Before September 11th we would see an occasional red, white and blue flying on a car antenna or a yard pole. But now, every vehicle and every lawn had a flag, or several. It was like America had gone flag crazy. But Patricia and I had already discussed that. So I wasn't sure what she was talking about.

She said, "People aren't smiling and waving at us like they did before."

Patricia was more cognizant of those things than me. Sometimes I got so caught up in where we were, that I forgot about the people driving by us. But not my wife. She always watched the windshields. Many times she said to me, "Those people just waved at us, and you didn't wave back. You need to be more friendly."

In the church parking lot, she said, "You know why people aren't being as friendly as before? It's because we aren't. We've let those terrorists get to us."

I had to admit, I didn't feel the joy walking out of Paducah that I did when we walked into it. Even though our trek in town had been a soggy affair, I was still filled with the thrill of being on the road in America. But on this sunny September 14th, I felt almost numb. Probably from a combination of the attacks and five days of the slaughter house.

Patricia agreed. "But we can't let it get to us. Now, more than ever, people need to see smiling faces. The news these days is all doom and destruction. It's overwhelmed everybody. We need to rise above it. Let's be a distraction for these people. Show them someone living their dream. America needs that right now. And we're the ones to do it!"

I felt like I had just been addressed by a motivational speaker. Patricia wasn't a cheerleader in school, but right then, on the outskirts of Paducah, she was. All she needed was a set of pom-poms as she said, "Let's wave at everybody that goes by–whether they wave at us or not. If they can go overboard waving their flags, we can go overboard waving our hands. Let's do it! Let's have some fun!"

When we set up camp that night, my left arm was worn out from waving. If it takes fewer muscles to smile, then why did my cheeks ache that night? But it was worth it. As soon as we started our little "friendly crusade" people began to reciprocate. And it seemed to gain momentum through the afternoon. Soon, every car had smiling faces behind wind-shields and arms extended out windows waving, and there were thumbs-up galore.

"It sure was refreshing to see you guys walking down the highway this afternoon."

Nan Donohoo, with her teenaged son and daughter, walked into our camp just as the sun was about to touch the horizon. We were on a hill above the highway between Paducah and Possum Trot. I had just put some brown rice in our pressure cooker when they stopped to visit. Nan saw us on the road when she took her son to soccer practice. So when it was time to pick him up, her daughter came along in case she passed us again. They had seen us on TV and read our story in the newspaper. "But that was last weekend. I thought you would have been long gone by now."

After we told her about Della's ankle, Nan asked, "Is there anything we can do to help you? Can I get you anything?"

People often asked us those questions. Unless we really needed some-thing, like hay or feed for Della, our answer was usually, "No, we're fine." But for some reason, this time I said, "I could use some new soles on my shoes."

When I said that, I meant it more as a joke. Not that I didn't need new soles. I had worn a hole in the heel of my right boot. In Paducah, we couldn't find a place to get it fixed. So I filled the hole with silicone caulk to get me by until we found a repair shop.

"Well I don't know about new soles, but my husband has a few old pairs of boots that he doesn't wear. Maybe he'll have something. What size do you wear?"

Immediately I was sorry I'd said anything. It's funny–I didn't mind asking for Della, but when I asked for myself, I felt like a bum, or a panhandler. So I said, "Don't worry about it. I'm all right with what I've got."

About an hour after dark, Nan returned with her husband, Jeff. "My wife said you wear size twelve. I don't have anything that would fit you. But when we get home I'll call around and see what I can find."

"You don't need to do that. Really, I'm fine."

It was a cool crisp night–the first since we hit the road. In the morning, a frosty dew was on everything. How great it was to feel that first hint of autumn. Finally, summer and all its steaminess was beginning to slip away.

The coffee had just begun to perk, when a car turned off the highway and pulled part-way up the hill toward our camp. When the door opened, Jeff got out with a large blue Walmart bag in his hand. He walked up to me and pulled out a box with a picture of a hiking boot on it. "They're cheap, but they ought to get you down the road a ways."

Speechless, I held the box and stared at the picture of the boot on the top. My emotions ricocheted from gratitude to guilt to humility and back to gratitude. When I looked up at Jeff's beaming face I stammered, "I don't know what to say. What I mean is, well, thank you. But I didn't expect you to buy me new boots."

"I know you didn't. But I think you're doing a really great thing here. This is my way of being a part of it."

⊰⊱

We had just finished eating lunch in a church parking lot near Possum Trot, when John and his chocolate Labrador, Beau, pulled up in a pickup truck. John was in his early thirties, about a head shorter than me, with the physique of someone who worked out in a gym every day. He owned an earth moving business, and had read our story in the paper. After he asked a few questions, the conversation turned to the terrorist attacks. He said, "Did you hear what the Chinese did?"

"No."

"They held a candle light service in Beijing yesterday for the 9/11 victims." Then he said, "This morning, I asked a couple of my dozer operators if the attacks had happened in China, would they have gone to a ceremony for those victims? They both said no."

John paused as he bent over, took a retrieved stick out of Beau's mouth and turned toward me. "Then I asked them, now that this has happened here, if it happens in China would they go to a ceremony for those people?"

John threw the stick for his dog as he said, "They told me they didn't know."

Beau romped toward us with the stick in his mouth as John sighed. "I had hoped this terrorist thing might make America a better neighbor in the world. But I don't know if it will. I just don't know."

CHAPTER 5

GOING TO
UNIONTOWN

꧁ꕥ꧂

WE FIRST THOUGHT ABOUT GOING to Uniontown, Kentucky, when Suzanne Tucker told us she wanted to drive from Hot Springs and visit us somewhere on the road. She was going to bring our former dog Spot with her.

We picked Uniontown as a place to rendezvous because it's on the Ohio River. When we were in the old river towns of Hickman and Paducah, Kentucky, Patricia and I commented several times how much Suzanne would have loved them. She's into antiques and old architecture, so we figured Uniontown might be a good place to meet her.

The first time we mentioned to anyone that we planned to go there, it was to a coal miner in Sturgis, Kentucky. We were in a city park camped next to a small lake where he, his wife and little dog had stopped to visit us. He pulled a pack of cigarettes out of his tee-shirt pocket and said, "You want to go to Uniontown?"

I replied, "Is there a problem with that?"

He lit a cigarette, took a deep drag and blew the smoke out before saying, "Oh, there's no real problem. It's just that nobody really *wants* to go to Uniontown."

"Why not?"

It was as if the miner was contemplating what he was going to say next as he took another puff. "Let me put it to you this way. A buddy of mine had a girl friend ask him to kiss her where it stinks. So he took her to Uniontown and kissed her."

I laughed. "It's that bad, eh?"

"It's that bad. Why do you want to go there?"

After I told him we wanted to rendezvous with a friend in an interesting place, he shook his head and chuckled, "It'd be interesting alright. But not the kind of interesting you're looking for. Meet your friend in Morganfield. That's a nice town."

It was September 23rd–the first full day of fall and my birthday. Patricia suggested we take the day off the road to celebrate. "This lake is a pretty place. Let's spend your birthday here."

"But what I really want to do is walk," I said.

So we packed up and headed out of town. On the edge of Sturgis we stopped at a supermarket where Patricia went in for groceries and I stayed in the parking lot with Della. While she was shopping, the fluffy cumulus clouds that had dominated the sky began to twist and swirl into ugly gray thunder-heads. By the time she came out of the store with a full shopping cart, the sky was completely overcast and the smell of rain was in the air.

Patricia opened the kitchen door of our cart, looked up and said, "Wow! I can't believe how much the sky changed while I was in that store." She shook her head and started stuffing supplies wherever she could. "This isn't looking none too good to me."

Sturgis is situated on a low ridge. And as we walked down it into the farm lands, lightning began to streak down into the valley and strike up on the hilltops all around us. Instead of rumbling about in the clouds, the thunder cracked and exploded across the sky. We were a little over a mile from the supermarket when heavy drops started splashing into the side of my face. So we pulled our rain suits on, and I had just snapped mine shut, when the downpour commenced. It was a loud storm, so I was yelling when I said to Patricia, "You climb in the cart! No sense in both of us getting soaked!"

For better than an hour Della and I trudged north along US 60 through the deluge that swept across the highway in curtains. We were about five miles out of Sturgis, when suddenly the air directly in front of us exploded with a blinding white flash. The boom made my ears pop, and Della reared up with a grunt and a snort. From the cart, Patricia screamed, "Holy Shit!"

Then she yelled, "Are you okay, Baby?"

"Damn, that was close!"

A mile farther we came to an abandoned farm on the right side of the highway. Out front was a huge spreading oak. We were pulling under it as the rain began to let up, and by the time we staked out Della, it was just sprinkling. So we took advantage of the lull and pitched the tent.

Ours was not an expensive state-of-the-art tent. It was a cheap dome that we bought at Wal-mart. No matter what we did to it, the seams on the bottom leaked. Then in Paducah, a zipper on one of the two front doors failed. So in Marion I sewed that door shut.

Under the Kentucky oak tree, as I staked the tent down, the sky opened up with another downpour. Patricia scrambled inside with her arms wrapped around our bedding. I was about to pound a stake down through the soggy grass, when I heard the tent door zipper stop abruptly. My wife screamed. "Not now!"

"What's wrong!"

"Now *this* stinking zipper won't work."

I scurried around to the front of the tent. The rain was tumultuous, and the door was wide open with the storm pouring in on our bed. It was a southern wind, but not a warm one. For the first time since we hit the road, I felt cold. Wet and cold, and it looked like bedtime wasn't going to be any better.

We tied a big piece of plastic across the top of the tent so it hung over the open door. It didn't keep all the rain out, but it was better than no door at all. After our bed was made, Patricia and I climbed into the cart and waited for the rain to let up.

In the middle of the downpour I announced, "It's toddy time."

For my birthday, we bought a bottle of bourbon. Our intention was to toast my birthday before we went to bed that night. So, as the storm raged on I pulled the bottle out from under the cart seat and poured some into a plastic cup. Then I asked my wife, "Would Madame care for a shot of water in her cocktail?"

"But of course."

I held the cup out in the storm for a moment.

After a toast, Patricia sighed. "I feel bad. Your birthday has turned into an awful mess."

Right then it seemed like the storm suddenly got worse. The sky sprang to life with staccato flashes of white light, and the thunder kept a sustained rumble overhead. For a few moments, I just stared out at the storm, then I turned to Patricia, lifted my plastic cup and said, "I can't think of a better celebration. How many men can say they spent their fifty-third birthday living their dream? Not many. No, Baby, I'm having a great birthday!"

After the miner told us what he thought of Uniontown, we decided to bypass it. We would meet Suzanne and Spot in Morganfield.

"You aren't going to Uniontown?"

She was a thin woman with white hair, and when she asked that question she was leaning out the driver's window of a mini-van on the outskirts of Morganfield.

Her name was Margaret and she was insistent. "But you've got to come to Uniontown!"

"Why?"

"It's the most wonderful old river town in the world. I wouldn't live anywhere else. It has the best people. You'll love it. I have an extra bedroom and your donkey can stay in the yard."

After I told Margaret we had already made plans to rendezvous with Suzanne in Morganfield, she said "Then after your friend leaves, you can come to Uniontown."

"Well, it really is out of our way. And—"

A desperate whine was in her voice. "Oh, please."

"We'll see."

Morganfield was a pretty little town of 4,000 people. Most of the homes were old Victorian or Queen Anne style houses, surrounded by manicured lawns with huge hardwood trees. The downtown buildings were mostly red brick, and looked like they had been built in the early 1800s. The miner was right. Morganfield would be a great place to rendezvous with Suzanne.

She and Spot met up with us at the American Legion Park on the east side of town. In the two and a half months since we last saw him, Spot had more than doubled in size. When he first hopped out of the motor home, Spot didn't seem to know who we were. That is, until he spotted Della. Then he went crazy running around her and us. He was obviously glad to see us, and until then, I didn't realize how much I missed him.

That night Suzanne took us out to dinner at the Feed Mill Restaurant. When the waitress first came to the table she asked where we were from. So I gave her one of our flyers. When she brought us the check at the end of the meal she asked, "From Morganfield where you headed?"

Patricia said, "We're going to Uniontown!"

The waitress made a face like she had just smelled something bad. "Oh, no." With her head she motioned toward the kitchen. "We all hoped you wouldn't say that."

She was shaking her head as she walked away from our table.

The next day, Patricia and Suzanne took off in the motor home to explore, while I stayed in camp to do some writing. Down the hill from our campsite was a football field with water spigots. I had just filled one of our jugs, when I saw a car pull up to our camp. A woman got out and carried a cardboard box to our picnic table. When she saw me toting the jug up, the hill she waved and yelled, "Hi. Remember me? It's Margaret from Uniontown."

In the box were canned goods like pork and beans, corn and potted meat. She also had a couple of loaves of white bread, a cake mix, macaroni and cheese, and a box of Hamburger Helper. After she showed me what was in the box, Margaret said "I thought you guys might get hungry before you got to Uniontown."

"I appreciate it, but we have plenty of food. I don't know where we'd put all this stuff."

She pulled a ten dollar bill out of her pocket and handed it to me. "Oh, you'll find room. And I know you have room for this–don't you?"

"Well, yes. But–"

"When do you think you'll get to Uniontown?"

I held the bill out to her. "You don't need to bribe us to come to Uniontown."

She took a step backwards and laid her hands across her chest. "I'm not bribing you. I just want to help you guys out. Please keep that."

I thanked her and stuck the bill in my pocket.

"You're still coming to Uniontown, aren't you?"

⊰⊱

Everyone in Morganfield said the B&M Café was the place to have breakfast. It's small and most of the seating was at a long L-shaped counter that faced the open kitchen. So the customers, cooks, and cashiers were all in the same space, and most conversations were café-wide affairs. We saw the same customers both mornings we ate there, and everybody knew everybody–except us.

Our second breakfast at the B&M was Thursday, just before Suzanne and Spot left to go back to Hot Springs. My butt had just landed on one of the stools, when a man on the other end of the counter yelled, "Hey, I figured out who you people are. When you left yesterday, we were all wondering. Then I seen your picture in the paper this morning."

A man half way up the counter asked, "They're in the paper?"

"They're walking to Maine with a mule."

The remainder of breakfast was interspersed with questions and comments about our journey. I was drinking my last cup of coffee, when the man at the far end of the counter yelled, "Where ya' going from here?"

With gusto my wife said. "We're going to Uniontown!"

The café erupted in laughter with some men slapping the backs of the guys next to them. Dishes and silverware rattled as several fists pounded the counter. Through the laughs and coughs could be heard, "Not Uniontown!" "Oh my God! Of all places."

When we walked out of the café, Suzanne said, "You know, you guys have no choice. You've *got* to go to Uniontown."

⊰⊱

I had to re-shoe Della that day. So it was almost three in the afternoon before we got on the road. At the edge of Morganfield, we passed a driveway where six teenaged boys were climbing into a Camero. They all had their ball caps on backwards and were waving at us, when one of them yelled, "Where ya going?"

Patricia shouted, "We're going to Uniontown!"

Simultaneously, they all burst into laughter.

The road to Uniontown was a flat straight ribbon of asphalt that parted fields of autumn brown soybeans ready for harvest. Interspersed through the fields were several oil wells, most of which were pumping. Not far from mile-marker thirteen, we came to the intersection of Highway 666. The mark of the devil on the road to Uniontown.

Not far from there, a farmer in a pickup truck pulled into a soy bean patch next to us. He yelled out the window, "I read about you in the paper today." Then he asked, "If you're walking to New England, how come you're going this way?"

"We're going to Uniontown!"

With thumbs-up, he drove ahead to a combine that was stopped in the soybean patch. He was talking with four other men beside the combine as we approached. When we got close, he strolled toward the pavement and shouted, "Are you guys crazy? You ought to ride in that thing."

I yelled back, "If we're crazy enough to go to Uniontown, we're crazy enough to walk!"

All five of them doubled over with laughter.

When we started down off the ridge into town, it was immediately obvious why everyone questioned our detour. Unlike Morganfield, with its well-kept homes and manicured yards, Uniontown had hap-hazard trailers on scruffy lots and buildings that begged the question, "Does anyone live here?" Everything seemed temporary. Parked in nearly every yard was a car with a door open and no one around. And in the streets along the curb, there were several junkers with their hoods up but no one was working on them.

Then we came to that unmistakable smell of a recently burnt building. It got stronger the further we descended into town. Unlike the smell of a campfire or fireplace that coddles feelings of warmth and well-being, a burnt building has the stink of strife. It was a derelict smell that got stronger as we walked further into Uniontown. About three blocks from the signal light in the middle of town, we came to the smoldering ruins.

It had been a house trailer on a rock foundation. Yellow plastic tape was laced through trees and shrubs marking the perimeter of the fire. At the center was a smoking rectangular pile of rubble, around which were burnt pieces of furniture and bright plastic parts of children's toys. A sense of melancholy was in the smell of that fire.

⊰⊱

A late model pickup stopped, and the driver asked if we needed a place to put down for the night. I said, "Thanks, but we're staying at Margaret's house."

"You mean Margaret on Third Street?"

"Yes. She said they have a big yard for our mule to graze in."

It was almost dark, so I couldn't see the driver's expression. But I could hear the reservation in his voice. "Okay. Do you mind if I wait for you there so I can take some pictures?"

When we got to Margaret's house, it was so dark it was hard to see her driveway. Normally, I would stop and check out the situation before I lead Della into a place like that. But that evening I just led her up onto the driveway and into the yard. Immediately I realized I'd made a mistake. Margaret's big front yard was barely large enough to play a game of croquet in. Even if it had been bigger you couldn't have played there because of all the shrubs everywhere. Della would tear the place up in no time.

Margaret's husband, Willie, said, "Don't worry about it! Just run those stupid little trees over. We don't care."

He was sitting on the front steps dressed in only shorts and sandals. A huge bundle of flesh hung over the top of the shorts and his thighs stressed their seams. Willie had a beer can in his hand and a New Jersey accent in his voice. "We didn't plant the damn things anyway. They just came up on their own. So you ain't hurting nothing."

The bushes weren't the problem, it was the fenced yard. It wasn't big enough to turn Della and the cart around in it. After I told him that, Willie stood and waddled toward me saying, "Aw, hell! We'll just take the damn fence down. It ain't much anyway."

"I'm sorry, but this just isn't going to work out for us."

Margaret grabbed my arm and pleaded, "Will you still be my friend?"

The guy in the pickup who wanted to take pictures of us was a big man. His friend was too. So they had the bulk to help Della back the cart over the curb and out into the street. Willie was bigger than anyone there, but he said, "My knees can't handle doing something like that."

Margaret's neighbor let us park the cart and stake out Della for the night in her unfenced yard. It didn't have much to graze on, but we had plenty of hay.

After we got her situated for the night, Patricia and I went next door to Margaret and Willie's house. She fixed us a dinner of cornbread, beans and cream style corn from a can. Willie brought out a couple cans of Busch beer.

Willie was fifty-three, and Margaret was ten years older. She described herself as, "A real mess. But I love people and I have fun!"

Willie was a salesman from Jersey City who followed a job to Kentucky a few years back. When the job came to an end he returned to New Jersey. "But I couldn't handle Jersey no more. I got spoiled here. You don't make as much money, but who cares. Here you can really live. In Jersey you just survive. You have to put bars on your windows and you don't look at nobody you don't know. Here everybody waves and says 'Hi.' Back in Jersey they'd think you was crazy, or trying to rob 'em or something."

Willie was a telemarketer and in awe of the people in Uniontown. "These are real men around here. If their pickup breaks down, they fix it right alongside the road. No calling Triple-A. If their roof blows off, they get the stuff and fix it. Back in Jersey City, nobody does that. Here they do it themselves. Now that's what I call real men!"

I told Willie about the negative remarks we heard about Uniontown. "Aw, that's all them people up in Morganfield. They think they're more sophisticated. They call Uniontown the ghetto. Hell, they don't know what a ghetto is. I do. They ain't never seen real sophistication. But I have. I'm from Jersey City. I know what sophistication is, and Morganfield ain't got it!"

Normally Willie and Margaret didn't sleep in the same room. If Willie was startled awake he would come up screaming and punching. One time, back when they did sleep in the same bed, he banged her up pretty bad. After that they slept in separate rooms. But the night we were there Margaret insisted we take her bed. She would chance sleeping with Willie.

"How do they know we aren't ax murderers?"

Patricia whispered the question as we laid in the dark bedroom. Everyone in the house had just settled down for the night. I whispered back, "What are you talking about?"

"I was just laying here thinking, they really don't know us, and yet they invite us to stay in their home. How do they know we aren't ax murderers?"

"*Invite*? It's more like she begged. Hey, that's it! Maybe Margaret's an ax murderer. That's why she made such a big deal about us coming here. She and Willie are going to get us while we're asleep."

My wife poked me in the ribs with her elbow. "Oh shush. They might hear you."

Then she pulled back the covers and whispered, "I've got to pee."

The door to the bathroom was halfway down the hall on the left. The door to Willie's room was directly across from it. In the dark, as Patricia tiptoed toward it, she could hear voices in Willie's room. When she reached for the bathroom doorknob, she heard him say, "How do we know they aren't ax murderers?"

⊰⧳⊱

In the morning, we moved our camp to the Uniontown city park. It's adjacent to a levee that protects the town from the Ohio River. On the other side of the levee, in the bottoms, was a dense forest. Hardwoods, willows and vines that were woven with bits of plastic, pieces of metal and debris of all description from high-waters gone by.

After we set up camp and staked out Della in a patch of lush grass, Patricia and I climbed on our bikes and took off to explore Uniontown. Before we left, we took extra precautions to secure everything we owned. We kept hearing how bad the thieves were in Uniontown. A seventy-two year old woman, who had lived in the area all her life, warned us. "Uniontown is a den of thieves! It's always been that way. They even stole an elephant here one time."

According to her, in the late 1800's one of the locals stole an elephant from a traveling circus. In the dead of the night he swam across the Ohio River with the pachyderm and sold it in Indiana to pay off a gambling debt.

Uniontown got its name when the hamlets of Francisburg and Locust Point merged as one community in the mid 1800's. The first settlers were trappers and loggers. Then coal was discovered on that part of the river.

The 1937 flood was a turning point in Uniontown's history. On February 1st, the Ohio River was 64.2 feet above flood stage. There was no levee then. But even if there had been, it wouldn't have made much difference. Willie told me when the Ohio flooded in 1997, he could sit on the top of the levee and slap the water.

"If we'd gotten another inch of rain it would have been all over for us down here."

In the 1997 flood the river crested eleven feet lower than it did in 1937.

Fire also shaped the history of Uniontown. In 1975 a blaze swept through most of the downtown historic buildings. They were replaced with un-ornate, single-story structures. Like the house trailers and parked cars we saw when we walked into town, these buildings had a sense of temporary about them.

That afternoon, during our tour, we stopped at the VFW for a beer. The bartender told us what really killed Uniontown was when the coal mines shut down. The first one was in 1988.

"We had five good mines with plenty of work for anyone who wanted it."

The man next to us at the bar said, "Now if you want work, you have to go to Morganfield, or Henderson, or over to Evansville. That's what's really killing Uniontown."

So why does anyone live in Uniontown? It will always have the threat of flood. You have to drive somewhere else to work. The crime rate is high and esthetically the place is hardly attractive. So why live there? To quote Margaret, "It's home. I'm comfortable here. I wouldn't live anywhere else."

⊰⊱

The next morning after breakfast, Patricia and I drank our last cup of coffee while we watched Della graze near the levee. Suddenly, two large dogs jumped up onto the top of it from the other side and started barking. It surprised Della and she bolted. With hobbles on her front feet she leaped away from the levee. In mid-air she came to the end of her rope, which made her flip head over hooves. When she hit the ground it was square on the top of her head, and as the rest of her body crashed down I heard something crack. For a frightening moment, she laid completely still as my body began to shiver. Had Della just broken her neck?

Patricia and I both screamed "Della!" as we scrambled toward her. But just before we got her Della shuddered, rolled over and up onto her feet.

When she flipped in the air the rope broke at her hobbles. So Della was loose. But when she whirled around to run away she was face to face with me.

"It's okay, Big Sis."

I threw my arms around her neck and tried to control her. But it didn't work. With me still holding onto her, Della spun back around to look for the dogs on the levee. My feet scrambled for footing like a marionette dancing across a stage.

Now there were two boys with the dogs on top of the levee. The dogs continued to bark, while the boys stood and looked dumbfounded at us. I yelled, "Get those dogs out of here!"

Della whirled around again to run away from the levee. But this time, she also had Patricia's arms around her neck. "It's okay, Sissy Belle!"

With both of us embracing her, Della began to settle down. I looked back up at the top of the levee. The boys and their dogs were gone. The event was over.

When we examined Della, all we could find was a cut gum in her mouth and a small tear inside one nostril. Aside from that, she was all right. A couple of hours later we had her hitched to the cart and on a residential street headed for the highway out of Uniontown.

We were a block from Third Street when I heard a clicking sound from the left rear tire. At first I thought it was a rock or a bottle cap stuck in the treads. But what I found was a huge tack. When I pulled it out air hissed. Our first flat tire of this trip would be in Uniontown.

It was a slow leak, so I was able to plug it before it went flat. Someone said there was an open gas station on the road out of town. On the way there, I began to smell something that I had smelled when we first arrived in Margaret's yard two days earlier. It wasn't the burnt building. This was different. When I asked Willie what it was he said, "You smell something? I don't. Oh, maybe it's the oil tanks. I'm so used to it I don't smell it anymore."

It did smell like oil, and when we got to the gas station the stink was really strong. The station was closed because it was Sunday. That meant the air compressor was turned off. So I got our hand pump out and went to work.

I was putting the pump back in the cart, when I remembered the coal miner in Sturgis who said, "My buddy's girl friend asked him to kiss her where it stinks. So he took her to Uniontown and kissed her."

So, there in the middle of all that Uniontown stink, I walked up to my wife, wrapped my arms around her and said, "I love ya' baby."

Then I kissed her.

On the road to Union Town.

CHAPTER 6

MISTER PARAGRAPH 18

"YOU WANT TO KNOW WHAT happened to this neighborhood? I'll tell ya. Niggers!"

I'm repulsed when someone uses that word–nigger. It ripples up my spine and makes me want to spit at the person who spoke it. I've never done that, and this man was not the one to start with. Don was six inches shorter than me and probably outweighed me by fifty pounds–and it was not fat. He looked like he could have been a wrestler. The Jessie Ventura type, but Don was shorter. His voice had that same gruffness that most of those guys have. He was not someone to mess with. Besides, I asked him about the neighborhood in his driveway. He had his right to free speech–especially in his driveway.

With more than 120,000 people, Evansville, Indiana was the largest town we had walked into. When we met Don, we were just east of downtown on Washington Avenue. From our camp on the east edge of the city, Patricia and I had bicycled in to explore the heart of Evansville. Della stayed in camp to graze on lush grass.

"It's a damn dirty shame," said Don. "There's some fine old homes here. But when the niggers started moving in, everybody else moved out."

Washington Avenue was a shaded thoroughfare with huge old oaks and elms in their early shades of autumn. Behind those trees were houses built between the 1920's and 40's–homes for the families of coal miners, mill workers and other middle-class types. Folks who could afford a two story house with a small front yard, neighborly porch and a driveway that led back to a detached garage. We also pedaled past some houses that were more like mansions–not the multi-millionaire type–but houses for people who were better off than most. The kind who didn't have to wear work-gloves on the job.

The closer we got to downtown, the more unkempt the houses and other buildings were. We saw people living in places with boarded up windows, busted front doors and peeling paint. It was about 1 p.m., the first Thursday in October. The sky was clear and temperature perfect for being outside. So, lots of those residents were on their porches, or hanging out on front steps and sidewalks. All sorts of folks, but mostly African-American.

We had stopped to look at an old church, when Don pulled into his driveway across the street. It was a simple buff brick Catholic church with weeds growing out of its cracks and crannies. Patricia and I were wondering if it was still being used. So I pushed my bicycle across the street to ask him. That's when I asked, "What happened to this neighborhood?"

After he told me, "Niggers!" Don said, "I know that makes me sound prejudiced, but I'm not. I've got black friends and they ain't the problem. It's the niggers!"

The house that Don's truck was parked at, and the ones on either side of it, were in good repair. "We lived in this house when I was a teenager. My dad moved us all over this town buying and selling houses. He'd get a good deal on one, and we'd live there a couple years. Then he'd sell it, make some money and we'd move into another one. We lived in this house the longest–probably four or five years. It was my favorite, and back then this was a great neighborhood."

Don was a Vietnam Veteran who did two tours–1967 and 1969. "My job was to get the body bags out of the field. Sometimes they were bagged and sometimes they weren't. Didn't make much difference. It was always a raw deal. I dodged a lot of bullets getting a bunch of dead guys home."

Between his tours in Vietnam, Don spent a few months on the streets of Evansville playing the part of a blind vet. "I had this Doberman I was real close to, and I took him everywhere. The only way I could get him in a bar was if he was a service dog. So I acted like I was blind. Wore dark glasses, got the harness for the dog, carried a stick–the whole bit. Told them it happened in 'Nam." He leaned against the tailgate of the pickup and folded his arms across his chest. A grin grew across his white-bearded face as he chuckled. "That sure was fun, and it got me a lot of free drinks."

Shortly after Don got home from his second tour, he was driving up Washington Avenue and saw a For Sale sign in the yard of the house we were standing in front of. "I thought, *Wouldn't that be sweet? I've got my GI Bill, hell, buy it!* So I went to the front door to find out what they wanted for it. When I knocked, a bunch of niggers came flying out and started wacking at me with straight razors."

When Don turned around to face the house, I spotted bits of several scars that disappeared into his beard. Then when he propped his forearms on the tailgate, and laced his distorted fingers together, it was obvious that they got him on his arms as well.

Don shook his curly white head and said, "I don't know why they did that. Just being niggers I guess. They didn't hurt me too bad, but it sure pissed me off. So I found the owner and bought the house. Then I came back with a tire tool and busted the windows out of the nigger's car. When they came out I chased them back in with my tire tool. They thought I was crazy. And they were right!"

Slapping the tailgate with his right hand, Don laughed as he put his foot on the back bumper. "After I got done busting the windows, I pushed the car into the street. Then I sat down on the curb and laid the tire tool next to me. When the cops showed up, they asked who I was. I told them I owned the house. Then they asked if I knew anything about the busted windows in the car. I told them no. Then they asked why I had a tire tool. Told them I found it laying in the street. Then I said I just got back from Nam and I was thinking about buying a car. I figured if I got one a tire tool might come in handy."

Obviously, Don had told this story many times, but it still cracked him up. "I couldn't believe it. The cops bought it. They told the niggers to get their car out of the street. Then they got back in the police car and drove off.

"The niggers were going berserk They were yelling at the cops, telling them I was crazy and stuff like that. When the cops were out of sight I told those niggers they was right. 'I am crazy. I've been to 'Nam twice and I'm as crazy as they come. And I've got guns—lots of guns and I love to use them!'"

Don stopped laughing and got real serious. "Then I told them that I now owned the house and I wanted all of them out by sundown tomorrow. One of them said they had thirty days. But I knew they'd already been evicted by the previous owner long ago. Just no one had come around to kick them out yet. I told them what I knew, then I said, 'It's up to you. But it's my house now and I'm going to start cleaning it tomorrow night. The first thing I've got to do is get rid of the rats. So I'm coming over with my guns and gonna clean house.' The next night this place was empty."

Don went on to buy more real-estate and at one time owned more than 200 rental properties. "I had some real dumps. So I've had to deal with lots of low-life scum. It seemed like I was always having to straighten out some smart ass. You know, show them what the program was. I learned early on, that if you let those bums know up front you won't take any shit, you have a lot less trouble."

All of Don's tenants signed a rental agreement in which paragraph eighteen stated, "If you can whip my ass, I'll sign the house over to you."

"A few years ago a judge asked me about paragraph eighteen. Said he never saw anything like that. I told him I put it in there so everyone knew I meant business. He asked me if I ever lost a house that way. I told him yes, a couple of times. But that was a lie."

"Why did you lie to him?"

"If I'd said no, he would have thought I was bragging. Nobody likes a braggart."

Don turned around, leaned his back against the tail gate, crossed his arms and said, "See, the thing is, I like to fight. I've done it enough that I'm good at it. That doesn't mean I always win. I've lost some."

Over the years, Don's fights had netted him more than one thousand stitches, and he couldn't remember how many broken bones. In one lost battle, all of his fingers were broken against a curb by his opponent stomping on them. "The thing is, if you're going to be a good fighter, you can't be afraid to lose. You don't never fight to lose. But hey, if you lose that's okay, too. I kind of like to lose. Because when you do, you get lots of attention. Sometimes they send you to the hospital, where you lay around and do nothing but get better. And you have pretty young nurses taking care of you. Then, they send you home where your wife waits on you, and brings you soup and stuff to make you feel better. A good fighter has got to have a good woman."

Don was married six times and had six children. "I never cheated on any of them. Don't mess around on my wife and I didn't dodge the draft. Who would ever think I'd be over qualified to be president."

Slowly, he walked along the driver's side of the pickup as he said. "Problem is, when you get my age it takes a lot longer to heal. So these days I bring a little extra help."

With that he yanked open the door and folded the back of the seat forward. Strapped into place was an assortment of firearms that would be the envy of any SWAT team. "Things are different these days. Punks don't carry razors and brass knuckles any more. These days, they've all got guns. And every punk in town knows I got more guns than them."

Don no longer owned 200 properties. "I got rid of the dumps. It wasn't worth the trouble. I was always on the run–hardly ever home."

Home for Don was a four level house on fourteen acres in rural Evansville. "So now I'm down to eighty-six places. I'd like to cut that in half. Just keep the nice ones–like these."

His mother-in-law lived in his boyhood home. "She's never had much of nothing. When her old man died, it looked like she was going to end up in the street. So I moved her in here. She gets enough social security to feed her. I take care of the utilities.

Don also owned the house next door, which his older brother lived in. "He got shot up real bad in 'Nam. He don't get around too good. The VA takes care of him. When they pay his rent, I give the money to him. That way he's got a little something extra to spend." Don had just returned from a shopping trip for his brother and mother-in-law. He started to pull the plastic bags out of the truck cab, then he stopped and turned toward me. "Here, this will show you the kind of shit I run into every day. I've got this little black gal that rents from me a few blocks from here. Real sweet little gal. She's got a baby girl that just started walking a couple of months ago. Cutest little thing. Of course she's got no husband, and she's on welfare. But she's no trouble. Late on her rent sometimes, but I work with her.

"This morning, I went by to get the rent, and there's this big buck Nigger sitting at her kitchen table. He had an empty forty-ouncer on the floor and half-full one in front of him, and her baby girl was running around the kitchen butt naked. When she gave me the rent, I asked her why the baby didn't have any pants. She said she didn't have money for diapers. Right then, this dude says, 'Baby, how about holding out ten bucks so I can get some more brew.'"

Don paused, grimaced and said, "That went through me like a shot. I walked over to him, pulled out a ten dollar bill, waved it in his face and told him, 'No, I'll pull out ten bucks and buy that baby some diapers. And when I get back with them, you aren't going to be here.' Then he said, 'Says who?'"

Poking himself in the chest with his forefinger, Don said, "'Says me!' I told him 'I own the place and I ain't renting to you. I don't know who you are but anyone who'd buy beer before diapers is not welcome in anyplace I own. And if you aren't gone when I get back, I will remove you.'"

Reaching under the driver's seat, Don pulled out a 9mm hand gun and tossed it on the seat. "I figured he'd be gone when I got there. But just in case, I stuck this in my pants when I took her the diapers. He was gone and she thanked me. Said she'd never have him over again. And she'd get the ten bucks to me next month. I told her not to worry about it."

For the past few minutes, as Don was telling us his stories, we had been watching a low riding, mid-80's Oldsmobile creep toward us. It was baby-blue, highly polished and headed east along the avenue. Because there was no parking lane, east bound traffic had to swerve across the yellow line to get around it. We heard a redundant base line from the radio long before we saw the car. Because the windows were tinted, we couldn't see who was inside, but every once in a while a black arm would gesture out the passenger window. And when a vehicle behind them honked, a black fist with the middle finger pointing upward would emerge from the driver's side.

Adjacent to them, on the sidewalk was a tall slender black woman pushing a stroller. She was in her early twenties with the figure and face of a cover-girl.

It was apparent that someone in the Olds was talking to her. And as they got closer to us, it was obvious she was not interested in talking to him.

They were about twenty yards from us, when the engine revved and the car roared on up the avenue. When she got close to us, Don asked, "Those guys harassing you?"

With a forced grin, she shrugged her shoulders and said, "It's no big deal."

Don knelt down in front of the stroller. "Will you look at this little man! I can't get over how much he's grown. How old is he now?"

"He'll be a year the end of this month?"

"Has he learned to say Grandpa yet?"

She blushed and giggled. "We're working on it."

Don stood up. "Tell your dad I said it's good thing this little guy looks like you instead of his grandpa."

While she walked away from us, the Oldsmobile stopped next to the curb across the street headed the other way. The radio was silent and a black man, wearing sunglasses, with gold dangling around his neck, leaned out the back seat window. "Baby, you and me could make some pretty babies together! Come on, baby!"

I could feel Don tense up next to me. I think the guy in the car, and the young mother did too. Because both of them suddenly turned to look at us. Immediately the man stuck his head back in the car, and it sped away.

Under his breath, Don said, "Niggers!"

I was thinking, *"Ass holes!"*

⇥⊟⊢⇤

CHAPTER 7

AUTUMN ON THE NORTH BANK

❧❦

WHEN WE CROSSED THE OHIO River into Evansville, Indiana, it meant we were out of Dixie. To runaway slaves the Ohio must have been the most beautiful river they had ever seen. Once they crossed it, they were free. That didn't mean they were out of danger. The north bank was rife with professional slave catchers. And southern Indiana was a strong hold for the Ku Klux Klan. But the north bank was also home to many slave sympathizers. Folks who opened their homes, cellars and barns to those on the run to freedom. When we walked along the Indiana side of the river, we encountered numerous historic markers and heard lots of stories about this network of abolitionists known as the "Underground Railroad". In Troy, we met the Efingers who, while renovating a house on the river front, uncovered a tunnel that had been part of it.

Of the large rivers that we had come to so far—the kind with barge traffic—the Ohio was by far the prettiest. The water in the Mississippi and the Arkansas Rivers was muddy. But the Ohio was shimmering and blue. Along the shore were bluffs and hills covered with oak, hickory and maples adorned in all shades of orange, yellow, red and purple. While we walked along the Ohio, it seemed like each day the valley got prettier. It was the Iroquois Indians who named it, "Oyo", which meant "beautiful." The French changed it to Ohio.

West of Troy, we camped in a roadside park called "Lincoln's Ferry." It was where the Anderson River empties into the Ohio. When he was fifteen, Abraham Lincoln got a job on a ferry that crossed the Anderson River near there. A couple of years later, he built a flat bottom boat and went into business. He rowed passengers and cargo to and from the steam boats in the main channel of the Ohio.

According to a historic marker in the park, it was this enterprise that piqued young Lincoln's interest in government. When he was seventeen, Abe was sued by a Kentucky ferry operator for operating without a license. Representing himself, Lincoln maintained that since he only rowed to the middle of the river he was not operating a ferry in Kentucky. The court ruled in Lincoln's favor.

Our camp at Lincoln's Ferry was on a bluff about thirty feet above the river. It was October 9th. So autumn was really showing its colors. Late in the afternoon, as the sun approached the hill tops, I began to think about the first people who saw the river. Natives who feasted from its waters and hunted game in the surrounding hills. Surely they saw the river as more than just a provider for their livelihoods. Like me, there must have been moments when they paused to simply marvel at the way the sun shimmered across the water. While they watched the sun slip toward the horizon they had to have been awe-stuck by the orange-red rays that splayed across the heavens like giant burning fingers.

On a day like that, with fall dabbed among the evergreens, those natives must have rejoiced in where they were. Especially when the wind was still and Oyo was reflecting all that magic on its surface. Like me, did they ever find themselves with their mouths agape– mesmerized by that spectacle?

And what about young Abe in his row boat? After he delivered his passengers to a big boat mid-stream, he must have had moments like this. While his little hand-made boat plied the waters by the power of his biceps, there had to have been autumn sunsets that so amazed him, he paused and lifted the oars up from the water. With the boat drifting and oars dripping onto the surface, he must have been mesmerized by the spectacle that the Iroquois called, "Beautiful."

⧊⧊

In my travels on foot, in a car, bus, plane and by thumb, I've had my heart stolen by the beauty of lots of places. The Rocky Mountains, Pacific Coast, Yellowstone—places like that where you expect to be wowed before you get to them. But Indiana? Never was I so surprised by the beauty of a place as I was with Southern Indiana.

When I was growing up in Oklahoma, our family often drove back and forth across northern Indiana to visit relatives in northeast Ohio. In the 1970s, as I toured America with my pack pony and dog, I crossed Indiana in the north, too. Mostly, it's flat farm land. Thus, that's how I'd always thought of Indiana—as flat.

So I was not prepared for the rugged high bluffs, steep valleys, lush wood lands and long breathtaking views of the shimmering Ohio. I had never been in a place with so many waterfalls. They weren't tremendous tumblers like Niagra, or those in Yellowstone. These were brooks and springs that fell over rocks and ledges down to the river. Most flowed under vines, trees and other vegetation. So, in a car you wouldn't have noticed them. But on foot you do. In Southern Indiana, there were times when the sound of falling water was all around us.

It was certainly that way at Camp Koch (pronounced Cook)—a Girl Scout camp east of Cannelton. My mother and step-father drove their motor home up from Arkansas and rendezvoused with us there. The camp was in a small dead end canyon across the highway from the Ohio. In the back of the canyon, plunging off a high sandstone bluff, was a long skinny waterfall—the sound of it reverberated throughout the canyon. In the middle of the canyon that stream had been dammed-up into a manmade pond with an arched wooden bridge over it. A picture perfect place to teach Girl Scouts how to swim and row a boat.

At the back of the canyon, in the face of the bluff, were several caves. One behind the water fall was big enough to put a small home in. Carved by centuries of water and wind, the bluff looked like giant fingers had molded the sandstone when it was wet. The sidewalls were steep and forested with switch-back foot trails that led to the top. Vines, as big around as my arm, looped up from ferns and moss into limbs adorned with autumn.

Camp Koch was named after the doctor who gave the land to the Girl Scouts in the late 1940's. Originally he offered it to the Boy Scouts, but they decided the terrain was too rugged for young boys. So the girls got it instead.

⚞⚟

The Ohio is a curvy river. In some places the river twists around so much that it nearly meets itself coming and going. Although the Ohio basically runs east to west, in lots of places it's a north/south river. In the nearly 1,000 miles that the river flows from Pittsburgh to the Mississippi there's only an eight mile stretch where it's straight. It's called "Schenault Reach", and it's on one of those north/south portions of the river. Named after a French military officer, Schenault Reach starts just north of Derby and runs south.

Derby, Indiana was one of those old river towns that had been burnt down, flooded out and carved up by ice. Before the Ohio was dammed and locked, moving ice was a big problem. In the winter and early spring, huge chunks–some the size of two city blocks – would sail down river and wreak havoc with everything in its way. In 1910, the heart of Derby was in the way. It was situated in a basin that was open to the river with bluffs and high hills around the rest of it. The wharfs, mills, warehouses and business district were all down there when a wall of ice sailed into town. It turned Derby into a giant pile of rubble. The splintered wood and busted brick was so jammed up against the hills and bluffs, that most of it was burnt where it landed.

Derby rebuilt. But twenty-seven years later came the flood of 1937. Again Derby was in the way, and most of it washed down steam. It never recovered.

When we were in Derby, there was still a bit of a town. It had a grocery store/gas station and a tavern up away from the river. The basin, where the town used to be, had been turned into a riverside park. Up on the hills were several homes. Some were lived in, but a lot of them were not.

We initially stopped at Ramsey's Tavern to have a beer and inquire about camping on a spot we saw on the south edge of Derby. It was a flat place, on a bluff above the river. They told us it used to be a night club that burnt down a long time ago. No one would care if we camped there for the night.

When we first walked into Derby, gray clouds were gathering. While we set up our tent the clouds got darker, and every once in a while a heavy drop or two would splash into us. The wind picked up and got blustery, which made it hard to pitch the tent. I piled rocks on the stakes to keep them from pulling up out of the dirt when it got soaked.

With the wind and rain it would be hard to fix dinner in camp. Plus, just down the hill was Ramsey's Tavern that supposedly had great food. So we stepped out for dinner. The special that night was two steak dinners for the price of one. I don't recall what kind of steak it was, but I remember it being good.

After dinner, when we climbed into our tent, the rain-fly was fluttering like a kite hung up in a tree. Patricia asked, "Do you think we'll be all right camped up here?"

"What do you mean?"

The wind was howling, with an occasional crack of thunder and flash of light. It wasn't raining hard yet, but the night was ripe with storm.

My wife said, "I sure would hate to get blown off this bluff."

"Do you have something else in mind?"

Patricia was silent for a moment. "No."

A few minutes later the rain got heavier, but the wind was easing up. Soon the evening settled into an autumn shower. The danger was past. I snuggled down into my sleeping bag and went to sleep.

In the background of a dream I heard someone say, "What's that?" Then I started shaking, and as I shuddered out of sleep, I realized it was Patricia shaking me. "Wake up Bud. Listen! What is that?"

Something was roaring up the river. It sounded like a locomotive, but then I remembered, there were no railroad tracks along the river.

In a loud whisper Patricia asked, "What is that sound?"

I've been in tornados before. The closer it got, the more it sounded like one. I was about to tell her that, when a huge burst of wind ravaged our tent. The poles bowed in, then snapped back as the nylon quivered and popped. That roar was no longer just down on the river. It was up on the ridge with us. The top and walls of the tent continued to collapse down on us, then explode away.

Suddenly, the tent was ablaze in white as the sky exploded with thunder. So much lightning flashed around us, that it was like a strobe light inside our tent. Then, as if in slow motion, by lightning-light I saw the corner of our tent blew up off the stake and billow in toward us. It looked like the tent was going to roll up with us in it.

Patricia screamed, "Bud!"

"Oh shit!"

Then the wind sucked the corner away and the nylon cracked like a bull-whip. I could hear pans and other metal blowing around the cart. Sitting up in my sleeping bag, I said, "I'd better go out and stake that corner back down."

Patricia grabbed my arm, pulled me down to her and yelled through the storm. "Oh no you're not! You're staying in here! Our weight is what's holding this tent down. If you get up and go outside it won't weigh as much. If this tent blows off this cliff with me in it, then by God, you're going with me!"

So I laid down and the two of us huddled together in our separate sleeping bags– both of us trying to be as heavy as we could. The tempest wailed on.

I don't know how long it was before it let up. It seemed like forever. But eventually the roar moved away, taking its light and thunder show with it. Soon the rain slowed to a steady soft shower.

I whispered, "You all right Baby?"

Patricia said nothing for a moment. Then she rustled a bit in her bag. "I'm okay."

"I think it's over."

Patricia mumbled. "I sure hope so."

A few moments later I said, "Can I ask you something?"

My wife was annoyed. "What?"

"Are you still enjoying your honeymoon?"

Patricia snuggled deeper into her sleeping bag and muttered. It was hard to understand what she said. I think it was "Yes I am." Or maybe it was "Go to hell!"

I didn't ask her to repeat it.

※

"You can't camp here! Now, pack up and move on down the road!"

When the police car pulled up, it was ten o'clock at night. We were camped on the side of the highway next to a roadside park east of Leavenworth, Indiana. I was in the cab of the cart typing on the computer when the cruiser stopped. The headlights blinded me, so I couldn't see the source of the voice.

"You want us to move now?"

His voice was nasal, with a Kentucky kind-of-drawl. "That's what I said. Now!"

Right then, the body stepped from behind the headlights toward the cart. It was huge. Not tall huge—round huge. "There's no camping here! Didn't you see the sign?"

The sun was sinking into the horizon when we came to the roadside park. It had lots of grass for mule grazing, picnic tables, restrooms and a hand pump with sweet well water. We would have loved to have camped there. But it had the "No Camping" sign. So we camped on the right-of-way nearby. Who would have a problem with that?

"I've got a problem with that!" He waddled a couple of steps toward the cart. "Citizens have been calling me and complaining about the gypsies camped in the park. I can't have that. Now pack up and get on down the road!"

"But it's dark. It's too dangerous for us to be out on that highway now."

When he moved closer to the cart, the light in the cab lit him up. He was rotund, his uniform unbuttoned and pulled back behind his holstered pistol. He pointed to the cart and said, "You got lights on that thing, don't you?"

"Yes, but it's still too dangerous. We aren't hurting anything here."

He crossed his arms above his mammoth stomach. "Oh yes you are. There's no camping here and my job is to–"

Patricia shouted, "Protect the public!"

She had gone to bed earlier. While the cop and I were arguing, I heard her unzip the tent door. Walking toward him she said, "I was in law enforcement for more than fifteen years, and that has always been job-one– protect the public! How in the hell do you think you're protecting the public by sending us out on that highway tonight?"

He was obviously taken aback. The cop's round face was suddenly red as he uncrossed his arms and took a couple of steps back. He was speechless as my wife demanded, "Well, how is that protecting the public?"

He stammered. "Well. . .uh. You were a cop? Where?"

"Northern Illinois. What's that got to do with anything?"

He sounded like he was pleading his case when he said "Look, I've got citizens calling and complaining about you being here. If you wanted to camp here you should have asked me."

I slid out of the cart and stood next to my wife. "It was almost dark when we got here. How could I ask you anything? I don't know you."

"Well," he blurted out, "Everybody around here knows me. You walked right by my house. You should have stopped and asked."

I said, "We didn't know this park existed until we got here."

He re-crossed his arms and started rocking back and forth on his feet. "That ain't my problem. It's against the law to camp here. You've got to go!"

The absurdity of this irked me. I got louder with each word, when I said, "Ok! If you insist that we move in the middle of the night, we will. But let me tell you this. If something happens to us, we'll make sure the whole world knows why we were in harm's way. We've had lots of press in Indiana, and we'll make sure they all know about this!"

I had his attention. "Well. . .uh. . ."

Patricia was softer. She walked up to him with one of our flyers in her hand. "We just want to spend the night. We'll pull out first thing in the morning." She handed the flyer to him. "This will tell you all about us. We are not gypsies, tramps or thieves. We're just walking across the country."

He was looking down at the flyer in his hands. "You'll leave in the morning?"

"After breakfast, we'll pack up and get on down the road."

"Well, . . ." When he looked up from the flyer, he had a sheepish expression and stammered when he said, "As long as you leave in the morning, I guess it'll be all right."

Patricia said, "We'll get out of here as soon as we can."

He got in the car and slammed the door. After he backed the cruiser around to pull onto the highway, he leaned out the window and said, "Now I don't want no trouble out here tonight. No parties or nothing like that! You hear?"

In unison we replied, "Yes sir."

While we watched the tail lights fade away, Patricia asked, "Were you planning on a party tonight?"

"Yeah. You want to come?"

⛥

While the year turned into November, nearly every morning we woke to frozen dew on the tent and ice on Della's bucket. On those days, we had to wait for the dew to thaw and evaporate before we could pack the tent. So we were getting on the road later everyday—sometimes past noon. And the days were getting shorter, so we were having to stop for the night earlier and earlier.

"You need a place to camp tonight?"

We met Ron on one of those days when it was after noon before we got on the road. We also had a lot of people stop to talk to us that day, so we'd only walked about three miles. The sky already had the orange of sunset creeping into it, and Highway 62 was rampant with homebound traffic. We accepted his offer.

Ron was a short man, a bit hunched over, with a pitted face and lumpy round nose. We were talking to a group of people in the parking lot of a convenience store when he pulled in, got out and joined the group. He didn't say anything until the others wandered away. When he spoke, he was timid. "How long did you think about traveling before you actually did it?"

I told him, "About twenty-five years."

He wiped the end of his nose with his coat sleeve, then jammed his hands into his pants pockets. "That's a long time. I've dreamed of living on the river for at least forty."

"Are you doing it?"

A tone of defeat was in his voice as he looked down. "Naw. Wish I was." Then he looked up with excitement in his blood shot eyes. "But I've got the boat."

That's when he asked if we needed a place to camp for the night. "My house boat is sitting on a lot that I own. You could stay in the boat. It's got a heater and beds."

A heated place to sleep sounded good to us. Ron said "It's nothing fancy. But it's livable. Wish I was living in it."

"Why aren't you?"

He pulled his right hand out of his pocket and wiped his nose on the sleeve again. "It's the wife. She won't do it. She used to like to go out on the boat, and sometimes in the summer we'd spend a night or two on the river. It was a lot of fun. When we were young we used to talk about doing it full time–after the kids were gone, and I was retired. But now she won't even go out for a day trip. I built her a fine home and she doesn't want to leave it. She wants nothing to do with the boat."

With his hands still in his pockets, Ron shrugged his shoulders and sighed. "Oh well. What can you do?" He pulled his right hand out and pointed down the highway. "Let me tell you how to get to my place."

Ron said his lot was about a quarter of a mile off the highway. It was three times that far. And when we got to it, had the hour not been so late, we would have turned around and walked back to the highway. Ron's "lot" was actually a junk yard full of old rusty bulldozers, tractors with wheels missing, banged up trucks, a few wrecked cars—some laying on their sides. And there were piles of parts for all kinds of machinery everywhere. The place even had a couple of beat-up port-a-potties. And right in the middle of it all, on a trailer with a flat tire, was Ron's house boat–The Island Queen.

It was a twenty-eight foot pontoon boat, with a cabin on it that looked like a travel trailer without wheels. "The Island Queen" was painted in brown letters across the back of the yellow cabin. Because of the flat tire, the boat was listing to starboard.

"Oh, my, God," whispered Patricia as we stood facing the back of the boat. Ron was closing the gate behind us. "This is it? What are we going to do with Della?"

When Ron first offered us a place to camp, we asked if there was room for Della. "Oh sure. The lot is fenced, so you can turn her loose. She can't hurt anything."

While I looked around at the twisted metal, shards of glass, tangled steel cable and all the other junk, I had to agree with Ron. Della couldn't hurt anything. But there were lots of things that could hurt her.

"You could tie her out across the road." Ron said. "Plenty of grass over there. They're going to subdivide it. No one will care."

After we got Della taken care of, Ron gave us a tour of his boat. Because it was up on the trailer, we had to use a six foot step ladder to get on board. When he opened the door, it smelled like dirty socks in a locker. Ron turned to me. "Been a while since anybody has been in here. I'll open the front door. It'll air out pretty quick."

He was walking through the cabin when he said, "My boy, and some of his friends, use it to play cards and drink beer every now and then. Keeps the wives off their backs."

The cabin had a set of bunk beds on each side. Ron leaned against the top bunk on the port side. "Every once in a while I'll spend the night here by myself. It's not like being on the river. But it's better than nothing."

By the time Ron lit the heater and left, it was dark. We decided not to use the bunks. "I don't know who did what on those things." Patricia said. "I want my own bed."

While I pumped up our bed, Patricia made cold cut sandwiches. I was detaching the hand pump from the bed, when my wife asked. "What would you do if you were Ron?"

"What do you mean?"

"Well, after all those years of dreaming of living on the river, and then your wife says she won't do it–what would you do?"

I had a feeling this was a loaded question. So I treaded lightly. "Well, that's hard to say. I mean, they've raised a family and–"

Patricia interrupted me. "I'll tell you what you'd do. The same thing he ought to do. You'd tell her, 'You live in the house, I'll live on the river. I'll stop and see you now and then. If you decide to come along, you can.'" She paused. "And you would be right."

I had to think for a moment. "Sounds like me."

My wife handed me a sandwich. "That's what I love about you. You've got the guts to be true to yourself. Most people are like water. They take the path of least resistance. Ron took the easy way out, and now his dream sits on a flat tire."

As the cabin got warmer, the stink got worse. It smelled like rat urine, or a dead rotten critter. Or maybe it was the decay of an old man's dream.

⇥⇤

Louisville from the north bank.

CHAPTER 8

A HOME FOR
THE WINTER

❊

"I am in love with America's old river towns.
. . For me the princess of the rivers
(sorry, St Louis, forgive me Memphis) is
unquestionably Madison, Indiana."

-CHARLES KURALT-

LONG BEFORE WE GOT THERE, we had fallen in love with Madison, Indiana.
We first heard about it back in Kentucky. Someone said, "If you liked those
old buildings in Paducah, you're going to love Madison!" The further up the
river we got, and the more we heard and read about it, the more we loved "The
princess of the rivers." It's a town of 13,000, and 133 blocks of downtown has
been designated a National Historic District–the second largest in America.
To quote travel writer Dennis Wissing, "There are enough pediments and columns and elaborate cornices in Madison to start a toga fad, . . ." In his book
Traveling The Ohio Scenic River Route, Wissing quotes a first time tourist who
said, "Madison is such a beautiful hip place, I half way expected the residents
to be snooty. But they aren't. . . (it's) the kind of place where people sit on their
front porches and talk to strangers." Who wouldn't love a place like that?

"Hello Patricia. How are you?"

My wife heard that question as she was bent over a produce case in the Jayco Supermarket downtown Madison. We had walked into town just the afternoon before, so she was shocked to hear someone call her name. When she turned around she found Sarah Green grinning at her.

We had camped on Sarah's property the night before we walked into Madison. She and her husband Gene owned a farm three miles west of town. On the bluff where Highway 56 began it's descent into Madison, their 150 acres skirted the edge of a bluff that overlooked the Ohio River

Sarah was a wisp of a woman with gray hair that was cut in a bob. For thirty-five years she'd taught home-economics at the local high school, and when she spoke there was usually a hesitation before the words came out. Sarah didn't stammer or stutter. It was more like she double-checked everything to make sure that what she said was what she meant to say. "So, are you staying somewhere in Madison?"

We were camped in a lot on the west end of the city's river front park.

"Are you going to be around here long?" Sarah asked

"We've fallen in love with this town," Patricia said. "We hope to find some place close-by to spend the winter."

The next afternoon, a reporter showed up at our camp to interview us for the Madison newspaper. He had only been there a few minutes when Sarah walked into our camp with a small baked ham and a bowl of home-made potato soup. While the reporter interviewed me, Sarah and my wife went to the other side of our camp to chat.

"Patricia, do you remember the old white house on our farm?"

Constructed in 1840, it was a grand two-story brick Federalist style home. A rectangle shaped house with a high pitched roof, a chimney on each end and a large porch with tall white columns on the front. Gene Green told us most of the building materials came from that property. The bricks were made from clay dug on the farm, and the timber in the house was harvested on the place. It had been built as a gift for a slave mistress.

"No one has lived in the house since my mother passed away three years ago," Sarah said. "That is, nobody except Katy the cat."

Sarah and Gene Green's home was about a hundred yards from the old house. The farm also had two large barns and several other out buildings. But the Greens were not farmers. Gene was an executive for a local company that built lifts for auto repair shops. No animals were in the barns, and the Greens leased out the crop lands to a local farmer.

"Gene and I talked about you last night. We keep the old house heated for mother's cat, and the water is on because I'm still watering her plants. And we have to keep the phone on for the alarm system. So if you don't mind living with Katy you're welcome to stay there for the winter."

⚞⚟

"Bud, maybe I should drive, Patricia said. "The speed limit is forty. Look at you. You're white knuckled and you're only doing twenty."

The Greens loaned us their Datsun pick-up to fetch supplies for winter house keeping. Had we been downtown, in Old Madison, my driving would have been fine. But we were on top of the hill, on Clifty Drive in New Madison. Walmart, Mc Donald's and all of the usual American joints were up there. My wife was right. I wasn't fast enough for that crowd. In the past five months that we'd been on the road, I hadn't driven a motor vehicle. The speed of my feet had been just fine for me. I wasn't sure I wanted to go any faster.

But the reality right then was that we were no longer traveling at the speed of our feet. We'd stopped to settle down for the winter, and we needed some things to do that. And a truck was the best way to get them.

It had been more than fifteen years since livestock had been on the farm. So fences needed mending, gates built and the barn had to be cleaned before Della could settle in for the winter. So a roll of barbed wire was among the things we fetched on our first trip to New Madison.

Although Sarah and Gene had maintained the house since Sarah's mother passed away, it had been three years since anyone–but cats–had lived in it. So there was cleaning that had to be done. Hence, cleaning supplies were also on our list.

Since we hit the road, I don't know how many parking lots we'd pulled into with Della and the cart. It didn't take long to establish a routine. First, we tried to find something to tie her to. Like a light pole, sign post, dumpster or—the best of all—a tree. If we didn't find anything, we just pulled into a parking space. Then I used Della's water bucket as a seat and sat on it in front of her holding the rope, while Patricia went shopping. We usually made a new friend or few doing that.

It got to be such a common thing for us to do, that we never thought anything odd about it. When I parked that pickup at the New Madison Walmart and we walked in together, now that was strange.

❖

The day after Thanksgiving, I went into downtown Madison to apply for a job driving a horse-drawn carriage in the historic district. The owner, Jim Macke, asked, "Where did you learn to drive a horse?"

Back home in Hot Springs, I owned and operated a tourist business called "The Mule Line." With teams of mules, we gave tours of the city and national park on twenty passenger wagons that looked like 19th century trolleys. When I told Jim about that, he said, "That sounds great!"

Then he paused for a moment. "Say, you're the guy walking across the country with a mule—aren't you? I read about you in the paper. I'd like to hire you, but I'm looking for someone for next spring. I shut this thing down after Christmas. You'll be on the road when I'm ready to reopen."

Jim operated a large carriage company in Cincinnati. He had fifteen carriages there, but just one in Madison. He wanted someone to run the Madison business so he could concentrate on Cincinnati. It took a couple of days, but finally I talked him into letting me run on the weekends through the winter.

It was a Cinderella carriage pulled by a big white horse named "Belle." When I asked Jim about using Della, he said, "A mule pulling a Cinderella carriage? That would look weird."

"She is one classy mule."

A few weeks later, Jim was in front of the Fudge Factory when Della trotted up with his carriage full of passengers. I had on a full length black faux fur coat that I bought for four bucks at the Salvation Army. On my head was a second hand top hat with a piece of red garland for a hat-band. Della's harness was decorated with gold garland, red ribbons and sleigh bells. After the passengers got off and went into the Fudge Factory, Jim walked up and said, "You're right. That is a mighty classy mule. You guys look like a million!"

After I went to work for Jim, we moved Belle to the farm where we lived. When I suggested it, Jim said, "I don't know. Belle doesn't get along very well with other horses."

But Belle and Della were fast friends. Whenever I took Belle out of the barnyard to go to town, Della would stand at the gate and call to her. And Belle would do the same when Della left. As a pair, they were like Mutt and Jeff. We called her "Big Belle." Not big as in tall–big as in broad. She was at least six inches shorter than Della, but she probably outweighed the Big Sis by two hundred pounds. Belle's legs were short and squatty, with long white hair that hung down over her hooves.

The barn closest to the house was built into the side of a small hill. It had a stone basement with doors that opened out to a small pasture at the bottom. I repaired that fence and cleaned out the barn so we had two stalls. But unless we closed them up separately in the barn, we usually found the girls together in the same stall.

When not in use, the Cinderella carriage was parked in front of the Fudge Factory on the west side of downtown. Jim Macke had a buckboard that we drove the horse, or mule, back and forth between the farm and town. It was a three and a half mile trip on State Highway 56. The first mile and a half to town was the descent from the top of the ridge into the Ohio Valley. It began at our driveway and was a beautiful route that traversed the face of the bluff in long graceful turns. In a couple of places the roadway cut through rock with high rugged limestone walls with cracks that wept water on both sides of the highway.

Usually we drove to town in the middle of the afternoon and returned late in the evening. Both the Cinderella carriage, and buckboard, had headlights and flashing red taillights. For the trip home I attached the flashing yellow beacon from our cart on the back of the buckboard. I wanted to be sure we were seen.

The downtown tour was a nostalgic and romantic thirty minute ride. At night, it was exceptionally romantic as clip-clops echoed through the old neighborhoods on our way down to the river. We would wind our way along dark narrow streets past 19th century homes at a 19th century pace. Homes with flickering gas lights in their yards and bay windows that glowed with parlor lamps. On the pavement at the intersections, street lights would cast silhouettes of mule ears, top hat and the pumpkin carriage And as we rolled through the intersections, those shadows would float beside us.

At the corner of Second and Vine I would rein the trot in. Slowly, as we made the left turn, I would growl, "Take me to the river, girl."

While we ambled down Vine Street toward River Front Park, my passengers would gawk at the Lanier Mansion on their left as I told them about it. Completed in 1844, it's a two story Greek Revival house with four massive thirty foot white columns on the portico facing the river. At the time it was built it was considered the finest home on the Ohio River. James Lanier was a native of Madison and a self-made millionaire. He made his fortune as a lawyer, banker, merchant and railroad financier. He was so rich, that during the Civil War he loaned the state a million dollars to keep it from going broke.

At the river front we turned left, and the equine of the night would trot along Vaughn Drive as it paralleled the Ohio. Unlike the residential streets, the water front was well lit and there seemed to always be people in the park—regardless the hour. Floating at the shoreline was the Wharf Restaurant, which had been built on an old barge. Across the street from River Front Park was Kiwanis Park, whose basketball courts always had at least one game going on.

The trot along the Ohio was extra special when there was traffic on the river. Lights from the boats would shimmer across the water as grumbling motors propelled them along. From the coachman's seat, no matter how many times I saw the barges and tugs, I always got excited. While we cruised along at a trot parallel to them, I always felt this nostalgic glow. Like I had done this before, and it was good to be back.

Over the years in my travels and enterprises with horses and mules, I've often been asked, "Do you feel like you were born in the wrong century?"

I've never had to contemplate my reply. "Hell no! This is the perfect time for me."

From the river, we turned left on Mulberry Street where the one pulling the carriage picked her own pace up the hill. On Mulberry were a couple of taverns with a winery around the corner on Second Street. So people were usually milling around in front of those 1830's buildings as we passed by. It was slow-going up the hill, so there was enough time for an exchange of chatter between those on the sidewalk and us in the carriage. Always there was laughter–always it was fun.

At the top of Mulberry, when we turned left on Main, suddenly we were plunged into a flood of light. Street lights and neon for the eateries, taverns and other Main Street merchants. When we made the turn, my voice would echo off the buildings. "Come up girl! Show them what you've got!"

Sometimes when we trotted onto Main Street, people on the sidewalk would clap as I called out to the equine in front of me. Every once in awhile, when Della pulled the carriage, someone on the walk–always a man in a group of folks–would start he-hawing. I'd point to him and yell, "Hey Della, there's your daddy!"

(A mule has a mare horse for a mother, and a jack ass for a father.)

The Madison tour was wonderful, but it wasn't an adventure like the trip back to the farm at night. Especially as we got further into winter. I kept adding layers of clothes and was always on the lookout for warmer gloves. When we plodded up the hill to the farm, many times my feet hurt so much from the cold I would climb out of the buckboard and walk up the hill beside either Della or Belle to get my circulation going.

But no matter how cold, or wet, or maddening the night traffic would be, I always felt a thrill and sense of pride when headlights projected our shadows upon the face of the bluff. The high-spoked wheels of the carriage, the steed in front of me, my huge fur coat and of course the top hat–it all looked very Charles Dickens. I loved casting that shadow.

One day, in early January, Patricia rode into town with me. That night, as Big Belle pulled up the hill toward the farm, I handed Patricia the reins. "You drive home."

At the top of the hill, a biting westerly started pelting our faces with frigid rain drops mixed with ice pellets. Belle's nostrils blasted mighty plumes of breath that in the carriage lights looked like steam from a loco-motive. Patricia pulled on Belle's left rein and guided her into the driveway as she shivered and said, "I can't wait to get in the house and have a cup of hot chocolate."

But first there were chores that had to be done. After Patricia stopped Belle at the hitching post, we climbed out from under the carriage blanket and went about our jobs. Mine was to unhitch Belle, strip the harness off her and carry it into the enclosed porch on the house. Then I rubbed her down with a towel, while Patricia went in the house to mix the feed. I lit the kerosene lantern, then with it in one hand and Belle's lead rope in the other we headed for the paddock and the barn.

Every night, when we returned from Madison, the ritual was the same. At the paddock gate, the animal who didn't go downtown would be wait-ing to greet it's barn mate. No matter which one it was, I'd have to negoti-ate her away from the gate, so I could get the one I was leading into the paddock. Then, we three would stumble down the hill over frozen mud ruts to the barn basement. The equine that didn't go to town would get ahead of us and go into the stall of the one I was leading. So I would have to chase that one out before I could lead the other one into her stall. Then I would have to chase the other one out again and close the stall door–it was always confusing. But we always worked it out.

That's when the bobbing glow of Patricia's flashlight would appear at the other end of the basement. While she made her way down the stairs with the feed buckets, the barn sprang to life with knickers and the shuffle of hooves in straw beds. My wife would sing out, "Hey girly pies, look here. Mom's got supper for you. Who's hungry?"

Wooden stall boards would bang with blows from bodies and hooves. The racket always crescendoed until the rattle of corn and oats poured into their feed bins. Then, the old stable would settle down to a gentle cadence of grain being chewed by giant jaws.

I have always found something sweet and satisfying in the sound of a large animal eating. Maybe because that's one of the greatest pleasures they know, and I'm the one who brought it to them. Or maybe it's the peaceful expression that's always on their faces as they chew their feed. Probably it's a combination of the two that made those moments in the soft lamp light so romantic. The four of us, in that old barn basement—man, woman, horse and mule—were more harmonious in those moments than at any other time. "Gently satisfying" best describes the feeling I had at feeding time, when we came home late at night in the carriage from Madison.

⋈

It was around 9 p.m. one night in early January when I turned Belle and the empty carriage onto Third Street. At a trot, we were headed for the east side of town. Third was a dark residential street of 19th Century row-homes, and half way down the first block someone had laid a Christmas tree beside the curb. It wasn't there the last time we passed by, and when we got next to it Belle suddenly stopped, turned toward it and snorted. Then, in one motion, she leaped from a standstill to a full gallop. She paid no attention as I pulled back on the reins and yelled, "Whoa, Belle! Whoa!"

She ran as fast as her stubby legs could go. We flew along the dark narrow street with the carriage fish-tailing back and forth. I tried frantically to rein her in and keep the carriage from side-swiping the cars parked curbside. Finally, I found the brake pedal. But when I stomped on it, the back wheels skipped across the pavement and the whole carriage began to buck up and down with a horrendous clatter. It sounded like the whole back end of the thing was coming apart. All of this only made Belle run faster.

I took my foot off the brake and quit yelling. The only thing I could do was ride it out and guide her so the carriage didn't hit anything. Thank God the street was one way, and Belle was running in the right direction. We had already run the stop signs at both Vine and Elm Streets–and Broadway was dead ahead. It's a three-way stop that's usually busy because it's the main route to the hospital.

When we got close, I could see head lights stopped at the intersection. I pleaded, "If you're going to go, go now!"

But they didn't move until we were in the intersection. Just as we got to the center of the boulevard they started across. I screamed, "No, dammit! No!"

Car tires screeched as the white sedan lurched to a stop. Belle bolted to the left around the front of the car with the carriage wheels barely missing the bumper. While we sailed through the intersection the driver laid on his horn, which only egged Belle on.

We had already covered three blocks in this runaway, and only two blocks further was West Street. It had a traffic light, and it's one of the main thoroughfare's that connects downtown with New Madison on the hill. Approaching the red light, I could feel Belle begin to run out of steam, but I still couldn't get her under control. Then, just as we got to the intersection, the light in our direction turned green. When we crossed West Street, Belle slowed to a trot and by the time we got to Mulberry I was able to stop her. But my heart was still racing.

When we turned onto Main, I heard loud creaking and it sounded like something was rubbing at the back of the carriage. When I pulled over and turned around, I found the pumpkin listing off to the right. The pumpkin frame had popped out of the brackets on the carriage frame, and was leaning on the back wheel. I couldn't see anyway to fix it right there. All I could do was drive it that way back to the Fudge Factory. Downtown was deserted so no one saw me drive that cockeyed Cinderella carriage through Madison.

A couple days later I fixed the carriage and never had another problem with Belle. I didn't say anything to her owner about it until a couple of months later. When I did, Jim told me that he had problems with her on the streets of Cincinnati. He brought her to Madison thinking a smaller town might be better for her. I was sorry I ever told him. A few weeks later he took her away and brought a couple of other horses. Neither of them was as good as Belle downtown, and Della hated them both. All of us were broken hearted when they took her away, but it was worse for Della. She searched and called for Belle for days.

⚜

It was the middle of January before Patricia landed a job. She had a couple of things working against her. Mainly she was overqualified for the jobs that were available. One was as a waitress at Clifty Inn at Clifty Falls State Park. After the manager read her application, she asked, "So why do you want to wait tables here?"

This is where my wife made her mistake. She told them the truth. Everyone who interviewed her had read about us in the paper. They were all intrigued, but no one wanted to hire someone who'd be leaving in the spring. "Jeez, it's not like I'm trying to be a CEO," Patricia said. "I just want to wait tables."

So, when Patricia applied for a job at Frisches Big Boy, she told them, "We moved here so my husband could run the horse drawn carriage downtown."

They hired her at the handsome wage of $2.30 an hour. She did such a good job, that a month later they gave her a raise. A nickel.

True, she got tips. But when you work in a restaurant that has a buffet, a lot of patrons feel just because you brought them drinks you don't deserve a tip. After all, they got their own food, didn't they? What most people don't realize is, regardless if it's a buffet or you're being served a five-course-meal, that waitress is taxed on eight percent of <u>your</u> bill. Whether you tip or not.

Patricia's favorite group included Grandma, her daughter and three grandchildren– Grandma was buying lunch. They had to have a highchair for one of the kids—the others were too big for a highchair but not old enough to be in school. Throughout the meal the five-year-old kept screaming, "I want McDonald's!"

Grandma and her daughter ate from the buffet, while the children got something off the kiddie menu. The one in the highchair ate what Grandma spooned into her mouth. After a few spoons full, the toddler spit half of it out and it drooled down her face, onto her bib and into the highchair tray. Then she started bawling.

The tears stopped when Patricia brought a couple of fresh damp napkins and helped Grandma clean up the mess. During the cleanup, baby's head wobbled about with wide eyes fixed on the newcomer in her life. She rewarded the waitress with a fat cheeked smile that had bubbles coming out of it. Then, as my wife went to the next booth to check on those patrons, the baby started to whimper.

To keep her quiet, Grandma laid a paper napkin on the highchair tray and plopped some of Junior's fries down on the napkin. (Junior was boycotting them and the burger because it wasn't a McDonald's Happy Meal.) Then, to keep the baby entertained, Grandma squirted a blob of ketchup on the napkin. That way baby could use the fries, or fingers, to decorate the highchair. Most of the fries—coated with ketchup—fell on the floor.

After one spilt Pepsi, a tipped over milk and a kiddie burger thrown on the floor, they were ready to leave. When Grandma got the bill she said, "It's Senior Citizen's Day. Where's my discount?"

Patricia showed Grandma where it was taken off her meal. "But I'm paying for their meals too. It should be taken off the whole bill."

My wife was just the Slave Waitress. Grandma had to take it up with the manager. "He's at the cash register."

They all scooted out of the booth as Mother thanked my wife for being so helpful. "We're sorry about the mess."

Grandma got nowhere with the manager, but Junior got his way. Grandma said, "Honey, the boy has to eat something! We'll just pull into the drive-thru at McDonalds. It's on the way."

I'm sure I don't have to tell you they didn't leave a tip. Not only did Patricia make nothing, but she had to pay income tax on $2.40 of their bill.

⚜

The best part of Patricia's day was the ride home. Madison had a public transportation system called "CAR" (Catch A Ride). It was a service that picked you up at your door and took you to most of the commercial areas. In the afternoon, she came home on a small bus with a dozen residents from Madison State Hospital. They did piece work for a couple of the local manufacturers and lived at the hospital.

Patricia was the only one on the bus who didn't live there, and she was the last passenger they picked up on their way home. Most of the time they would get to the restaurant before Patricia was off the clock. So they'd wait in the parking lot–sometimes as long as half an hour–for her to come out. The patients were assigned seats on the bus, so Patricia was too. She sat in the back seat with Chucky who was in his mid-twenties, had light red hair and Downs Syndrome. In the parking lot at Friches, he would wait outside the bus to help her get on. Angel, who sat in the seat behind the driver, would always call out, "Here she comes. Here comes Patwisha!" Then she'd start clapping her hands, squirm in her seat and giggle as my wife stepped up into the bus. In un-unison chorus they'd all say "Hello, Patricia!"

"Hello, everybody!"

No matter how bad a day it had been, no matter how upset she was walking out of the restaurant, it all melted away as my wife looked down at the faces that welcomed her aboard. Some were contorted, there were those with nervous twitches and others just weren't normal. But they all had a separate sweetness to them. Some would wave up to her, others would touch her hand or pat her on the leg as she went by. And then there was Bert.

118

Bert was wiry, in his mid-twenties, with thick black eyebrows and a feisty grin. He was in the fourth row in the seat next to the aisle, but he could never just sit there. It seemed like Bert was always up to something. When my wife walked down the aisle, he'd wink at her in a Casanova sort-of-way. Then, when she got next to him, he would reach for her hand. "Hey Patricia, you can sit with me."

Chucky followed her and would always slap Bert's hand away. "No she can't! She sits next to me. Stay away from him, Patricia. Bert's nasty!"

After they sat down in the back seat, Chucky hardly said another word the rest of the way home. Bert, on the other hand, would turn around every few minutes, wink at my wife and give her a thumbs-up. Sometimes he would blow her kisses and point to himself as he nodded his head. But he never got out of the way with Patricia.

Bert was the jokester on the bus. He would slip out of his seat, sneak up behind someone and pinch them. Or maybe drop something down their back, then scurry to his seat. Every time, he would turn around, wink at Patricia and giggle. Chucky would always say, "That Bert! Nobody likes that Bert. He's no good! He's nasty!"

Then there was Gloria—the matriarch of the bus—who sat two seats ahead of Bert. She was at least ten years older than him and outweighed him by at least a hundred pounds. Several times on the way home she would yell, "Bert, grow up!" One time he leaned over the seat in front of him and stuck a cold bottle of Dr. Pepper on the back of Gloria's neck. She whirled around, slapped him hard across the face and screamed, "Grow up!"

Bert laughed, then turned and winked at Patricia with his thumb up.

One evening, on the way home, the guy in front of Gloria was complaining that he felt sick. Every time he said something about it, she would reach around, put her palm on his forehead and say, "Yup, you're sick all right. Sick in the head."

Late in the winter, Patricia got bronchitis and couldn't go to work for two weeks. Her first day back, when she climbed into the bus, it was pandemonium. They were all cheering and clapping. And the girl in the front seat cried as she bounced up and down yelling "It's Patwisha! It's Patwisha!" On his feet, in the middle of the isle, Bert was doing the twist with his thumbs up.

Patricia turned to the driver, a semi-retired man with a big grin on his face. "You've got yourself a fan club," he said. "They asked about you every day."

But the one who touched her the most was the man in a seat two rows ahead of her. He was always by himself, curled up in a ball, pressed against the wall of the bus. He never looked at or spoke to anybody. A couple of times Patricia saw him look at her as she walked toward her seat. When she smiled at him, he turned away and drew into a tighter ball. But that day, after she sat down next to Chucky, this young man slid out of his seat and shuffled to the back of the bus with his eyes cast down. He stopped in front of my wife, and without a word, leaned over and kissed the top of her head. Then, silently, he turned around and shuffled to his seat where he turned back into a cocoon.

⇥⇤

We made lots of friends while we were in Madison. Among them were John, Cheryl and their twelve year old son, Dylan. We met them while camped on the river front when we first got to town. John was a boat builder and ran Eagle Hollow Marina a mile east of Madison.

I wanted to put a lighter back axle on Della's cart, and John offered to help. The plan was that when we started traveling again, we would walk from the farm to Eagle Hollow on Friday, May 17th. On Saturday, John and I would replace the axle. then Monday we would hit the road headed east.

Cheryl home schooled Dylan and was active in a local home schooling group. She asked me if I would put on a poetry show for the group at Eagle Hollow. We set the time for 7 p.m. Friday night.

Thursday night when we said goodbye to the Greens, there were lots of tears. During the past six months we had become part of the family. Sarah said, "Next winter, if you don't find a good place to stay, just give us a call. We'll get a horse trailer and bring you back here."

Friday morning after everything was packed, the house cleaned and thank you cards set on the kitchen table, Patricia and I walked down to the barn to get Della. When my wife led her out of the barn, my attention was drawn to Della's right rear hoof. It had only half a shoe on it. She had broken it, and the outside half was gone. I would have to re-shoe her before we went anywhere. It was early enough in the day to do that and still hike to Eagle Hollow in time to do the show.

Della was in no mood to have her feet worked on. She had watched us get the cart ready. We were highway-bound, and she knew it. Being shod was not part of Della's plan.

She and I danced around for a bit, but finally she settled down and I got both feet trimmed. Then, as I reshaped the new shoe, I broke it. I didn't have another one road-ready. On the phone from Eagle Hollow, John said, "Bring it over and weld it back together."

So, I borrowed the Green's truck, drove across town and welded the shoe. While I was getting ready to put the shoe on, Patricia said "Shouldn't we take her for a walk first?"

It was mid-afternoon. I still had to get both shoes on Della, we had a six mile hike ahead of us, and then we had to set up the stage and put on a show. "I don't have time to take Della for a walk. We need to get going."

"But she's been standing here a long time."

I snapped, "She'll be alright!"

After I got the fourth nail in the right shoe, Della started to fidget and lean on me. So I poked her in the ribs with my elbow. "Straighten up!"

I had just finished the last nail, when she leaned so hard on me we both nearly fell down. I elbowed her again. This time she jumped so far the other way that I couldn't get under her. So I walked around to the other side of Della to push her back in place.

I was directly behind her when it happened. It came quick—deliberately and precisely. Della's left rear hoof slammed into my right thigh. I flew through the air and landed in a painful heap four feet away.

Patricia screamed, "Oh my God, no! Bud, are you okay?"

When I landed on the ground it knocked the wind out of me. Literally, I saw stars, and I couldn't breathe—much less answer my wife. She was frantic, "Bud, are you okay?"

A couple of days later, as Dr. Steve showed me the x-rays of my thigh, he said, "You have a bruised femur. Sometimes a bruised bone can be more painful than a broken one. You need to stay off this thing for a while."

"How long?"

He knew about our journey. "If you stay completely off it for two weeks, you could start using it slowly. Then, in another week you may be ready for the road."

He paused, "Don't push it. You'll just make it hurt longer."

I followed doctor's orders and just sat for two weeks with my leg propped up as spring got prettier. The longest string of perfect-for-traveling days we'd had, were those three and a half weeks that I was laid up on the farm.

Sarah Green said, "Maybe Della kicked you because she doesn't want to travel."

I could fill a couple of chapters with stories about how Della proved to us she loved the road. Like the way she'd paw the ground as we packed the cart in the morning. Then, as we hitched her to it, Della would get so excited that she could hardly stand still long enough for us to get hitched up. While we were walking, she was constantly looking from side to side checking out the scenery. Patricia called her "the perennial tourist."

Sarah asked, "So why did she kick you?"

"Because I had it coming. I got in a hurry and none of us were having fun. So Della slowed me down."

⌁⌂⌁

Downtown Madison with Belle.

CHAPTER 9

INTO THE HEARTLAND

❧❧

"HEY, WHAT GIVES OVER THERE?"

He had just sat down at a booth close to ours in a Bob Evans Restaurant near Aurora, Indiana. His was next to one of the front windows, and his stomach came close to keeping him from getting into the booth. He was inching his way across the vinyl seat, when the waitress said, "What's that Charlie?"

Out of breath, he stopped scooting and jerked his left thumb toward the window. "That over there–across the highway. What the hell's going on? Somebody open a campground over there?"

We had left Madison three weeks ago and took our time following the river. Later today we would cross the state line into Ohio. Now we were camped in an open grassy area next to the busy four lanes of US 50. It was a good distance off the highway, but everyone in Bob Evans had a view of our camp. A very fish-bowl sort of place.

The waitress was kind of cute, in her mid-thirties with a touch of Kentucky in her voice. She poured Charlie's coffee and said, "I read about them in the paper. It said they're walking across the country with a mule. Goin' east somewhere. I think Maine."

She pulled out her order pad. "So Charlie, what are ya' having? The usual?"

He nodded and stirred his coffee as the waitress scurried off. The way he stared out the window at our camp, I sensed something about it bothered him. When she brought his food, Charlie looked up at the waitress and grimaced. "So why are they doing that? They walking for cancer or something?"

"Naw, nothing like that."

While we listened to her, Patricia and I were impressed with how much of our story she retained. She told him we were poets, that I was writing a book and we planned to travel on foot for several years. The waitress ended with, "But mostly they just wanted to do it. I've got the paper at home. Want me to bring it tomorrow?"

He turned toward the window and shook his shaved head. "So they're just wandering around camping anywhere they damn well want, eh?"

She shrugged. "I guess."

When he turned back toward the waitress, his fleshy face was puckered with disapproval. "Who said they could camp there? Probably nobody. Just squatted. Sounds like a bunch of damn freeloaders to me." He picked up his fork and pointed it at the waitress. "They got a home somewhere?"

"I don't know. I'll bring you the paper."

"Don't bother. I got it figured out."

Dumping salt on his hash browns, Charlie laughed and shook his head. "In other words, they don't really have a life."

⌁

We decided to bypass downtown Cincinnati. It seemed like the safe thing to do. When I walked across the country in the 1970s with the pack pony and dog, I never hesitated to trek through a city. I walked into the hearts of Cleveland, Chicago, Portland, San Francisco and Denver. But it's like a lot of people kept telling me, "That was thirty years ago. Things are tougher now!"

I was also younger then, and I was single. But now I had a wife to think about. And Cincinnati had all those race riots. I saw it on TV. White guys being pulled out of trucks and clubbed in the streets.

"And you ain't even got a truck," said one good-ole-boy back down the river road. "They'll kill you, rape your wife and barbeque your mule!"

So I thought it best to go through the northern suburbs instead.

Jeff Swinger said, "They'll love you in Cincinnati."

We met Jeff as we walked into Aurora, Indiana. He and his wife passed us on their way home to Cincinnati from Madison. He was a photographer for the *Cincinnati Enquirer*. "When we drove by you, I told my wife, 'There has got to be a story here.'"

When we first saw Jeff, his face was behind a Nikon with a long white monster lens. He was in front of us, walking backwards, snapping away when he asked if we were going downtown. I told him why we weren't.

"Every city has its problems. And none are trying harder to fix them than Cincinnati. It's a great town. Come see for yourself."

That night in the tent, Patricia said, "If we're not going downtown because you're looking out for me, forget it!"

"Well–"

"Listen, I told you I would do this trip however you wanted to do it. And if you want to walk downtown, let's go!"

It first felt like we were coming into a big city when we camped in the town of Cleve on the west edge of Cincinnati. We spotted a big grassy spot next to a NAPA auto parts store, and they gave us permission to camp. In front of the lot, next to the highway, was a deep ditch with water in it. At the back of the lot was a row of trees, and behind them was several sets of railroad tracks. A few hundred yards to the west of our camp, was a switch yard for some sort of industry. Nearby, to the east was a crossing. So every train had to blow its whistle several times as they approached, and the tracks were busy throughout the night. So was the highway in front of our camp. And every once in a while a jetliner would fly low over us. We were definitely coming into a city.

"Hey, you've got a phone call!"

The guy who yelled that at me had just come out the side door of the NAPA store and was walking toward us. He was halfway between the store and us when he stopped, cupped his hands around his mouth and yelled. I hollered back, "For me?"

He nodded. "Yeah. It's inside the store."

I was dumbfounded. Who would call me at the NAPA store in Cleves, Ohio? We'd only been camped there an hour. When the parts guy and I walked back toward the store I asked, "Are you sure it's for me?"

"You're the only one around here traveling with a mule."

"Hi, I'm Chris Hursh with WKRC-TV Channel 12 in Cincinnati. Could we come out and interview you? We'd like to get it on this evening's news."

In the backroom of the parts store, with the receiver to my face, I was still awe-struck that I got a phone call. "How did you find me?"

The newsman chuckled. "I've had a lady tracking you all day."

⊰⊱

Cincinnati grew up in a basin on the river. It's where the Miami and Little Miami rivers run into the Ohio. A semi-circle of ridges and hills encompass the north side of the basin. Most of Cincinnati's residential neighborhoods and suburbs were up in those hills. Downtown is in the bottom of the basin.

Our route into town was Highway 50, which paralleled the river with railroad tracks between us and it. The closer to the city, the heavier and more rapid the traffic. Highway 50–a.k.a. River Road–was hard to walk on. Sometimes we had a shoulder, but most of the time we didn't. In some places it was a four lane, in others it was not. Almost all of it was pot-holed with wide spots of crumbled pavement. None of that deterred the speed of the traffic. Front-end alignment had to be big business in that part of town.

The farther we went, the more big trucks we saw. And it seemed like there was always a train on our right. On the other side of the tracks, perched along the river, were miles of giant oil and chemical tanks behind rusted chain-link fences. We passed several manmade mountains of coal, and a couple of times we saw huge white piles that looked like salt. The

127

acrid smell of industry, with a hint of sulfur, was the predominate bouquet of that neighborhood. And the reds of rust, with the yellows and blues of corrosion tinted everything made out of steel.

In the middle of all that industry, we pulled onto a wide dirt area beside the highway. It was lunch time. Patricia opened the kitchen compartment on the cart and began to make sandwiches, while I sat on Della's bucket and held her rope. She was grazing on a small clump of grass, when a mid-1980s brown Pontiac pulled in next to us with four young black men in it. The car had a few spots where it had been painted primer gray, and the right front hub cap was missing. From the front passenger seat, a guy with sunglasses and dread-locks leaned out the window and said, "Say Man, what 'ch you doin?"

I held up Della's rope so they could see it. "I'm holding onto my ass!"

The car was silent as they looked around at each other. Then the one who asked the question looked back out the window, pointed toward Della and blurted out, "I got it!" A huge grin was on his face as he mimicked my grip on Della's rope. "He's holding his ass!"

Instantly, they all burst into laughter. The Pontiac was rollicking as high fives made their way around the inside of the car. With a chuckle still in his voice, he leaned back out the window. "No, really man, what 'ch you and your woman doin'?"

"Right now we're walking to the coast of Maine."

"For real? You're walking all the way to the coast?"

"Sure am."

"So, you walkin' for cancer, or Jesus or something like that?"

"Oh, you want to know what our cause is?"

"Yeah man. What's your cause? Why you doing this?"

I stood up from the bucket and walked over to them. "Be-cause we damn well want to do it. We're just taking our time to see America. That's all there is to it."

A wide grin bloomed on his face. He took off his sun glasses, and a sparkle danced in his brown eyes as he extended his up-turned palm toward me. "Wow! Now, that's really bad man. I mean, *really* bad!"

Everyone in the Pontiac nodded and grinned as other hands emerged from the windows. When their car started to pull back into traffic, the one in the front seat leaned out and yelled. "Hey dude, you're in The Queen City now. Welcome to Cincinnati!"

Longfellow was the first to call Cincinnati, "The Queen City".

⧫

Further in town, Highway 50 took us through a neighborhood with narrow row-houses and old skinny buildings. Some of the houses were in good repair, but most were not. A lot of the buildings were empty with broken windows and graffiti. Weeds grew out of cracks in the buildings, sidewalks and curbs. It seemed like anywhere there was a crack, mother nature was trying her best to take over. Some sidewalks had chunks of concrete and bricks laying on them that had fallen from building facades And there were bits of glass glistening everywhere.

"Hey! I want to pet your donkey!"

It was a little white girl. She was four or five years old, jumping up and down and screaming at us from across the highway. A young black boy, probably a sixth grader, ran up and stopped behind her. He had the whine of the ghetto in his voice when he yelled, "Hey, mister! Wait up!"

Behind them were at least half a dozen more kids. All colors and sizes, running and screaming. I yelled at them from across the street, "Wait! We'll come over there."

The older kids kept the little ones from darting out into the traffic. By the time we got across the four lanes, the group had grown to fifteen— including a couple of young mothers with babies in their arms. When we pulled across the highway onto their street, the kids surged toward us jumping up and down and screaming. I held my hand up and roared, "Whoa! Stop right there."

They did. I had their attention. Loudly and slowly I said, "You will all get a chance to say hello to Della. But you can't jump or scream. That will scare her and make her jump and she could land on you."

They all said at the same time, "Oh." Then in unison they took a few steps back, as the oldest boy said, "Oh man, that would kill you!"

An older girl, who was holding the hand of one of the smaller ones said, "Baby Girl, if she stepped on you, there'd be nothin' left!"

Finally I got them to calm down. Then Patricia started escorting the little kids up to Della—a couple at a time. Each one of them squealed when her big mule nose first got close to their little faces. But within moments, all of them had relaxed and were giggling when she breathed on them. They all fell in love with Della.

"What's she eat?"

"She loves ice cream."

"Naw man, for real?"

"Yeah, she does. But she likes hay and grass and stuff like that, too."

Within moments kids were pulling weeds out of those urban cracks and feeding them to Della. After about twenty minutes, I said, "We need to get going. We've got a lot of miles to walk before we stop for the night."

"Dude, you can stay at my house," the sixth grader said. "People crash there all the time."

⧗

While we walked on Central Avenue toward the heart of the city, it was obvious Cincinnati knew who we were. Every couple of minutes from the windows of passing cars, or from people on the sidewalks, we heard "I saw you on TV the other night." or "Read about you in the paper this morning." And there were a few who yelled, "Hi Della!"

A block before we turned off Central, a man walked out the side door of an Italian restaurant with a handful of long carrots. They were scrubbed clean, with the lacy green tops still attached. Patricia was in the cart running the brake. When he handed them to her, he said, with an exuberant Italian accent, "I saved these for Della. I read about you's in the paper this morning. I knew you's come by here. God bless!"

On Fourth Street, we turned toward Fountain Square. Jim Macke, who owned the Cinderella carriage in Madison, picked up passengers for his Cincinnati carriages in the square. He told me when we got downtown to look for him there first.

In the middle of the square was the Tyler Davidson Fountain. Dedicated in 1871, it was a huge bronze sculpture more than forty feet high. On top of it was a woman with outstretched arms. From her hands water rained down on numerous bronze figures who were using or looking for water. They ranged from a fireman on a burning roof, to a boy strapping on ice skates.

It was mid-Saturday afternoon as we walked toward the fountain. Traffic swirled all around us, with cars, buses, taxis and delivery trucks jockeying for position. All around us was the unrelenting racket of revving motors, squealing brakes and intermittent horns. But above all that, was the sound of the water falling from the bronze woman's hands. It made the other urban noise much more palatable.

While we made our way through the chaos, Della was a princess. She just plodded along and responded to my every request. When we started into Fountain Square, the road surface went from pavement to metal grating. As we approached it, I began to get nervous. I hadn't walked Della across anything like that before. What if it freaked her out and she wouldn't walk across it? But she didn't even hesitate. With her shoes clicking across the steel grating, she acted like she had done it every day of her life.

Then suddenly, something exploded under us. A huge blast of steam rushed up through the grates and enveloped Della and me. We both lunged forward to get out of the steam. But as soon as we were out of it, Della immediately went back to plodding along.

When I tied her to a street sign in front of the Westin Hotel, it only took a moment for a small crowd to gather around. Some of them knew about us, and those who didn't were soon filled in by those who had read the story in that morning's paper. Among them was a young woman who asked us to autograph the article.

Patricia stayed with Della and the crowd, while I went in the Westin to find a phone to call Jim Macke. It took about twenty minutes to track him down and get directions to his carriage barn. When I walked out the hotel door, I discovered Della had done her part to beautify downtown Cincinnati. She'd nipped off a limb from the young urban tree in front of her. Part of it hung out the side of her mouth as she chewed. And behind her was a perfectly stacked pile of dark green mule turds.

Up to now, I haven't said anything about the poop aspect of traveling with a mule. We had a scoop shovel and a leaf rake to take care of it. But rarely did she do it while she was in the harness. In front of the Cincinnati Westin was the first time. What a classy girl!

⊰⊱

We spent three nights at Jim Macke's farm across the river in Kentucky. On Sunday he showed Patricia and me around Cincinnati in his BMW. Monday we toured the city on our bicycles. Then Tuesday we hitched up Della and were back on the road.

It was around noon when we stopped for a traffic light at Sixth Street and Vine downtown. A pack of pedestrians flowed from the sidewalk into the crosswalk in front of us. Among them was a tall woman, dressed in a tight fitting business suit, with amber hair draped about her shoulders. She had a cover-girl kind of face with a wide glossy red smile. With long grace-ful strides, she quickly got to the front of the pack, and it seemed like she was determined to get to us before the rest of the pedestrians—and she did. Then, stopping directly in front of me, she said, "Thank you for coming to Cincinnati."

She said that with such sincerity that I was dumfounded at first. I stumbled through, "Oh, uh, well. You're welcome."

While the rest of the pedestrians scurried past her, the woman stepped closer to me, reached over, took my left hand and held it with both of hers. "I really mean it. I read about you in the paper the other day. It was such an uplifting story. We talked about it at church Sunday. It's a wonderful thing that you're doing. You're living your dream."

She stepped closer and caressed my arm to her chest. Tears were in her eyes when she said, "Thank you for showing us that people can still do this in America!"

Then she dropped my arm and disappeared into the downtown crowd. When the light changed and we started through the intersection, I recalled what Jeff Swinger said when he talked us into going downtown. "They'll love you in Cincinnati!"

⁂

That afternoon as we hiked out of the valley, up through the suburbs, I often found myself thinking about what that woman said. I kept asking myself, "What did we do that was so special? All we did was walk through town. I don't get it."

"Oh, I think you do," Father Terry said, as he poured me another glass of beer from the pitcher. "If you don't, you should. It's really very simple."

The hike up to Silverton had been a long, hot, urban affair. So we appreciated it when they told us we could camp in the shade on the grounds of St. Vincent Ferrer Catholic Church. We especially appreciated their offer to open the church beer-tap after their meeting that night. The priest, a couple of nuns and a few parishioners, brought cold glasses and frosted pitchers full of beer to our camp just after dark.

I asked the priest, "What do you mean, it's very simple?"

"You're living your dream. Just seeing you walk down the street, it's obvious that's what you're doing. So *that's* what you did. You brought your dream to Cincinnati–a place where it's easy for dreams to get lost. People in a place like this need to see that."

I looked up at the illuminated bell tower with the silver half-moon shimmering above it and tried to think of a response. All I could come up with was, "Oh."

Father Terry put his hand on my shoulder. "You say you're walking just because it's something you've always wanted to do. But it's more than that. You're a sign of hope that there is more to life than just the everyday grind. It's your way of doing God's work."

How do you respond to something like that? I was speechless. It just seemed natural to look back up at the bell tower. After a few moments of silence the priest said, "And I would like to thank you for something, too. Thank you for camping here." He motioned toward the moon. "I have never seen the prayer tower look as beautiful as it does right now. I don't take the time to come back here at night to just sit and enjoy it."

He held up his beer glass in a salute. "Thank you. I will certainly do this again."

⧼⧽

I yelled to eager faces across the highway. "Do you want to come meet Della?"

They were the urban black faces of two young mothers with six small children huddled around them. The oldest child was about ten. When I told them to come over, the street corner sprang to life with squealing little kids jumping up and down clapping their hands. One of the smallest hopped off the curb like she was going to dash across the four lanes. But each mother grabbed a shoulder and yanked her back onto the sidewalk. One of them bent over and swatted the little girl's bottom as she scolded her. The ten-year-old grabbed his little sister's hand and held it as she stood on the sidewalk bawling. But, by the time traffic was such that they could get across, she was bright faced and skipping her way toward us–with big brother still holding onto her.

Like most little kids that first met Della, they were all in a hurry until they got close. About six feet from her they had slowed down to a nervous shuffle. Little sister, who was only as tall as Della's knees, was still bubbling with excitement, but she too was afraid to get closer. And the mothers stayed with their kids.

134

"It's okay, you can pet Della," Patricia said as she stroked our mule-girl's neck. "Just come up to her slow so you don't scare her."

While they were scooting closer, the ten-year old, with little sis in hand, suddenly veered away from the others toward Della's rear end. I yelled, "No! Don't go back there!"

My wife whirled around, lunged in front of those kids and guided them toward the others at Della's head. "You can get hurt back there. Stay up here with everybody else."

The children giggled and squealed as they ran their little hands up and down Della's front legs. Both mothers were petting her neck, when one said, "I never touched a real horse before."

"Really? Me neither. She sure is soft!"

Right then, a small school bus turned off the highway and stopped on a side street near us. I had seen the bus earlier back down the highway. What drew my attention to it then, was the beaming round face and enthusiastic waving of the woman driving it. When the bus door opened, she was the one who got out. A short, plump, white woman who walked up to us in hasty steps and said, "I just had to stop!"

The words bounced out of her. "We have a few disabled children on the bus who'd love to meet your mule. Could we bring them over?"

A few minutes later, two other women got out of the bus and began to lead five girls toward us. They were about ten years old, and each had some sort of impairment in their movement. A couple used metal crutches that wrapped around their arms just below their elbows. Another girl–without a crutch–dragged her right leg with each step, and there was one who limped like both her left leg and left arm were frozen stiff. Then there was the girl who had no physical problem, but she just couldn't seem to keep her mind on where she was going. She'd take a few steps with the rest of the group, then suddenly turn and go another way. The women guiding the girls toward us spent most of their time keeping track of that little wanderer.

When they got close to us, it was obvious the black mothers were getting nervous about that group. They thanked us, hastily collected their children and left before the girls from the bus reached us.

While the girls stroked Della, one of the women said, "We have one more girl, but it takes longer to get her off the bus."

A few minutes later, the driver stepped out the bus door with a folded wheel chair. One of the other women said "I'd better go help with Lilly."

It took both women to carry her off the bus and situate her in the chair. Lilly was much bigger and older than the other girls. I figured she was probably in her early teens. It was hard to tell from the way Cerebral Palsy contorted her body and face. Her head constantly bobbed about in the headrest on the chair, and her curled hands twitched every few moments. They told me Lilly was blind and couldn't speak.

"But she can hear and understand just fine," the driver said as she pushed Lilly's wheel chair closer to Della.

At first, the Big Sis didn't know what to make of it--the wheel chair with this bobbing and twitching girl in it. She had been patient with all of the children so far, but this was a lot different. Della wasn't sure she wanted anything to do with it and side stepped away from the chair. So I motioned to the bus driver to stop. "I don't think Della has ever been around a wheel chair. Let her figure it out before you come any closer to her."

The bus driver leaned over and said, "Lilly, the mule hasn't ever seen a wheel chair before. So we're going to sit still so she can get used to it. We don't want to scare her."

A series of excited grunts came out of Lilly, as she tried to nod. That piqued Della's curiosity. Slowly she moved her regal head toward the girl and sniffed the air around her. Then, Della took a step toward the chair while she continued to sniff. After another step, she stretched her neck out until her muzzle was next to Lilly's cheek. The air from her nostrils blew strands of the girl's blond hair about her face. Lilly squealed with excitement. Della drew back a bit as the bus driver said, "Lilly, be careful not to scare Della."

Our big mule girl was more surprised than scared. She slowly moved her face toward the girl again. But this time she didn't sniff. I could tell Della desperately wanted to make contact with Lilly. When her whiskers touched the girl's cheeks, Lilly squealed again. But this time Della didn't pull back.

"I think Della has figured it out," I said. "Push Lilly closer to her."

When she did, Della stood still and let the chair come up beside her. Then the driver guided Lilly's hands to those big mule shoulders. While she helped the girl pet the soft fur the driver said, "This is Della the mule. She likes you, Lilly."

Right then Lilly leaned forward and laid the side of her face on Della's coat. For those few moments the bobbing and twitching stopped. Tears began to roll down her cheeks, as she cooed like a baby. A sweet peaceful expression lit Lilly's face.

My vision began to blur. When I took off the sunglasses to wipe my eyes, I found the other adults wiping their eyes too.

When people asked us why we were walking, our standard reply was "Because we want to." But when pressed with, "Why do you want to?" I found myself stymied–unable to answer. The truth was, I really didn't know why. Over the past two and a half decades, I asked myself countless times, "Why are you so consumed with this journey?" The answer was always the same. "It's just something I've got to do." Standing on that urban sidewalk in America's heartland, with Della and Lilly, I saw a new depth in that answer.

⌘

"Child, what are you doing out in this weather?"

When Arlene Justice opened her back door and found Patricia on her stoop, a churn of clouds was overhead and a few fat drops were splattering on my wife. When the front rolled in from the north, we were about five miles southwest of Springfield, Ohio, on Highway 68. It looked like this was going to be a rough storm. So, when we spotted the big barns behind Arlene's house, we pulled in to ask if we could hunker down in one.

"Honey, I don't own those barns. But you and your husband come on in here before you get soaking wet! They say we're in for a lot of rain."

Arlene was short, in her mid-seventies and a bit bent at the shoulders, with silver hair curled close to her head. She wore a sack-shaped dress made out of a light, flowery material.

In her back yard was a sprawling elm tree. It would be good shelter for Della, so I tethered her under it with hay, feed and water. Then, just as I stepped up onto Arlene's stoop, the sky let loose. The clouds couldn't hold back anymore.

"The Lord was looking out for you," Arlene said, as I scrambled through her kitchen door. She handed me a big fluffy bath towel. "You come on in here and make yourself at home. It ain't much, but at least it's dry."

Patricia was sitting at the cluttered kitchen table with a steaming cup of tea in front of her. I was rubbing the rain off my head, as Arlene said, "Like I told your wife, I'm sorry for the mess. But since I lost my husband, there just doesn't seem to be any reason to put all this stuff away. He's been gone a year."

The table was cluttered with boxes of paper records, photos and old newspapers. There was also a stack of that sort of stuff in a corner on the floor. Arlene insisted on fixing us dinner. "But we'll have to clear a place to eat. I usually just sit at the counter."

While I helped her move some of the boxes from the table to the floor, Arlene said, "I'm trying to get this all sorted out so my kids don't have to mess with it when I'm gone. Should have done it a long time ago. But my husband got sick, and . . ." She sighed, and slid the last box across the table to me. "Well, one thing about it, now I've got the time."

Dinner was going to be hot dogs, home baked beans, apple sauce and angel food cake. Arlene was at the stove fixing it as she told us her oldest son lived on the other side of the hayfield next door. She was dropping hot dogs into the steaming pot when she said, "He comes by a couple times a day. His wife stops in a lot too. And so do my grandchildren. They all want to take care of me. But I can take care of myself."

Arlene put the lid on the hot dog pot as she said, "Lord, that's all I've got left to take care of, is me. And that's no fun."

After she said grace, Arlene looked across the table at me with twinkles in her eyes. Her face was beaming. "I just can't believe it! I saw you on TV last night, and now here you are. It's such a blessing!"

She handed Patricia a glass bowl of apple sauce. "Sometimes my husband comes to me and tells me things. Most of the time it's in my dreams.

But sometimes it's when I'm awake in the middle of the day. And he'll be just as alive as you or me."

With the spoon that she was about to stick into the bean pan, Arlene pointed across the table at me. "When I came out here this morning he was sitting right where you are. And he was smiling as big a smile as I ever saw on him. He told me I was going to have a great day today. And that tonight was going to be extra special. He said it was something I really needed. But he wasn't going to tell me what it was. He just started laughing."

Shaking her head, with a chuckle in her voice, Arlene plopped a small pile of beans on her plate. "When he was alive he used to do that to me all the time—tease me like that. Tell me I was going to get something, then wouldn't tell me what it was. He'd just laugh and say 'You'll see.' That's exactly what he did this morning."

She handed the pan of beans to Patricia and said, "Now I know what he was talking about. You can bet he's getting a big kick out of this."

When Arlene invited us in, she said she had an extra room with a double bed already made up. "I changed the sheets on all the beds today."

I figured Patricia and I would sleep in the extra room. But when it came time for bed, Arlene insisted that we take hers. It was king-size with a big screen TV at the foot of it. We hadn't watched TV in ages. The last time in bed was back in the hotel in Paducah. We decided to live it up and watch Jay Leno's monologue. But we barely made it through the local weather. It was going to be clear in the morning.

Patricia turned off the bed lamp, then whispered, "Isn't this something? Here this dear lady took us in out of the storm, fed us, gave us her bed, and she acts like we're doing her favor."

"Yeah, I know. And I keep asking myself, 'What did we do?'"

Slowly my wife said "We knocked on her door."

I pondered that for bit. "I guess she really needed that."

"Bud, lots of people need someone to knock on their door."

⊰⊱

Crossing the Ohio in Cincinnati

CHAPTER 10

WELCOME TO COLUMBUS

❧❧

"GIT THAT ANIMAL OUT OF here," the security guard's voice squeaked. "Now, git!"

It was a steamy Friday afternoon in the suburbs of Columbus, rush hour was in full swing and the smog was at choke-level. We had just pulled into the parking lot at Westland Mall, when the security guard emerged from the building. It was a huge parking lot with barely any cars in it. I wanted to give Della a drink of water and rest her a bit, so we stopped in the shade of a small tree close to the highway. The security guard had to stomp a long ways to squeal, "Now git!"

At the beginning of this book, I told you all the people in this story were real, but I changed some of their names. This is one of them. From here on, that pasty little pear-shaped security guard will be known as "Officer Pinky."

I fear Pinky must have said "Git!" at least half a dozen times before he got close enough for me to understand him. Rush hour was drowning him out. But long before I heard him, I could tell he didn't want us there. Sweaty Pinky was huffing and puffing when he reached us. If you could have heard his voice, and seen his face, you would understand why I call him "Pinky."

"We just stopped to give our mule a drink of water," I said.

He pointed toward the parking lot entrance, puckered up and snorted, "I don't care what you stopped to do. We don't want you here. Now git!"

"But—"

"No but's about it," Pinky squealed. "This is private property. You're trespassing! We don't want you here. Now git!"

At first he was comical. But now he was pissing me off. I stepped toward him. "Are you telling me that if my wife wanted to shop in that mall, I couldn't wait for her?"

For the moment that he pondered that thought, I could see the pulse in the veins on his pale pink head. The man's heart was racing. Then, as if his index finger was the barrel of a pistol, he aimed at me and squeaked, "I told you, we don't want you here. Now git!"

He was shaking. Whether it was with fear or anger, it didn't matter. A shook up man with a badge, a walkie talkie and a loaded finger is not someone to mess with.

So I untied Della. When I turned around to lead her away, I came face to face with Pinky. I made sure he knew I was reading his name badge as I glared down at him and said, "Let me tell you something Officer Pinky, I've walked all over this country–coast to coast and half way back again. That's a lot of miles. And I've never had anyone be so rude, or . . . or stupid as you are right now!"

He took a couple of steps back, put the walkie talkie to his mouth and screamed. "This is Pinky! Call the police! He just threatened me!"

"I didn't threaten you. We're leaving."

With that we started toward the next exit.

"Not that way," Pinky squealed. "The way you came in."

"But that way is easier."

"We don't want you crossing our property. Go out the way you came in" Repeatedly he jabbed his finger in that direction. "Now git!"

At the entrance to the parking lot, as we waited for a spot in rush-hour traffic, I turned to my wife and said, "Welcome to Columbus."

It was the first Friday afternoon in August, and it felt like it. Everything was hot. The sun, the air, the pavement, the traffic, the exhaust, my temper–it was all hot. We needed to get off the highway and into some shade.

A little farther down the road, we came to a large manufacturing plant owned by the Delphi Corporation. I never did find out what they made there. I was more interested in their shade. They had a row of huge oak trees along both sides of a long driveway. It was the entrance for shipping, receiving and employees. The factory was surrounded by several acres of green grass. A hundred yards before the security shack was a shady place, with picnic tables and a small pond that had ducks swimming on it. It would be a perfect place to camp. While I waited there with Della, Patricia hiked to the security shack to see if we could stay there for the night.

They weren't able to find the person who had the authority to say "yea" or "nay." But the shift manager said we were welcome to rest in the shade and wait for rush hour to slow down. So we did.

In that shade, I kept rehashing what happened with the security guard back at the mall. What did we do to provoke him? To be honest, sitting in the shade on Della's bucket, my feelings were hurt.

While I sat there pouting, I heard in the distance a woman's voice on a public address system call out, "Parts department, line one."

Then, from another direction it was, "Steve Brown to customer service, please." Hardly had that voice hung-up, when another one clicked on across the highway. It had a nasal tone. "Jim Williams, call accounting." Somewhere closer, a seductive woman's voice said, "Paul Tucker, Paul Tucker. Please report to the body shop."

Nearby, both sides of the highway were lined with car-dealerships. Places with names like, "Westside Dodge–The Home of Trader Bud," "Lyman's Chevrolet–Save thousands Bobby's Way" and at least half a dozen more were within earshot.

Listening to this flurry of announcements, I began to mellow out. Because if someone had said, "Bud, go here or call there!" I knew it wasn't for me.

Then my brain conjured up, "Officer Pinky, call security!"

My imagination could hear resonating throughout the mall, "Officer Pinky, we have gypsies in the parking lot. You go out there and tell them to git!".

The thought put a smile on my face.

⌐◻╠

We camped that night in a vacant lot at the end of Huron Street in the Hill Top District. The next morning we walked on Broad Street toward downtown Columbus. The heart of the Capitol City is on the Scioto River. From Hill Top it was a steady descent into the heart of town.

People didn't stop us to visit, like they did in Cincinnati. The stories I told you about our walk through the Queen City were just a sampling of our encounters there. But on our walk through downtown Columbus, not much happened.

We did have three twelve-year-old black kids accost us at a traffic light. They were getting kicked out of a church as we walked by. A big wedding was going on inside, and these boys obviously weren't on the guest list. All of them were crazed with laughter as they scrambled down the church steps toward us. One of them screamed, "Hey man, let me ride that donkey!"

The kid in front of him yelled, "I'm going to ride it first!"

"No you're not, nigger! I said it first!"

Right then our light turned red. We had no choice. I was going to have to deal with them. Unlike little kids, this pack didn't stop running until they got to us, and it startled Della. She shuffled a little to the left, while I whirled around to the right side of her head, pointed to the boys and roared. "Don't! Stop there!"

They all froze for a moment. Then, as if on cue, they sprang back into action. One leaped onto the cart, and the other two sprinted up to Della's side. I jumped in front of those two with my fist up. "Get back!"

In the cart, Patricia stood on the brake petal, and with one of the wooden wheel chocks in her hand, she hissed in the kid's face, "Just try it, you little bastard!"

He jumped back off the cart and whined, "Hey, all I want is to go for a ride."

Patricia shook the piece of four-by-four at him. "Stay back! No one goes for a ride."

The two boys in front of me shuffled back a little as one of them said, "How come we can't go for a ride? How much you charge?"

The kid next to him burst into laughter and slugged him in the shoulder. "Dude, what are you talking about? You ain't got no money."

I said, "We don't sell rides."

The one who tried to climb in the cab said, "Then take us on a free ride."

They all started laughing and dancing around on the sidewalk giving each other high-fives. This was getting tedious. How I wished that light would change.

"Come-on, dude. Take us for a ride." The tallest one strutted up to the curb half a dozen feet in front of me. He had his left hand on his crotch, while he gestured like a rapper with his right one. "You ain't doing nothing but standing here. We want to ride."

Whenever I see a man grab himself in public like that, I feel like saying, "You hoping something will show up down there?" But I didn't. I just stared at the traffic light.

"I'm talking to you." His voice was angry. "What, you too good to talk to me?"

Right then the light changed. I didn't have to tell Della to get up. She was ready to go. The kids started into the cross walk beside us. "Say man, where you going?"

"Don't!" was all I said. But the word came out with such conviction, that it even startled me. All three of them immediately stopped in their tracks in the crosswalk. No one said a word. They just turned around and walked away.

⌘

"Hello, Della. Hey, you guys. Welcome to Columbus! It's Annette."

We were less than a block from Franklin Park, on the east side of the city, when Annette pulled up to a stop sign on a side street. She was driving an older white convertible Volkswagen Rabbit with the top down. From across the highway, her silver-haired-head and excited face were above the windshield, while she waved wildly and yelled, "Bud, pull into the park!"

Three days earlier–west of Columbus–we met Annette Kuss in Lafayette, Ohio. It was at the Red Brick Tavern where we had lunch with her and some of her friends from Springfield. Her friends had read about us in the newspaper, saw us on the road and invited us to lunch as we were walking past the tavern. She lived in the Columbus suburb of Bexley and knew nothing about us. But after she heard the story she invited us to stop and spend a night at her house when we walked through the city. "It's on the east side of Franklin Park. You can put Della in the back yard."

She paused, then said, "That is, if it's all right with the town. I need to check with the mayor and make sure it's okay."

"You probably ought to check with your husband, too."

"Steve?" She waved off the notion. "He'll love it."

When Annette got out of her car at the park entrance she was effervescent. "I talked to the mayor and he said it was fine if Della spends the night at my house."

"How far is that from here?"

"I'd say a mile and a half or so. No more than that."

It was a hot afternoon. The heat radiating up from the pavement was miserable. We needed to get off the road and into some shade for a while.

Annette said, "There should be a shady place in the park."

Unlike downtown, the park was alive with activity and the parking lots packed. But eventually we found a shady spot and pulled into it. I had just opened Della's water bucket, when I spotted a golf cart headed our way. It had a sign on it that read "Security Guard."

Oh no, not again?

I couldn't call this security guard "Pinky" because this one was black. He was short, his hair gray at the temples and he had a pleasant expression on his face when he asked, "What are you folks doing?"

I was still feeling the sting of the security guard the day before, so I was defensive when I replied, "We just stopped for a few minutes. I need to give our mule a drink and cool off in the shade. We won't be here long. Is that okay?"

"Sure. But I can show you a lot better shade than this."

I thanked Ernie, then told him, "This is fine. We just stopped for a few minutes."

Annette sounded like she was bragging when she said, "They're going to spend the night at my house in Bexley."

After answering his questions about our journey, I gave Ernie one of our fliers and he drove off. A few minutes later he returned with a man and woman on the back of the cart. The woman said, "Ernie told us about you, and I read your flyer. I think this is wonderful! Could we buy you lunch?"

Barb Jenks Tiffan was director of the Franklin Park Conservatory. Besides buying us lunch at their café, she offered us a free tour of the conservatory. The original glass pavilion opened in 1895 and has been in operation ever since. In it were botanical gardens and rooms with habitat that ranged from desert to tropical. In the Pacific Island Water Garden, the air was alive with butterflies from Asia, Africa and South America. It was a treat that thrilled all the senses.

You could spend a whole day at the conservatory and not see it all. But we only stayed two hours, we had Della to think of. We had moved her to the "better shade" that Ernie told us about. He had me tie her to a "No Parking" sign, where I hung her a bag of hay. While we were in the conservatory, Ernie and his partner, Gary, kept an eye on Della. Even so, two hours was a long time to be away from our girl. We knew she'd be excited to see us. Especially when we showed up with two Hagen Daz ice cream bars.

Bexley was *the* suburb of the well to-do on the west side of Columbus. Even the Governor's Mansion was there. Annette and Steve lived in a stately old home, with ancient oak trees that shaded a lush green lawn. When I warned them about the damage Della could do to their yard, Steve said, "I plan to re-landscape the backyard anyway. She's fine."

The next morning, when we left Annette's house, she accompanied us on her bicycle. She wanted to take our picture in front of the Governor's Mansion. It was a gothic stone house, with a huge manicured lawn, majestic oak trees and beautiful flowerbeds. All of it was surrounded by an iron and stone fence with massive gates and a stone drive that curved up to the front door.

After Annette snapped a few pictures in front of the house, we went around the corner and stopped in front of two iron gates. Inside those gates, behind the mansion, was a smaller house with a State Highway Patrol cruiser parked in front of it. Two uniformed officers were close at hand, keeping their eyes on us.

I had just turned toward Annette, so she could take a picture, when I heard a man's voice behind me. "Say, what's going on here?"

He wore Bermuda shorts, a t-shirt and ball cap. The man was about my height and around the same age as me. I figured he was a gardener. "We just stopped to take a couple of pictures."

Both officers stepped up beside the man as Annette said, "It's the Governor!"

I asked, "You're the Governor?"

Bob Taft grinned as he put his hands on his hips and chuckled. "Last time I checked. So who are you? And what are you doing?"

After I gave him a brief rundown, the Governor said, "You walked here from Arkansas? My wife is from Arkansas."

While I was telling him about our trip, a younger man walked up beside the Governor. He was Bob Taft's nephew. The Governor told him, "Go up and get Hope. She'll want to meet these people."

Then he turned to me. "Have you got a few minutes? I want my wife to meet you."

He motioned for the patrolmen to open the gate. I was leading Della up the driveway, when Ohio's first lady came out the front door of the mansion wearing a pair of Burkenstocks, blue jeans and a frumpy shirt. At her side, was their daughter Anne. Hope Taft shook my hand as she said, "I know who you are."

The Governor asked, "You do?"

"Yes. I read about them in the *Cincinnati Enquirer* a couple of weeks ago. Bob, have them come up to the front of the house. I want to get some pictures."

With that, Ohio's First Lady turned around and trotted back into the mansion. We had just stopped in front of the house, when she came out with a camera and a clipping of the article about us from the Cincinnati paper. She handed it to her daughter. "Here Anne, I cut this out for you while you were on your trip."

The Governor had a hurt look on his face. "Why didn't you show it to me?"

Hope shrugged her shoulders. "I don't know."

Then she put the camera up to her face and motioned for the Governor to move closer to me. "Get next to Bud, so I can get you both in this picture."

We visited with the Tafts for better than an hour and a half. I gave the Governor and his family a tour of the cart. Then Mrs. Taft said, "Come in and let me show you around the mansion."

"I need to tie Della up to something first."

"Tie her to that tree." Bob Taft pointed to one on the manicured lawn.

"She might paw up the grass."

"We've got people to take care of that. Come on in."

He was in the middle of his first term. Before he was governor, Bob Taft represented Ohio in the US Senate. He was an avid bicyclist, and had ridden all 1,000 miles of Ohio's Rails-to-Trails.

During our visit, the Governor pulled out a state road map and we talked about our route. "You've got to go through Holmes County. It's the largest concentration of Amish in the world."

"In the world? You mean even more than Lancaster County, Pennsylvania?"

The Governor nodded. "The countryside is beautiful. Rolling hills with lots of farms—all of it tended to with horses. They'll love you."

He brought us ice water in old jelly glasses. And Hope kept asking Patricia if she needed to use the bathroom. "We have several."

The governor, and the first lady, walked with us down their driveway toward the street. While we approached the gate, I could see that the patrolman was having a problem with the gate motor, so he manually tried to open it. When we got there, both Bob and Hope grabbed hold of it and helped him push the gate open.

When we walked past him, Governor Taft saluted me. "If you come back through Columbus, and I'm still here, give me a call and let us know you're coming."

In our guest book Governor Taft wrote "Thanks for coming to Ohio!"

Showing Ohio Governor Bob Taft the cart.

CHAPTER 11

AMONG THE
PLAIN FOLK

⚜

WHEN WE WALKED ACROSS THE Kokosing River on the US 62 Bridge, I looked down and spotted a wide gravel bar at the base of the southern bank. It had lots of shade, good graze for Della and a long gravel beach next to clear flowing water. A perfect place to camp for a few days. It was time to re-shoe Della, and this would be a great spot to do it.

Patricia said, "I don't know if we should take the cart down there."

"Why not?"

Long ago someone had bulldozed a short narrow driveway down through the bank onto the beach. My wife pointed at it and said, "It looks too steep."

"Get in and ride the brake. It'll be all right."

She climbed in saying, "I'm not worried about going down."

It was steep, and going up would be a tough pull. But it was nothing Della couldn't handle. Besides, it was dirt and gravel, so she'd have lots of traction. I signaled like a wagon master leading a train of covered wagons headed west. "It's no big deal. Let's go!"

And down we went, me slowly leading Della around the ruts and holes—creations of storms gone by. Halfway down, a cart tire skidded in loose gravel. Patricia gasped, "I don't know about this."

A minute later, we were down on the beach rolling smoothly along the gravel toward a perfect spot to camp. In less than an hour we had the tent up about twenty feet from the water's edge, with a fire flickering in a circle of charred rocks that had held many previous fires. It was the perfect spot for a vagabond camp.

The Kokosing wasn't a wide mighty river. It was a canoe kind of stream, with rapids that looked like undulating wrinkles where they flowed in and out of long smooth pools. Our camp was next to a still pool that was about a hundred yards long. The newest Highway 62 Bridge was at the upstream end of it, and the downstream end flowed into rapids under the old bridge.

Of all our campsites so far, this one was the most pleasing to the ears. There was the water that babbled and chattered over stones as it flowed in and out the pools. And then there was the sound of the crackling fire, whose flames leaped up between the logs to ignite the night with an orange glow. Every-so-often there was an explosion of sparks that spewed into the night sky like fireworks. I think small fires, and jabbering rapids, are more meditative than major conflagrations and roaring cascades. The senses aren't overwhelmed. Your spirit is free to be carried away by the flicker and babble of it all.

Another treat for the ears was the sound of hoofs and carriage wheels up on the highway. Into the late hours of Friday and Saturday night, carriages with flashing lights rolled across the bridge above our camp. Sunday morning it was often like a parade of buggies. No doubt about it, we were in land of the Plain Folk. This was Amish country.

We met lots of people during our three days on the river. None were Amish, but most had lived around there all of their lives. Men and women who grew up playing on that gravel bar. One middle aged man said, "I sure drank a lot of beer on this beach!"

Sunday, late in the afternoon, a crowd of people came down to the river for a baptizing—the Pentecostal kind, where the baptized, and the preacher, wade into the river in their Sunday best. Bending them backwards, the preacher dunked them completely under, while on shore, the congregation sang, clapped, cried and testified. It was very exciting. But not as exciting as that evening.

It began about an hour after sundown. Patricia and I were sitting next to our riverside fire, when a huge rain drop landed on one of the burning logs. It sizzled, spattered and steamed away before it could drip down into the heart of the flames. Then another, and another, followed by several more. Through orange steam my wife looked at me and asked, "What's the forecast?"

"Last time I saw the Weather Channel—"

Suddenly, a jag of white ripped across the night sky. Like the report from a dozen sharp shooters, the heavens sprang to life with flashing. It sounded like bullets ricocheting all around us as we scurried to the tent. After a few moments of fighting with the door zipper, I yanked it open just as Mother Nature tipped her bucket over.

"Got it!" I screamed, then pushed Patricia inside, with me tumbling in behind her.

After zipping it shut, I turned toward my wife and said, "Rain."

Patricia was rubbing her head with a towel. "Huh?"

"You asked for the forecast. I think it's going to rain."

And it did, all night long. It was an hour past dawn before it quit. When I stuck my head out the tent door I was shocked at what I saw. "Oh-my-God!"

My wife rustled around in her sleeping bag as she said, "What?"

"The river is coming up. We need to get out of here!"

Instead of twenty feet, our tent was now less than six feet away from the river. The clear sweet ripples had become churning brown rapids frothing around boulders that earlier had been high and dry on a gravel bar midstream. The once babbling Kokosing now was grumbling.

We broke camp, packed the cart and hitched up Della faster than we ever had. Even so, by the time we got moving, the water was up to our wheels. Della had to step into the river to turn the cart around. When we got to the steep driveway, without hesitation, Della lunged into the pull. I had to trot to keep up as sturdy mule legs climbed up the hill. The rain had loosened the bank gravel, so each of her steps slid backwards a bit. Still she steadily kept moving.

We were almost to the top, when the right rear wheel dropped into a rut, and everything jerked to a stop. I yelled, "Get up, Big Sis!"

She leaped forward and popped the wheel out of the rut. But Della couldn't get traction in the wet gravel. Gravity took control, and the cart started pulling Della toward the river. I helped her guide it back down to the beach.

At the bottom, with hands on her hips, Patricia shook her head. "I knew coming down here was a bad idea."

And I knew *that* was coming. It sent a flare up my spine, but I ignored it and simply said, "Della can do it. If the wheel hadn't hit that rut we'd be on the top right now."

Patricia's rolled her eyes and arched their brows. "I don't know about that."

After Della rested for a few minutes, we tried it again. "Come-on Sis, let's go!"

Della leaped up the hill, and got up it faster than before. But the right rear wheel dropped into the same rut and jolted the cart to a stop. Before I could say anything, she lunged and popped the wheel out. But gravity, and the soft soil won. Again we backed down to the bottom, where the gravel bar was getting smaller—and the river wider.

"I knew it!" Patricia stalked around the cart with hands on her hips. "I knew we shouldn't have come down here." She stopped face to face with me, shook her trigger finger at me and yelled, "Didn't I tell you she couldn't make it?"

"If it wasn't for that rut she—"

Patricia exploded, "Rut, smut!" She aimed her finger at the cart. "She can't get it up there because we've got too much shit!"

I wanted to yell, "If I didn't have you, I wouldn't need all this shit!" But I kept my mouth shut and just stood there seething.

Exasperated, Patricia threw her hands up in the air. "So, now what do we do? Eh?"

One of the locals that we had met was a volunteer fireman, Don Brunner. He lived about a mile away and had a four-wheel drive pickup. He told us, "If you have trouble getting up the hill, come find me. Unless I'm out fighting a fire, I'm usually home."

So I took my bicycle off the back of the cart to go find Don. I was strapping my helmet on when Patricia said, "Don't take too long. The river is still coming up."

At the top of the driveway, I climbed on my bicycle and headed toward the village of Millwood. Although the road was badly pot-holed, it was smoother than things back on the beach. When I looked down from the old bridge to where Patricia, Della, and the cart were stranded, I started sputtering to myself, "It's bad enough we've got this problem, but I have to put up with her attitude too."

The further from the river I got, the more relaxed I felt. My legs were enjoying the smooth aerobic exercise and my spirit relished the lack of confrontation. *Man, this is living! Just me and the road. I should have made this a bicycle trip. It would have been a whole lot easier than dealing with a wife and mule.*

Then a familiar voice from deep inside me said, "Hey, you've got a hundred bucks in your wallet. Go for a ride. Man, you deserve it. Get away from all that negative bullshit."

When I got to the road to Don's house, I stopped and gazed at the highway ahead of me as that inner voice sang, "Go for it! Life is too short to be miserable."

Standing at that intersection, straddling my bicycle, I felt like I had been there before. Not the location, but the situation. A juncture where one direction would prolong my misery, while another offered hope for a better way. Every one of those times I took that vow ". . . for better or worse . . . ." I meant it. But damn it, if worse is all I'm going to get, then it's time for me to get going.

Suddenly, a shiver raced through me. *What the hell am I doing? My family is stuck beside a flooding river, and I'm going for a bike ride?*

-᠊᠊⧾⧿᠊-

In less than thirty minutes we had the cart chained to the trailer hitch on Don's truck. He shifted into four-wheel drive, then let out the clutch. At first, all four wheels spun in the gravel, but then they grabbed hold and everything began to creep up the hill. Patricia was standing next to Della at the top watching, while I walked beside the cart.

Don tried to miss the rut at the top, but the right rear cart wheel slid into it anyway, and it stopped the truck just like it did Della. So he revved the engine and let out the clutch. Sand and gravel flew as the cart wheel popped out of the rut with a loud bang, and the truck raced up the hill–but the cart did not. It was rolling back down the hill. Instinctively, when it passed me, I reached out to grab hold. But better sense made me step back and just watch it careen toward the river.

Patricia screamed, "No!"

I was helpless. All I could do was watch everything we own roll away.

Then, just a few feet from the bottom, the right front tire hit a big rock. The cart jack-knifed, and when it did, the back end crashed into the dirt embankment on the right side of the road. Teetering on just the two down-hill wheels, the cart looked like it was going to roll over.

I prayed, "Lord, please don't let this happen!"

And it didn't. In slow motion the cart came down on all fours and bounced a couple of times. Not until it stopped completely was I able to inhale. Then I clasped my hands together, touched them to my lips and whispered, "Thank you, thank you, thank you."

Except for some cosmetic damage, everything on the cart was all right. A repair link in the chain had come undone. This time we used a bigger chain, and I rode in the cart. If it did come loose, I could stop it with the brake. But it didn't. Don missed the rut and we made it to the top.

I tried to pay him, but he wouldn't take it. After Don left, we hooked up Della and walked back out onto Highway 62 headed east. On the bridge I stopped and looked down to where we had been camped. Now it was under water.

Patricia was standing beside me as I said, "What a great campsite."

"Not now."

"Yeah, but it was. Admit it, we had a great time down there."

My wife shook her head and scoffed, "Yeah, yeah, yeah, I had a great time down there. But I still say–"

I jumped in, "You were right. We shouldn't have taken the cart down there."

With her arms crossed, Patricia just stood there looking rather smug for a few moments. Then she grinned and said, "Thank you."

I couldn't help it. I had to say, "Some adventure, eh baby?"

⊰⊱

Many of the hills in Holmes County looked like big loaves of bread. Hills are not something that normally comes to mind when most people think of Ohio. But Holmes County had some beauties. And, although I was born in the Buckeye State, I didn't know Ohio had oil. But we saw several wells pumping in the middle of corn fields. Another thing most folks don't associate with Ohio, is logging. But in those Ohio hills, several log trucks passed us loaded with hardwoods.

In Holmes County I did expect to see plenty of Amish buggies on the road. But our first day there, we only saw one. Lots of Amish people passed us, but they were all in motor vehicles. We could see their hats, bonnets, beards and faces. The Governor said we'd be a hit with the Amish, and gauging by the expressions we saw, he was right.

A crew-cab pickup truck, full of Amish men, went by us twice that day. The second time a young man, with long blond hair streaming out from under his straw hat, leaned out the window and gave us a thumbs-up, as he yelled, "Keep on rollin'!"

The Amish weren't the ones doing the driving. It was either a Mennonite or an English person behind the wheel. Around there, if you aren't Amish or a Mennonite, you're English–regardless your nationality.

The Amish and Mennonites are part of an Anabaptist movement that began in Switzerland and migrated to Germany in the late 16th century. They didn't believe in childhood baptism. The ones who drove the horse and buggies were Amish. Mennonites dressed the same as the Amish, but they own motor vehicles. The Amish hired Mennonites and the English as their chauffeurs.

Our second day in Holmes County, as we were taking down the tent, a van pulled up, and two Amish women–who looked to be in their

157

late sixties–got out. The English woman driving was about twenty years younger and she accompanied them as they approached our camp. She was the one who asked, "Do you mind if we stop to visit a bit?"

The Amish women, Mary and Elsie, were both plump with round faces that beamed out from pleated white bonnets. They almost looked like sunflowers. Mary's voice was chatty, when she said, "The whole community is buzzing about the English people traveling with a mule. But no one seems to know what you're doing."

Elsie was the tallest and most assertive of the two. "We had Brenda stop so we could find out for ourselves." Then with the kind of smile you'd expect from a Walmart greeter, she said, "Is that all right?"

Their husbands were brothers who owned a farm together near Brinkhaven. While I told them about our trip, they listened intently with their hands clasped in front of them. I finished with, "I've had this dream for a long time, and now we're making it come true."

Mary was bubbling with excitement. "I think this is just wonderful!" She turned to Elsie. "Don't you love it? They're traveling like people used to in the olden days."

Elsie rolled her eyes and shook her head. Then she turned to me and asked, "What do you think of the Amish in Holmes County?"

Patricia said, "You're the first one's we've met."

Mary squealed, "Really?"

Suddenly Elsie was exuberant. "You haven't talked to any of the men?"

"Some have waved," my wife said. "But that's about it."

Elsie's fingers laced her hands together under her chin as if she were about to pray. But a mischievous laugh came out instead. "I just love this! The men always think they know so much."

Mary bounced as she giggled. "This will be such fun!"

With an air of brinkmanship, Elsie said, "They just hate it when we know something before they do."

Originally, they weren't from Holmes County. They sold their family farm near Middlefield, in northeastern Ohio, and moved down to Holmes County ten years ago. Elsie said, "It got too crazy for us up there."

Mary had a hint of disgust in her voice. "It got so commercial. They treated us like we were some kind of freaks. Always wanting to take our picture."

Elsie said, "One time, our neighbors were eating Sunday dinner and an Englishman just walked into their house with a camera. He didn't knock, or anything. Just walked in and started taking pictures."

In the early 1970's while I lived on a horse farm in Lancaster County, Pennsylvania, one of our Amish neighbors–a woman–had a man barge into their outhouse with a camera and take her picture.

The Amish first migrated to America from Germany around 1720. They came to escape religious persecution. Now they move due to the lack of shutterbug diplomacy.

⊰⊟⊱

A few days later found us walking into the village of Berlin. It was a gray and blustery Friday afternoon. The date was August 23rd, and the area was rampant with tourists. Sometimes Highway 62 was bumper-to-bumper with them, and I was getting fed up with how inconsiderate they were toward the Amish on the road. I was shocked at how often I saw buggies get cut off in traffic. Everyone wanted to see the Amish, take their pictures, buy their handiwork and eat their cooking. But, God forbid, they should get stuck on the road behind a buggy.

We were on the west edge of Berlin, headed into the village, when I saw a carriage waiting for a spot in traffic. It was at a stop sign on a side street on the other side of the highway. Even though it was nearly fifty yards ahead of us, it was obvious that the driver wanted to get in our lane and head toward town. But no one would stop and let the carriage get out onto road. They just gawked, took pictures and kept on going.

While we approached the intersection, I found myself getting angrier with each step. *Why won't they give this horse a break.* When we got close, I eased us out into the eastbound lane. Traffic behind us had no choice but to stop. Then, when we got to the intersection, I stepped to the yellow line,

159

held up my hand and motioned for the other lane to stop. They were going slow, but they kept coming. So I yelled at an approaching motorist, "Stop right there!"

He stopped for a moment, then started to move. I roared, "Don't you dare!"

His brakes jarred the car to an abrupt stop. I yelled. "Stay right there!"

Then I motioned to the man in the carriage. "Right this way, sir."

At first, the Amish man just sat there with a look of shock on his face. The carriage was packed with his family, and they were all just staring at me. Again, I gestured for them to pull in front of us, as I said, "Please, sir, we'll all wait for you."

His bearded face beamed as he urged the horse out onto the highway. When the carriage passed in front of me, he nodded and said, "Thank you, sir. God bless you."

While the carriage rolled away from us, its open back window was filled with smiling young, wide-eyed faces—each one framed with a bonnet. All of them were waving as their horse clip-clopped off toward Berlin.

⧏⧐

"Are you staying here tonight?"

I was unpacking the tent from the top of the cart, when Ferman asked me that question. This young Amish man stood at least six-foot-four, and because he wore a beard, he had to have been married. (Only married Amish men wear them.) And if there was such a thing as a "trophy Amish husband", Ferman would have been it. He was slender and muscular. His closely trimmed dark beard accentuated the sharp, strong angles of his face.

We were in Berlin Village Park and it was starting to rain. I had Della pull the cart up next to a picnic shelter where we planned to pitch the tent inside. When we first got there it was just sprinkling, but it was steadily getting stronger. Before long it would be a heavy shower, so we were in a hurry to get the tent up.

Ferman asked, "Can I help?"

"Thanks, but we've got ourselves a routine."

"So, I'd probably be in the way, eh?"

Three things made Ferman stand out from other Amish men. One was his looks. He was Johnny-Depp-kind-of-handsome–sans the mustache. (Amish don't wear them.) Besides being the best looking Amish man I had ever seen, Ferman was also the most outgoing I'd ever met. He oozed the confidence of a successful politician.

The third thing that made Ferman different from other Amish men, was the cell phone clipped to his pants pocket. "I'm a fireman. This is how they get hold of me."

An Amish fireman. Okay, here was another first for me. Looking at his chiseled features beneath his straw hat, for an instant my mind replaced the hat with a firefighter's helmet. And instead of farmer's work clothes, Ferman was in a yellow fireman's-suit. No doubt, he could have been cal-endar material.

Berlin Village Park was in a rolling valley. The picnic shelter was on a knoll on the west side, about a hundred yards from the park's boundary. At that boundary were the back yards of a dozen homes. Ferman, and his pregnant wife, lived in the one directly behind the shelter. She was due anytime, and this would be their first.

The houses at that side of the park were various types, sizes and age. Ferman's was the newest–a brown brick, split level, with three bedrooms. It was so new, the dirt around it hadn't been leveled into a yard yet.

Ferman's father, Jonas Miller, lived in the oldest house adjacent to the park. It was about a quarter of a mile from the shelter, at the park's north-west corner. A plain two story farm house, with several outbuildings, a barn and paddock for his road-horse and a pony.

Jonas was my age–in his mid-fifties. We met him just as Ferman was about to leave for home. Had Ferman not said, "Hey, here comes Dad!" I never would have guessed they were related. While Jonas was certainly not an ugly man, he was no looker like his oldest son. And Ferman didn't get his height from his father either. But there was no doubt where the young fireman got his smile and personality. When Jonas limped into the picnic shelter, it felt like a long lost friend had just dropped in.

"I trust my boy gave you a proper welcome." Jonas patted Ferman on the back, then extended that hand to me. "Jonas Miller. It's a pleasure to have you in the neighborhood." Then he aimed his thumb over his shoulder, and said, "I live in the place at that end of the park. If you need anything just come on over. Do you want to put your mule in a barn?"

It had been a hot, muggy day, and it looked like Della was enjoying the rain. So I said, "Thanks, but I think she'd rather be near us. And the rain will do her some good."

Jonas nodded as he sat down at one of the picnic tables. "My horses have the choice of being inside or out, and they're all out in it right now."

Hoisting his right leg up onto the bench, Jonas said, "Every veterinarian I've known says, the more they're outside the healthier they'll be."

For the first thirty years of his working life, Jonas had been a horseshoer. "But it was getting to my back." So he went to work in the logging woods driving a team of horses. Last February he got his leg caught between a skidding log and a tree. It shattered the leg, so he was laid up for several months. When we met Jonas, he had recently gone to work as a tour guide at nearby exotic animal farm. He drove tourists around the eighty-eight acre farm in a wagon pulled by a team of horses.

"I didn't think I'd like dealing with tourists all the time." Jonas pushed his straw hat back and laughed. "But it's the most fun job I've ever had. I love going to work. Too bad I had to cripple myself up to find a job that I like so much."

It rained most of that night, then off and on throughout Saturday. So we spent most of the day in the picnic shelter. Because of the rain, there were no wagon tours at the animal farm. So Jonas had the day off–he spent part of it visiting with us. As you would expect, I asked him a lot of questions about Amish life.

"What I don't understand is, if you are against modern things, like cars and telephones, how do you justify riding in somebody else's car–or Ferman carrying a cell phone?"

"We aren't against those things," Jonas said. "It's what those things can do to our families and our community that we don't like."

I had just perked a pot of coffee on the camp stove, and was pouring Jonas a cup when I asked, "Like what?"

"The most important thing to us Amish is our family. We believe if our families fail, so will our community. So we avoid anything that threatens to tear our families apart. We see things like cars, telephones and televisions as a threat to our families."

Jonas's spoon clinked against the insides of his coffee cup as he said, "Cars carry people too far away from their family. With a horse and buggy, you have to stay pretty close to home. And when there's a telephone in the home, children don't talk to their parents, or brothers and sisters. Instead they're talking to someone who isn't there. With TV, rather than being involved in their own lives, they sit and watch somebody else's."

Jonas paused and laid the spoon on the picnic table next to the cup. Then he said, "How can a family survive, when the people in it are not living in the present?"

I sat down on the bench across the table from Jonas. "Okay, but I see Amish riding in other people's cars all the time. How do you explain that?"

Jonas chuckled. "I knew you were going to ask me that. Like I said, we aren't against cars. We don't see them as evil. They're tools that sometimes we have to use. I ride back and forth to work in a van every day. But we hire someone who has one. It's part of their family, not mine. When I'm done using it, it's gone. It's not sitting in my yard so we just can hop in it and buzz around. If my children want to visit their friends, they can walk or ride a bicycle. The older ones use the horse and buggy. My youngest has his own pony. So it's not like they don't have a way to get around."

Bringing the cup to his lips, Jonas said, "Keeps them closer to home."

"What about Ferman and his—"

"Cell phone," Jonas finished my sentence. "That was a big event in our community. Everyone in the district, the Bishop, all of us talked that over for nearly a month."

A district consists of twenty to forty Amish families who live in close proximity. They have services every-other Sunday at a different home, which is usually led by the Bishop, or a minister that he appoints. Bishops preside over several districts.

"Ferman had his heart set on being a fireman. Since he would be helping the community, we decided he should do it. When there's a fire, they have to be able to get in touch with him. So he had to have a cell phone. It's good for the community."

⚞⚟

That Saturday night we had visitors from one Mennonite and three Amish families in our camp. While it rained outside, the picnic shelter rang with stories and laughter until nearly midnight. Stories told by men with wide brimmed hats, suspenders and mustache-less beards. Ivan Moore was one of the Mennonites. He was in his early seventies, squatty and the first person in Holmes County to ask if I was a Christian. His house was one of those that bordered the park, and his son lived next door. They both visited us a couple of times while we were there. It was on the first visit that he popped the Christian question. I guess he was all right with my reply. Both he and his son came back and were part of the Saturday night crowd.

The funniest topic of the evening was tourists. After seeing how inconsiderate the motorists were, I would have thought the Amish would be as disgusted as I was. But this group was more amused by them than anything.

"My daughter had a real corker a couple of days ago," Ivan said. His daughter worked at the Berlin Visitor Center. "A woman came in and asked where she could find the Amish. My daughter gave her a map and showed her which roads she most likely would see some."

Ivan's short, thick body began to heave with laughter as he said, "She threw a fit and said, 'You mean they're just out running loose? Isn't that dangerous?'"

The picnic shelter reverberated with laughter as Jonas piped in, "Oh, that's us. Dangerous Amish. They really should lock us all up."

"And throw away the key," Ivan added.

A little later Ivan stood up and announced it was time for him to go home. Then he turned to me and said, "You're welcome to join us for church in the morning. I know none of these Amish invited you to their service."

"You know good and well we don't have service until next Sunday." Jonas said.

Ivan laughed. "See, we Mennonites aren't nearly as good as the Amish. They only have to go to church every other Sunday. Us poor Mennonites have to go every Sunday."

The picnic shelter exploded with laughter again. The Amish and Mennonites seemed to laugh a lot. Every time I saw them greet each other, or us, it was always with good humor. It wasn't just the adults. Several times Patricia and I remarked how happy Amish children seemed to be. And they were always polite.

Earlier that night, as rain pelted the roof of the picnic shelter, Ivan read a poem to the group. The gist was, "Always greet your neighbor with a glad face."

<hr />

Sunday, instead of going to the Mennonite Church, we had dinner with Jonas Miller and his family. It was a great honor to have Ohio's governor invite us into his mansion, but it paled in comparison to being invited to an Amish home for Sunday dinner.

It was at one o'clock and fifteen people showed up, too many to sit around the table. So folks sat on chairs, sofas, stools and the floor with their plates in their laps. In the middle of the Miller's kitchen table was a platter piled high with pork chops. Some were barbequed, others baked and a bunch were fried. Big bowls with two different pastas, steamed corn and a heaping pan of tossed salad were also on the table. Before everyone helped themselves, we all went into the living room, held hands in a circle and said the traditional Amish grace—a few quiet moments for silent prayer.

I think "quiet grace" is a perfect way to describe the Amish. They go about their lives simply, without pretense or trying to impress the rest of the world. I have never known an Amish person to push their religion, or their way of life, on anyone. They just live their lives the way they think they should.

"Can someone who isn't born Amish become Amish?"

I asked that question of Esther Mullet. She and her husband Bennie drove up to our camp Sunday morning in a two-wheel cart pulled by a pair of Haflinger horses. Esther said, "Yes. But as an adult, it would be a hard thing to do."

"You mean giving up their worldly ways?"

"No. I think the language would be the hardest part."

Esther went on to explain that the Amish in America speak three languages. Growing up they learn English, "Pennsylvania Dutch" and High German. Actually Pennsylvania Dutch is not Dutch at all. It's a type of German. Originally it was known as Pennsylvania Deutch (Deutch meaning German). But Englishmen mistook the word Deutch for Dutch. So these days even the Amish call the language Pennsylvania Dutch. That's what they speak in their homes and within their community. High German is used in their church services. It's the type of German that was spoken in the fifteenth century. Esther said, "These days most Germans don't understand High German."

When we were at Jonas Miller's house, I mentioned how happy all of the Amish children seemed to be. He said, "Most of them are. That doesn't mean we don't have problem kids. But they either straighten up or they move on."

Excommunication and shunning wasn't just reserved for those who choose the outside world. Habitually disrupting the family, or the community, could get you kicked out too. But that's not to say the Amish were quick to give up on their own.

Bennie and Ester were members of the same district as Jonas. So they wouldn't be going to services that Sunday either. Bennie said, "But I've got plenty of church business to take care of today."

A member of their district committed suicide last October. He left a wife and seven children behind. A few years earlier, he had been diagnosed as paranoid schizophrenic and was institutionalized for a while. That was when the Bishop appointed Bennie as the family's guardian, and he set up a committee to oversee their finances.

"They never really had anything," Bennie said. "He and his boys worked at a dairy, so they had money coming in, but he was always complaining that his wife wasted it. She said he never brought it home and no one knows what he did with it. We had to take over so the family could pay their rent and have food to eat."

Soon after his release from the mental hospital, the man hung himself in a calf barn at the dairy farm where he worked. He left a note that said he was dying so Jesus would take care of his family. Bennie shook his head. "That's crazy talk."

So the church used some of its money and solicited donations from area businesses to set up a trust fund for the family. Someone in the community donated five acres. So, on the weekends, the community got together and worked on building them a new house.

"It's important to keep that family together. That's all they have now. If they fail, we all lose. That's how it is with Amish."

Amish Brotherhood Publications puts out a newspaper that goes to Amish homes around the world. It doesn't have news of war, politics or world affairs. It publishes stories about things that happen to Amish families–like the one Bennie was guardian of. That's how the Amish find out where to funnel money and other resources to those in need.

Isn't that crazy? Instead of tithing the church to build a better house of worship, they send it to those who are down on their luck. Instead of spending it on religious tracts, missionaries and other forms of evangelism, they invest in their brethren in need. Are the Amish wack-o or what?

Because all the shops and tourist traps were closed on Sunday, the highway had very little motorized traffic. Most it was horse drawn, and we met lots of Amish people that afternoon.

One was a lanky twenty-year-old man, named Eli. He was clean shaven, wore a straw hat and suspenders, and he was riding a twenty-one speed mountain bicycle with wire baskets on the back. Eli was on his way to hit a few balls at the batting cages west of Winesburg. After I answered his questions about us, Eli started talking about what it was like to be Amish at his age.

"There's a lot of pressure to go out and run around. Nearly everyone I know, who's my age, wants to go out and party. You know, get a car, drink and do drugs–the whole bit. But I'm just not into it. I was just a little kid when my brothers were in rumspringa, but I remember it. And it didn't seem to me that they were very happy then."

Rumspringa is a period of Amish adolescence, beginning at the age of sixteen, that worldly behavior is tolerated. They're allowed to own cars, be a part of modern society and still live on the farm. But then comes a time, usually by the mid-twenties, when they have to decide between their family or the rest of the world. If they don't choose the Amish faith, they are shunned by the family and the rest of the community.

"Both of my brothers had cars, but my father wouldn't let them keep them at the farm. They rented a parking space behind a gas station that had hitching-rails. That way they could leave the horse and buggy there when they were out partying."

Coasting beside me on his bike, Eli had a bit of a chuckle in his voice. "I remember when they'd come racing into the yard with the buggy in the middle of the night whooping and hollering, you'd thought they was having the best time. But the next morning they'd be hurting. I mean, in real pain. Sometimes, it'd be so bad they couldn't get up and do chores. My father would say, 'If you want to burn the candle at both ends, that's your business. But don't be burning my end up!' Then he'd pull them out of bed and make them go to work– whether they wanted to or not."

I stopped Della on the highway shoulder, and Eli held her lead rope as I took the lid off her water bucket. While she drank he said, "My oldest brother got into drugs."

"What kind?"

"I'm not sure what all he took. I know he was on Meth when he wrecked his car. They found some on him when they took him to the hospital. He went to jail for that one."

I snapped the lid back onto the water bucket. "So what became of him?"

"When he got out of jail, he came back to the family, repented and got baptized. Both of my brothers did." Eli's voice had a bit of a lilt to it when he said, "They're both married and my oldest brother has a new baby boy."

Patricia had been in the cab working the brake on the down-hills. Now she was at the kitchen compartment, spreading honey on a piece of bread for Della. She screwed the lid back on the honey jar as she asked, "So the community didn't hold his going to jail against him?"

"No. He repented. Now he has a family and they're part of our community."

Eli laughed at Della as she lapped her tongue around her honey coated mule lips. He rubbed her neck, as he said, "Drugs and cars, to me, it just doesn't seem like they're worth the trouble." Then he patted his bicycle seat. "Bikes and baseball, that's more my speed."

⌐⊐⊏¬

We camped that night on the west side of Winesburg in a vacant lot that had once been the site of a grocery store. Most of the traffic was horse-drawn, and there were lots of Amish walking along the highway too. Several stopped to visit.

The sun was about to touch the horizon when two white haired men, one Amish the other Mennonite, walked into our camp and welcomed us to

Winesburg. I was showing them our cart when a carriage pulled by a high-stepping black horse approached from the west. Della was grazing less than twenty feet from the pavement, and the horse's eyes were fixated on her. His trot became erratic and his nostrils flared as he got closer. He was almost adjacent to Della when he abruptly side-stepped into the eastbound lane. The carriage, which was packed with a family of six, swerved across the double yellow line. Frantically, the man pulled on the right rein. The horse's head turned that way, but the rest of him kept moving further into the wrong lane.

A pickup truck in that lane screeched to a stop about fifty feet ahead of the horse. Suddenly the horse reared up and began to paw the air with his front feet. The carriage shook violently as the horse, up on his hind legs, twisted from side to side and squealed. The driver's face was fraught with horror as he yelled, "Whoa!"

The Amish man in our camp calmly turned to the Mennonite and said, "Do you suppose we should do something?"

Equally as calm, the Mennonite replied, "I don't know. Maybe we should."

Right then the horse came down on all four feet, then lunged forward. The driver yanked back on both reins and the horse reared up again. When he did, a young teenaged girl tumbled out the back of the carriage onto the pavement, as her father desperately screamed, "Whoa!"

When she got to her feet, the girl's bonnet was dangling on her back from the ribbon that had been tied under her chin. She pulled up the front of her skirt as she scurried around to the front of the carriage. Her father yelled, "Grab his bridle!"

The horse was back down on all fours, but he was getting crazier by the moment. He thrashed around in the shafts, as the girl's panicked face turned back and forth from her father to the horse. Her father hollered, "Grab the bridle!"

She took a timid step toward the horse; he squealed and reared up again. The girl screamed, jumped back, tripped over her skirt and fell backwards onto the road.

The Mennonite standing next to me calmly said, "I think they need a hand."

When I turned toward them, neither he nor his Amish friend moved. So I dashed out onto the highway and got the horse just as his front feet landed on the pavement again. When I grabbed his bridle, he tried to strike me with his right front hoof. I jumped out of the way, then kicked him in the knee. He stumbled, and for an instant, I thought he was going fall down. But he recovered and stood there shaking.

With a hand on both sides of his bit, I stood in front of him and said, "Whoa, big boy. It's okay."

A mighty snort exploded from his flaring nostrils, and with it came a spray of horse snot in my face. It was gross, but I couldn't let go to wipe it off. I had to ignore it. Then, in as soothing a voice as I could muster, I said, "It's okay, big boy. Settle down. You're going to be all right."

It worked. Although he was still shaking, he let me take control. I stroked his neck as I looked over at the girl who was getting to her feet. I asked her, "Are you okay?"

She was pulling the bonnet back up onto her head. "Yes sir. I'm fine. Thank you."

I turned to her father, whose face was void of color, and I said, "Let me lead him up the road a ways past our camp."

He nodded. Then I told the girl, "I'll wait till you get back in."

By the time I had led him fifty yards down the highway the horse had settled down. When I looked back at the family in the carriage, I could see they were all still in a state of shock, but the color had returned to the father's face.

I asked, "Do you think you can handle him now?"

He nodded. "I think so. Thank you, sir."

I let go of the horse's bridle, and when the carriage pulled up beside me I said, "I'm sorry my mule scared your horse."

"It's not your fault. Thank you, sir. God bless you!"

The girl was facing out the back of carriage as the horse began to trot down the road. Her face beamed as she waved and called out, "God bless you!"

That spot where we were camped was up on a ridge. After sunset, I walked to the other side of the road with my tape recorder and sat on the ground to work on my journal. In the valley below I could see the lights of several carriages as they wound along the back roads. The evening air was filled with the clip-clopping of homebound horses. Soon they would be unharnessed, fed and bedded down. And before long their owners would say their evening prayers, and they too would retire for the night. No late night TV, or internet chat, nor video or online games. Just simple prayers of thanksgiving, wishes of "Good night" and then, sweet slumber.

Tomorrow we would walk out of Holmes County—out of the land of the Plain Folk. Away from these people of quiet grace. The thought made me a bit sad.

CHAPTER 12

IN THE LAND OF OLD KING OIL

OUR FIRST CAMPSITE IN PENNSYLVANIA was a wide spot beside US 62, west of Mercer. It had been eighteen grueling up-and-down miles that day. The Allegheny foothills were beginning to feel like mountains. When we crawled in the tent, I was so tired Patricia had to undress me. It was fun, but it wasn't a lengthy affair. We were both too beat–she soon fell asleep. But it was past midnight before I did.

On the other side of the hills, not far away, was a race track. It was Saturday night, so the stock cars were running. The sky over the hill tops glowed from the lights around the track. We were so close, that most of the time I could understand what the announcer was saying. And when the cars weren't too loud, I could hear the applause and cheers of the fans in the stands.

While the hours rumbled by, I was drawn back to the days following my 1970's cross-country trek with the pack pony and dog. After I finished that journey, for more than a year I lived in the woods near Bismark, Arkansas. It was a peaceful little place–except on Saturday night. A few miles away was a stock car track, and every weekend through the spring, summer and fall, Saturday night would be wild with the roar of the races. Motors grumbled, growled and roared for hours as they propelled cars and drivers around a circle.

Back then the buzz words were "conserve energy." "Turn down your thermostat!" Ever since then, for more than three decades, every winter has been ushered in with warnings of home heating oil shortages. And yet, in the past thirty years NASCAR has grown to be the second biggest spectator sport in America.

Petroleum truly is black gold! When you think of all the things we use it for, oil is actually more important than gold. Besides its use as fuel, consider what's made out of it. Plastics, chemicals and medicines are derivatives of petroleum. The keys I'm typing on, the lenses of my glasses, the fabric of our tent, Della's harness: it's all made out of oil.

In western Pennsylvania, among the Allegheny foothills, was where the world's first successful oil well was drilled. It was in1859 near Oil Creek, and Col. Edwin L Drake only had to go down 69 ½ feet to strike it rich. A year later, and fifteen miles down stream, where the creek flowed into the Allegheny River, Oil City began to boom. Distilleries, refineries, and wharfs for shipping sprang up along the river.

Eight miles down river from Oil City was Franklin. It was a timber town long before oil was found in those hills. In the early 1800s timber barons built magnificent homes on the hillsides overlooking the Allegheny River. Then, as petroleum took over as king, oil tycoons moved in. They made their fortunes in Oil City, but made their beds in Franklin.

We had heard a lot about how beautifully the old homes and buildings in Franklin had been preserved. Like Madison, Indiana, it sounded like our kind of town. So we looked forward to exploring it, but as we walked into town our interest began to wane. By the time we reached downtown, we felt down-right unwelcome.

It all started on Highway 62 where it began to descend into Franklin. The road was narrow and it had little—and sometimes—no shoulder. So we had no choice but to be in the lane of traffic. It was early Thursday afternoon, the road was busy and every time we came to a place where we could pull over and let traffic get by us, we did. Usually it was a wide gravel spot, with a guard rail on the right and traffic to our left. Beyond the guardrail was a drop off into the Allegheny River Valley. Sometimes we stood in those spots for ten minutes before we could get back on the road. But that wasn't good enough for those motorists. Twice when we pulled over, the first car to pass us honked their horn and gave us the finger. Then there was the man in a primer gray Datsun pickup. He was in the other lane going uphill when he stopped at the yellow line and yelled out his window, "Who the fuck do you think you are? You got no business being on this road! Get that Goddam animal off the highway!"

Black smoke belched out of his tailpipe when the man stomped his accelerator.

Patricia was in the cab working the brake, and as the truck sputtered up the hill, she yelled, "What's his problem? We're not in his way."

"Got me."

She yelled back, "This is the most unfriendly road we've been on so far!"

We were walking into downtown Franklin when we passed an auto repair shop. In the open garage doorway stood five men dressed in matching green mechanic shirts–all with their arms folded across their chests. Obviously they had assembled to watch us walk by. So I waved and yelled, "Howdy!" But they all just stood and stared, except the man at the end of the row. He glanced to see if the others were watching before he quickly uncrossed his right arm and waved at us twice. Then he immediately re-crossed it.

Franklin was indeed a pretty little city–very Victorian. Downtown was mostly two and three story redbrick buildings that had either been restored or well cared for down through the years. It was the kind of town that we liked to explore. So when I spotted an open parking space, I guided Della into it. I was tying her to a sign post when Patricia climbed out of the cart and walked up to me. "Why are we stopping?"

"This sure is a pretty town. Isn't it?"

She shrugged her shoulders. "I guess so. But there seems to be a rash of broken arms around here."

"Huh?"

Patricia waved at me, then let her arm go limp and grimaced.

"Oh, yeah. Folks aren't too friendly," I said. "Do you want to explore?"

For a few moments my wife didn't say anything as she turned around and surveyed our surroundings. Then she looked at me with a frown on her face. "I don't feel welcome here. Let's move on."

On the northeast edge of Franklin, we pulled into the parking lot of the Giant Eagle supermarket. The last three times we stopped to get groceries, I ended up selling a poetry book or few. Patricia said, "You aren't going to make anything here."

Just as my wife walked into the store, a bent old woman with a huge purse hanging from her shoulder shuffled off the sidewalk and up to me. With a scowl she mumbled, "This is for the donkey."

From the purse she pulled two red and white striped peppermint candies. Then, without looking up, she handed them to me.

I said, "Thank you."

She grunted, then turned back toward the street as she grumbled, "Make sure you give those to the donkey." Then she shuffled down the sidewalk headed for town.

⋇⊟⊩⋇

Jerry said, "Yeah, well, that's the way it is around here".

He was a reporter for two local newspapers–Franklin's *The News Herald,* and Oil City's *The Derrick.* Jerry was in his early twenties, blond and immediately likeable. When he got out of his car, he had two cameras dangling from his neck, a note-pad in his left hand and a smile on his face. "Welcome to Franklin."

I couldn't help it. I had to say, "That's a nice change."

"Huh?"

Then I told him about our reception so far in Franklin. "It's a pretty town, but folks sure have been unfriendly."

He sighed. "Most people around here are real conservative. If they don't know you, they're not going to wave."

Originally from Marshall, Minnesota, Jerry had worked at the newspapers for a little over two years. "Doing this kind of work, I deal with lots of local people. And I've met some really great folks around here, but they're just not very open to strangers."

When Patricia stopped her shopping cart in front of the reporter, she shook Jerry's hand and said, "It's certainly refreshing to see a smiling face around here."

Then she turned to me. "I just met the rudest checkout person ever. I'm telling you, it was–" Patricia waved her hand over her head and said, "Never mind. I just want to get out of here!"

Jerry interviewed us and took pictures while we loaded provisions into the cart. After everything was packed, he said, "I'm going to drive ahead and find a spot to get some shots of you walking toward me."

Highway 62 to Oil City paralleled the Allegheny River and most of it was four lanes with a shoulder. We had walked quite a ways from the supermarket when I spotted Jerry ahead of us on a corner across the highway. A policeman was standing next him as he aimed a huge telephoto lens at us. He and the cop smiled and waved as we walked by.

About two hundred yards further, I heard the sound of a car motor directly behind the cart on the highway shoulder. Then there was a short bleep of a police siren followed by an amplified man's voice. "Would you please stop?"

Patricia said, "Now what?"

Behind the cart was the police car we had seen earlier. The officer was climbing out of it as Jerry pulled up behind him. Quickly, the reporter got out and scurried toward us with pen and pad in hand.

The officer was about the same age as the reporter–in his early twenties. A handsome, dark haired man who was smiling as he first approached us. I figured this was going to be a photo-op for the paper. But as he got closer, that smile began to fade, and his face looked strained when he said, "You have to get off this highway at Reno."

Officer Ryan didn't have demand in his voice. It was more like he was just passing information on to us. So I calmly asked, "Why?"

I sensed reluctance in his voice. "My supervisor said you can't walk through Reno on US 62. He says you can't have a horse on a four-lane highway."

Patricia snapped, "She's a mule!"

I put my hand on Patricia's shoulder to calm her down as I said, "Your supervisor is wrong. We can't be on an interstate highway. But we can be on a US highway, no matter how many lanes it has."

He was almost pleading when the cop said, "Look, I don't know what the problem is. I told him you weren't hurting anything. But he says that if you go into Reno on this highway, I'm supposed to arrest you."

In unison Patricia and I yelled, "What?"

Officer Ryan stepped back a bit, looked down at the ground and began to shake his head. His hands were on his hips as he said, "Look, I'm just doing my job. That's all. I don't want to hassle you people. I think what you're doing is really cool."

This young man was quickly winning both mine and Patricia's hearts. Back when she was a cop, several times Patricia was sent to do something that she didn't want to do. My wife was gentle when she asked, "So what are we supposed to do?"

"You want to go to Oil City, right?"

He pulled a note book out of his shirt pocket and said, "These are the directions they told me to give you."

Throughout this exchange, Jerry had been circling around us taking pictures. Then when Officer Ryan read me the directions, both the reporter and I wrote them down. "Take the first left in Reno and go to the stop signal. Then turn left on Walnut Street to Shafer Run. Take it to Route 428, that's Holiday Run. Go right–"

Jerry blurted out, "Holiday Run? You've got to be kidding!"

"I'm just telling you what they said."

When Officer Ryan pulled away in his patrol car, Jerry said, with delight, "Boy, have I got a story! The boss is going to love this. I can see the headline now, 'Sugar Creek Cops Stop World Travelers. Reroutes Them Onto Holiday Run.'"

I asked, "What's the big deal about Holiday Run?"

"Driving it is anything but a holiday. It's a nightmare! It's steep, narrow and busy. I can't imagine walking it."

After we made the first two turns that the police prescribed, I spotted a two story house with a hose in the yard. We needed water. So I grabbed Della's bucket, one of our blue jugs, and hiked up the dozen concrete steps that ascended the front yard. It was littered with four or five bicycles, a torn-apart go-cart, a couple of plastic rifles and a few big pieces of cardboard. When I stepped up onto the front porch, big dogs began to bark on the other side of the front door. Suddenly, it swung open and two huge Rottweiler's lunged at the screen door. I feared they were going to bust through the screen as they growled and barred their teeth at me.

A ten year old shirtless boy smacked each one on the top of their heads with his hand as he yelled. "I said, shut up! Sweetie, you git back and sit down. Knuckle Head, that means you too. Now sit!"

They both did. I was thrilled.

With a bit of a hillbilly drawl, the boy said, "What do you want?"

The question was barely out of his mouth, when a taller thirteen year old version of the boy walked up behind him. "Say man, what's happening?"

"I'm traveling with that mule down on the street and we need some water."

The younger brother yelled. "Wow, look at that! He's got a big-ass donkey."

The screen door slammed against the front of the house as the boy sprinted past me and bounded down the concrete steps in bare feet. "Hey, how much for a ride?"

Right then, one of the dogs barged past the older brother, out the screen door and began to sniff my bare legs. The wetness from his nose dripped on my calves as the huge head moved around me. My skin, my muscles, my bones, all of me cringed. His canines were too close.

"Sweetie, get back in here!"

The older brother was shirtless and barefoot, too. He grabbed the choker around the dog's neck and yanked her back into the house. Then he pointed at a spot next to where the other dog sat. "Now sit down and shut up!"

She did. My flesh and bones felt much better. I said, "Maybe I should move on."

This boy had the same drawl as his brother. "I'll ask my grandma if we can give you some water. Wait here."

Whenever we went to someone's door to ask for water, or a place to camp, we always took one of our flyers with us. I handed one to the boy. "It explains who we are."

"Cool! I'll be right back." He was already reading it when he turned around and headed back into the house yelling, "Grandma!"

While I stood on the porch waiting for Grandma, I surveyed the situation. Two barefoot boys, yard full of junk, a house in need of paint and repair–it felt very Appalachia. Grandma reinforced that feeling when she showed up at the door without her teeth. She was wearing a moo-moo, had our flyer in her hand and a toothless grin on her face. When she pushed the screen door open she said, "Well sir, the boy here says you need some water for your mule."

"Yes ma'am, but if it's a problem I–"

She had a chuckle in her voice. "No honey, it's no problem."

Her vacant grin got bigger as she eyed me from head to toe. It felt like she was undressing me as she held the door open. "No sir, not a problem at all. Just come on in here and make yourself to home."

When I stepped past her, I thought I heard her mutter, "Said the spider to the fly."

She turned to the boy, "Go git the basement key from your mama. She's upstairs in bed watching the TV."

When the boy left the room, both dogs got up, walked over to me and began to sniff my legs. Grandma said, "Don't worry about them. They won't hurt ya as long as one of us is around. Would ya like to sit down?"

Even if I had wanted to sit, I don't know where I would have done it. Every piece of furniture had something on it. Clothing, newspapers, books and toys were everywhere.

"Thanks, but I'd rather stand. Look, if this is going to be a hassle we can—"

"It's all right honey. The spigot for the hose is in the basement. We keep it locked so's the boys don't wander off with the tools or leave the water running. My daughter has got the key."

The boy was running down the stairs as he said, "Mama says to get water out of the sink in the kitchen."

Saliva spewed out of Grandma's mouth. "What is she talking about? Even if there weren't dirty dishes in it, there ain't no way he can git a bucket in that sink."

She handed the boy our flyer. "Now take this up and tell her we need that key."

The boy dashed up the stairs as I said, "I think we'll find some other—"

"You just wait right here," Grandma said as she grabbed my arm with her sweaty palm. I felt violated. I wanted to leap out the door and run away. She smacked her gums together as she spoke. "I'll get this straightened out."

She waddled toward the stairs. "Now don't go nowhere. I'll be back with that key." Ascending the steps she yelled, "Honey git out of that bed! Ya want to pet a mule?"

As soon as she was out of sight, I turned toward the door. Both Rottweiler's were sniffing me as I steadily moved myself out onto the porch. When I closed the screen door, both dogs were still inside. I said, "Sit!"

They did. I was delighted.

I had just stepped down off the porch, when the younger boy appeared at the top of the stairs from the street. A mean pout was on his face. "That lady said I can't have a ride!"

"We don't give rides."

"That's what she said." He stomped past me, up the porch steps and yelled, "That stinks! I'm just a kid. I ought to git to go for a ride!"

I was putting Della's empty water bucket in the cart when Patricia said, "What was that all about? Who does that kid think he is?"

I held up my hand. "Let's just go."

On Shafer Run we came to a buff-brick ranch-style home with a nice yard. A twelve year old boy was in the garage rolling up a hose, so I asked, "Could we get some water?"

"Sure. Let me hook it back up."

While I filled our jugs and Della's bucket, I told him about our experience with the police. When I finished, he shook his head. "Sugar Creek Cops. They're all rotten."

After a mile or so, the road led out of a residential area into a forest. Woodlands laced with rusted pipes, old oil pumps and gray tanks stained from where black gold had spilled down them. Shafer's Run was a gradual uphill route, in a narrow valley, with a clear tumbling brook running through it. It would have been a beautiful place if it hadn't been littered with old oil-field machinery. We saw a couple of pumps working—the kind that look like grasshoppers bobbing their heads up and down. So oil was still being pulled out of the ground around there. But most of the equipment was idle pieces of metal and tangled coils of cable with tall weeds and saplings growing up through it. The property on both sides of the road was all fenced off with sagging, rusty barbed wire and locked gates.

The sun was low in the west when we finally we came to an open gate with no signs saying we couldn't go in. So we did, and the drive led us back into a scruffy place with lots of brush and dead equipment, but there was enough room to tether out Della and pitch our tent. That night we fell asleep to the tap-tap-tapping of a distant pump pulling Old King Oil up to the surface.

Early the next afternoon, when we got to the top of Shafer's Run, the woods gave way to a suburban neighborhood, where each house had at least an acre of ground. We were walking by a ranch-style home with ladders leaned against it, when the man on the roof yelled, "I read about you in the paper this morning. How do you like our local Gestapo?"

From behind me Patricia said, "I can't wait to see what Jerry wrote."

A couple of blocks further, a lady walked out her front door with a newspaper in her hand. "Could I have your autograph?"

I didn't have my glasses on, so I couldn't read the caption under the front page picture of me looming over Officer Ryan. When I handed the paper back to the woman she said, "I'm so sorry for the way the police treated you."

And so it went throughout the rest of the afternoon. Person after person stopped to apologize. Many of them had us sign their newspapers. We had just turned right on Holiday Run when Patricia said, "What a difference a newspaper story can make. Yesterday, no one would even look at us. Today, it's like we're heroes."

When we first got on Holiday Run, it wasn't too bad. The traffic in both lanes was heavy, but there was room for us to get out of the way. That all changed when the road began its descent toward the Allegheny River. The shoulder disappeared, the pavement narrowed and we were out in the traffic lane as the highway twisted down the side of a ravine. To our immediate right was the rock face of the hill. Across the road was a guard rail and a drop off. Jerry was right, there wasn't room to pass, but that didn't stop people from doing it. They'd rev up their motors, tires would squeal, then a whoosh of steel, glass and exhaust would roar past us within inches of my body. I couldn't tell you how many times that afternoon Patricia and I yelled, "Oh my God!" or "Oh Shit!" or "Son-of-a-bitch!" Of the two of us, Patricia was the most vocal–but Della just kept plodding along. The only vehicle that bothered her was the school bus.

After all the thousands of miles I've hiked along this nation's roads, I've come to recognize the motor of a school bus. They all have a universal rattle in their motors, and in a blind curve I heard one rattle up behind us. I couldn't see if anything was in the approaching lane, so the bus driver couldn't either, but that didn't matter. The horn blared as the long mass of yellow and black careened into that lane, and charged past us. When the bus swerved back into our lane, its tires spun grit up into mine and Della's faces. Had I not side stepped into Della, the bus's back bumper would have snatched my left thigh. Della reared back when I bumped against her. As the bus disappeared around the corner, my wife screamed from the cab, "Can you fucking believe that?"

With my arms wrapped around Della's neck I prayed, "Lord, please help us get down this thing alive."

A few minutes later, a police car from Oil City stopped in the uphill lane with its blue lights flashing. The driver and his partner looked to be in their mid-thirties, and both of their faces were beaming as the driver leaned out the window and said, "You want help getting across the highway at the bottom?"

I felt like I was pleading. "What we need is help getting down there!"

Patricia's voice was frantic. "Could you follow us? These people are crazy!"

I said, "Someone needs to stop them from passing us on the curves."

The officer behind the wheel saluted me. "We can do that. I'll follow you the rest of the way down. See you at the bottom."

While the patrol car pulled in behind us, I looked up to heaven and said, "Thanks."

When we got across the highway at the bottom of the hill, I led Della onto a side street where we stopped beside the curb with the police cruiser behind us. After both officers got out, I said, "Thanks guys. It was scary up there."

The driver shook my hand. "Glad we could help."

His partner said, "Read about you in the paper."

"Yeah, we had quite a day yesterday."

"Sounds like it. They sure picked a rough way to get you here."

"But hey," The driver said. "Welcome to Oil City!"

⊰⊱

From Oil City, Highway 62 climbed up into the Alleghenies and it was a ridge road for ten miles or so. Then it descended down to the bottom of the valley and became a river road all the way to Warren. For more than forty-five miles it twisted along the east shore with lush green slopes all around us.

The Allegheny is a National Recreational River all the way down to Pittsburgh. Everyone we talked to said the most scenic part of it was from

Oil City up to Warren. For thirty miles the river and the highway were in the National Forest–but we were not in a wilderness. Big homes, small trailers, rustic cabins and camp grounds were all along the route. It seemed like nearly every flat dry place had some kind of shelter on it. That could have posed a problem for us finding campsites, but it didn't.

Socially, getting kicked off the highway at Reno was the best thing that could have happened to us. Because of it, our first day out of Oil City we were invited to a pot luck dinner and given a riverside campsite in Clark's Campground at President, PA. They read about our scrape with the law, were outraged and eager to have us join the party. We stayed two nights.

In Tionesta, Mark and Paula Cook, who owned Eagle Rock Motel and Campground, also read about it. They invited us to stay in their campground on the river's edge. They also ran a canoe and kayak service, and treated us to a seven mile float trip.

The Allegheny flows through the oldest river bed in America. It has a sheet of bedrock more that one hundred feet thick. Because it flows over rock instead of mud or sand, that part of the Allegheny is clear. On most of our kayak trip, I could see the bottom.

If you've never floated a big river in a kayak, you need to know it's not always rapids and white water shooting you downstream. They all have places where the water relaxes in long sleepy pools–places where the current takes a nap and lets you take control.

Patricia and I were floating in just such a place, where the banks were at least a quarter of a mile apart. My wife was paddling toward the western shore to get a good shot of a bald eagle with our camera. He was perched high in a poplar tree that leaned out over the Allegheny. Carefully, she dipped the paddles in and out of the blue water trying not to scare the eagle away.

I kept my boat next to the opposite shore, and just watched this scene unfold. Here was this huge black bird with its brilliant white head and tail, roosting on one of the upper limbs of an ancient white barked tree that was decked out in the yellows of late September. Behind it rose a green Allegheny mountain whose rounded top looked like it was holding up the baby blue sky. Below the tree was its reflection on a shimmering pool with my wife gliding across it in a little blue plastic boat.

In the midst of all that natural splendor, as I watched my wife get steadily closer to the eagle, I was suddenly struck by the irony of it all. Back in those hills, less than twenty miles from here, and less than a hundred and fifty years ago, Col. Drake's well was the beginning of the demise of lots of places like this. Worldwide, many pristine waters and lush woodlands have been spoiled to harvest Old King Oil.

Patricia was almost under the eagle and was putting the camera to her face, when with two flaps of his wings he sprang up from the tree and soared down river. A long stream of white poured from under his tail and rained down into the Allegheny as he flew away.

My wife yelled, "Holy eagle shit! I'm glad I wasn't any closer."

⁂

The cops kicking us off the highway also garnered us an invitation to the 20th Annual Johnson Barbeque. It was a clear, full moon night, and more than fifty people showed up for chicken cooked on spits over an open fire. Everyone brought a covered dish, and this potluck was one the lady folk took seriously. The food was tremendous and the camaraderie grand. They also had party games. Every man there, including me, tried to weasel out of the Newly Wed Game. But I was glad we played. Patricia and I won. Neither of us missed a question. First prize was a twenty-five-dollar gift certificate to Walmart.

But the highlight for me was talking to Cal—the hero in the family. He was a stock car driver, and they called him their "Rising Star." To which he said, "Yeah, well, I'm NASCAR certified, but that don't mean I'm going to Daytona anytime soon."

He was strawberry blond, in his mid-twenties, with a daughter who was learning to walk. His thin little wife's hair hung just below her shoulders and was the same color as his. She also had long pink fingernails and a face that looked like it belonged on the cover of *Seventeen* Magazine.

His little girl, Cally, stumbled around the living room in a tee-shirt with a color picture of him in his racing suit on the front of it. On the back was his race car.

While Cal's wife stretched her arms out to her approaching daughter, she said, "Don't let him kid you. He's better than Petty, or any of them!"

"Come on," Cal said as he blushed and shook his head. "I am not."

"He is too!" His wife, Angel, lifted Cally up onto her knee. "He may be quiet when he's around people, but he's a tiger on the track. Ask anyone who's seen him—or raced against him. They'll tell you."

Cal's father snatched a framed picture off the mantel and shoved it in front of me. It was of Cal in his racing suit, and he was kneeling next to a three-foot silver trophy with a stock car on top. Behind him in the picture was a wall full of trophies and ribbons. His father said, "That was over a year ago. He's got a bunch more since then."

Angel set her squirming little girl down to toddle across the carpet. "The only thing holding us back is sponsors."

"But that's changing." His father handed me a picture of the car zooming past a big grandstand filled with fans. "With the way he's winning these days, they're going to be lining up at the door to get their logos on that car."

Later that evening, I ran into Cal at the beer tub. He seemed a lot more relaxed than he was earlier in his father's living room. When he pulled his arm out of the ice water, he held out a bottle of Miller Lite to me. "That okay for you?"

I twisted the cap off the bottle and said, "Your family is mighty proud of you."

I expected a blush like before, but this time there was none. Cal was serious as he nodded his head. "I'm a very lucky man. I wouldn't be where I am now, if I didn't have my family."

He was taking a swig from the bottle in his right hand when I asked, "Do you make a good living racing?"

"No. I've been winning a lot of money lately, but most of that's eaten up getting there. Got to pay the pit crew, mechanics, parts, and transporting it all to the track."

I interjected. "And the cost of the gas!"

Cal choked a bit on his beer. "Yeah, fuel! It's not getting any cheaper. It takes a lot of money to race. No, I don't make a good living racing. Not now, anyway. But like my wife said, once we get ourselves a few good sponsors, we'll be doing all right."

At that moment a hint of cockiness emerged from him as he tossed the empty bottle into the nearby trash. "You know what it cost to get your logo on Robert Yates hood?"

"Not a clue."

He pulled another bottle out of the ice water as he slowly said, "More than ten million dollars."

"Wow!"

"That's just for the hood!" He flung the bottle cap in the trash. "A stock car has a lot of space for advertising. And when you're winning, they pay big bucks for a spot on it."

He held up his Miller Lite bottle. "Wouldn't I love to have that logo on my hood."

I saluted him with my beer, then we clinked bottle necks as I said, "Someday."

"Hopefully, soon," Cal sighed, and we both tipped our bottles up.

After swallowing, I asked, "So, what kind of mileage do you get with that car?"

He nonchalantly shrugged his shoulders. "A couple miles a gallon."

"So it's not cheap to run a long race like Daytona."

Cal took another swig of his beer before he said, "What you burn in the race ain't nothing compared to what it takes to get there. You've got time trials, qualifying rounds, and practice, practice, practice. A guy has got to do a lot of driving to get to Daytona."

I tipped the bottle toward my lips, as I asked "How many homes do you think you could heat each winter?"

"Huh?'

CHAPTER 13

UP THROUGH BUFFALO

❦

FROM THE DARK, HE STUMBLED into our camp and blurted out, "I need your help!"

It startled us. We were inside a picnic pavilion in Fireman's Park at Kennedy, New York. And this man was so drunk he had to lean on a picnic table to keep from falling over. We didn't hear him walk up because our pressure cooker was making so much noise.

I snapped, "What do you want?"

He was middle-aged, wore a rumpled brown suit coat and needed a shave. Still leaning on the table, he wobbled as he slurred, "I've got a bet on the bar at the steak house that says you're the kind of people who would bring your mule in for a drink!"

The village of Kennedy only had a few businesses in it. One was the Cross Roads Steak House. Although it was on the other side of the highway, a couple hundred yards from our camp, every now and then the scent of grilling beef would waft through the pavilion. Earlier, while cutting up sweet potatoes for the pressure cooker, Patricia said, "I sure wish we could afford a steak."

I told the drunk, "I'm not taking my mule in a bar."

He flopped his butt down on the bench, then leaned over and pounded the top of the table with his fist as he slobbered through, "I've got forty bucks over there that says you will! It's yours if you'll do it. And they'll buy you both a steak dinner."

Patricia slipped her arm around me. "Honey, maybe we ought to consider this."

189

This was trouble. The money was one thing, but a steak dinner? I knew my wife wouldn't let me pass it up. She turned to the man. "What do you want us to do?"

"Just take your mule over there and walk in the bar with it. That's all."

She turned to me and started rubbing my forearm. "Sounds easy enough."

"It's not worth getting Della hurt for a couple of steak dinners."

Patricia drew back from me as if I had insulted her. With hands on both hips she snapped, "In no way would I ever put her in danger! You know that!" Her tone softened. "I just think it wouldn't hurt to check it out. If we get over there and you think it isn't safe, we'll turn around, come back and have sweet potatoes and cabbage for dinner."

We decided to lead Della over, and if it looked safe—and she went in on her own accord—we would do it. I insisted, "But it's up to her."

When we walked into the brightly lit parking lot, all twenty patrons at the Cross Road's were in it clapping. While we walked toward the barroom door I heard, "They're really going to do it." "This is awesome!" and the usual, "Man, that's one big-ass mule!"

The plan was for Patricia to go in first and check the place out. It had three wide wooden steps up to a large landing. Then we would have to turn left and go up two more steps to get in the barroom. I was standing at the foot of the first three steps, holding Della's lead rope, when my wife came out and said, "I think it's okay. But maybe you should check it out."

Still holding onto Della's lead rope, I stepped up onto the landing to see what it looked like. When I turned around to hand the rope to Patricia, the Big Sis put her right front hoof on the first step and climbed up onto the landing. I had to leap into the barroom to get out of her way. Then she spun to the left, and the next thing I knew Della was standing at the bar beside me.

The place went crazy. Through the laughter, cheers and applause I heard, "Did you see that?" "Holy shit, she did it!" "Buy that mule a drink!"

Della sure knows how to make an entrance!

I knew she didn't want a drink. But she liked the peanuts and potato chips a lot. And after a couple bags of each, she calmly turned around and faced the door. She was ready to leave. Then, as if she had done it every day of her life, our big girl stepped down to the landing and gracefully leapt to the ground. Enough slumming for her!

⁓❦⁓

For us, every state line was a cause for celebration. New York's was extra special because it's the state that Patricia was born in. I was traveling with a broad from the Bronx.

When we crossed into New York from Pennsylvania, the most obvious difference for us was the roads. The ones in New York all had wide shoulders—many of them paved. It sure made walking a lot easier.

We also noticed that more people stopped to visit with us along New York's highways than they did in Pennsylvania—maybe because it was safer for them to pull over.

Another thing we noticed was the appearance of poverty. In New York it looked like people were poorer than they were back in Pennsylvania. More homes were in disrepair, and many of the farms had tumbled down fences with barns that leaned in one direction or another. I was particularly struck with how many homes had been added on to and never painted to match the rest of the house.

Lots of Amish live in western Cattaraugus County. The appearance of poverty was even more pronounced among them. Although it was October, nearly all the women and children we saw were bare foot—many in ragged clothes. And we didn't see the cheerfulness in the children's faces like we saw in the Amish communities back in Ohio. All of the Amish kids in New York seemed to be sad. Not once did any of them wave at us from the back of a carriage.

The few Amish adults we did talk to were much more serious than any we had met so far. Back in Ohio, it seemed like every Amish person we met had a spice of humor about them. They all seemed happy, but in New York the Amish we met were mostly solemn.

In the Buffalo suburb of Lacawanna, we camped behind the Lake Erie Italian Club. The club house was a large, flat roofed, red brick building that looked like it could have been a bowling alley. Surrounding the club was a paved parking lot that could hold four-hundred cars. On the back-side of the parking lot were several grass covered acres with shuffle board courts, bocce ball lanes, a huge covered barbeque pit, picnic shelters and places to play volley ball. Behind all of that was a wide open grassy area adjacent to a small forest. A perfect place for us to camp. Patricia went in to ask, and the manager was quick to say, "Sure. Make yourselves at home!"

Patricia and I had just finished pitching the tent, when I looked toward the club house and saw a group of four men sauntering across the parking lot in our direction. All wore suit coats, but none had ties on. They were all dark complexioned, with slicked-back hair at varying stages of gray, and everyone had a drink in his hand. It was the thickest of the men, the one with the cigar who said, "Louie was telling us about you, and showed me that paper yous gave him. I'm president of the club."

"I hope it's all right if we camp–"

A large ash fell off the cigar as he waved both arms. "Oh sure, sure, sure." His voice had the deep rattle of a long time smoker. "No problem! Stay as long as ya want! This is real interesting, this thing yous are doing."

They all spoke in that Italian/American dialect which demands the use of hands. While we talked, I couldn't help but wonder, who among them was *the man* to know in Buffalo? They all told us if we needed anything, to let them know. It was the president who said, "Go up to the bar and have a drink on me. Tell Louie I said so."

Lots of grass for Della to graze on, a good distance from the highway, water nearby, and drinks waiting for us at the bar–A perfect place to camp.

"Just watch out for the poacher." Anne said.

She lived next door to the Italian Club and had read about us in that morning's edition of the *Buffalo News*. "Some nights there's more than thir-ty deer out here," she said. "And there's a poacher who drives back here in the middle of the night with his lights off. Then he shines a spot light on the herd, blinds one and shoots it. We don't know he's here until his gun goes off. By the time we get up, he's got his deer in the truck and driving off."

Patricia asked, "Have you called the law?"

"Oh, sure. But what can they do? They said they'd start patrolling back here. But what's the chance of them showing up when he's here?"

When we were on the road we hung our folding chairs on the back of the cart over our bicycles. On the backs of each one I stitched a piece of bright orange material. On one I wrote our website address. The other had "Mule Ahead" on it. I took the Mule Ahead chair and set it up between Della and the parking lot. Then we hung our florescent safety vests out in the area, and we put orange banners on Della's halter, mane and tail. It would take a pretty stupid poacher to think she was a deer.

Just before sunset, we went to the Italian Club for cocktails. The main topic at the bar was the local news–Lacawanna was the center of an international story. Seven local men, of Yemeni descent, had recently been charged with running a training center for the Taliban. They were known as the "Lacawanna Seven." That afternoon they were in court for a bail bond hearing, and one of them got out on bail.

"Oh, great! Now we got a terrorist running loose." The bartender said. "Just what we need, eh? How's you supposed to feel safe with someone like that out on the streets?"

When we went to bed that night, I wasn't concerned about a foreign terrorist. We were worried about some local with a shotgun out to fill his freezer. Patricia and I both had a hard time getting to sleep.

"Did you hear that?"

When Patricia nudged me with her elbow, I was already awake. I had been listening to it too. Either a car, or a pickup, had pulled into the parking lot with its lights off. It stopped behind the club house and sat idling for a while. Then I heard the tires slowly roll across the grit on the asphalt. It sounded like it was headed our way. When it got to the edge of the asphalt it stopped.

That's when Patricia asked me, "Did you hear that?

Just as I said "Yes" the motor revved a bit. Then the tires started to creep out onto grass in the direction where Della was grazing. I already had my jeans on, and was reaching for the flashlight, when a floodlight suddenly blazed on.

Patricia screamed, "It's him! It's the poacher!"

Headlights came on and engulfed Della with light, as I tripped and stumbled through the tent door. Waving my flash light, I yelled. "Hey, stop! Over here!"

Suddenly, the vehicle made a sharp right turn and its headlights blinded me as it came my way. It wasn't until it stopped next to me that I realized it was a police car. The officer asked, "What's going on here?"

I pointed toward the club house. "They told us we could camp here."

"This ain't no damn campground! What's with the mule and all this stuff?"

He was moving his floodlight back and forth on the tent and the cart while I said, "We just stopped for the night. We walked here from Arkansas, and we're headed—"

The cop blurted out, "Hey. Hey! Hey!!" Each "hey" was crisper and louder.

"Yous was in the paper today! I read it just before I came to work. You've got the mule and walking to the East Coast. Then yous are going around the world or somethin— right?"

He shook my hand and wished us luck. Then he said, "You know there's been a poacher back here."

"We heard."

"Don't worry about it. I'll keep an eye on things tonight. Welcome to Buffalo!"

⚜

We got lots of press coverage everywhere we walked. We never asked for it. It just happened, and I had mixed feelings about that. Most of them good. But sometimes it was nice to encounter people on the street who didn't know anything about us.

Patricia always said, "I think the press is good. Because when people read about us first, then they know we're not gypsies, tramps or thieves."

I had to admit, being in a big newspaper like the *Buffalo News* did have its advantages. After reading our story Roy Haller, a member of the Upstate Mule and Donkey Association, took the route the paper said we were on when he drove into Buffalo that morning. He was going to try to find us winter accommodations in western New York.

Because of the article, Blasdell's invited us in for pizza. The next afternoon the owner of the Malamute Saloon yelled at us from his side of South Park Avenue. "How about a beer and something to eat?"

Farther into the city, a baker gave us two bags filled with fresh bread and other goodies from his one-hundred-year-old brick oven–the only commercial brick oven in Buffalo.

I think being in the newspaper and on the evening news helped us in city traffic too. Cab drivers all read the newspaper–that's part of their job. It gives them something to talk about. So usually they knew who we were and what we were doing. Walking in a city we always want the cabbies on our side.

Obviously it helped with the police. You always want them on your side no matter what you're doing, especially in city traffic.

It certainly helped to have that recognition with drivers who were jockeying for position in the heart of downtown. That's where we were Wednesday afternoon at 4 p.m. Of all the greetings and gestures we got downtown, none were ugly. Some of the hands that waved at us only had one digit up, but none of them was the middle finger.

Buffalo's City Hall was the most impressive municipal building I had ever seen. It's a massive tan brick art deco structure with more than twenty floors and six wings. On top was a dome of multi colored tile. Acid rain had stained the brick, but the dome was still brilliant.

If I were superman just passing through Buffalo, I would have to stop and fly out of City Hall just because it's such a classy building. Metropolis' *Daily Planet* looks mighty plain compared to Buffalo's City Hall.

We got a real good look at it because we walked around the same block three times before we got on the right route–but we weren't the only ones lost. During the work day, barricades had been erected for street repairs. So when people got in their cars to drive home, they found themselves going in directions that they weren't used to taking.

Here again, being in the newspaper helped. A policeman, who'd read our story, escorted us a few blocks and headed us in the right direction.

The Buffalo News article helped us get through downtown and helped us meet some nice people. But I've got to say, some of our most memorable Buffalo encounters were with people who knew nothing about us.

Like the young black man standing at a bus stop on South Park Avenue. We were headed toward downtown, and as we approached him I could tell he was doing his best to ignore us. With his arms folded across his puffed-up chest, the man's eyes were focused straight ahead at the street. I knew he saw us coming, but he was intent on ignoring us.

So when we got in front of him I said, "Whoa Della."

The young man didn't look at me, until I said, "You waiting on the bus?"

"Uh, yeah."

With a straight face I said, "Well, it broke down. So they sent us to pick you up."

Every shred of coolness dissolved, and his arms melted down to his sides as he slowly turned to survey the situation. While he panned from me to Della to the cart his whole body began to slump. He looked straight into my eyes and asked, "What?"

I tried, but I couldn't keep a straight face. He was quick to catch it and a wide toothy smile sprang to his face. "No, man. That ain't right!"

Laughing, we brushed palms. "You got me dude. You *really* got me!"

From City Hall we took Elmwood Avenue north. Nearly everyone we encountered while we walked up into Buffalo said it was the coolest part of town. Both Buffalo State College and the Buffalo campus of State University of New York were nearby. It had art galleries, a couple of museums and lots of boutiques. People told us the coolest coffee houses and hippest bars were on Elmwood. It sounded like a good street to walk a mule on.

But what they didn't tell us was that it's a main commuter route out of downtown. It was a little after 5 p.m. when we finally got onto Elmwood and we became part of the gridlock–not the cause of it, just part of it.

With everyone else, we were at a standstill for several minutes in the five-hundred block. Traffic had just begun to move when I heard a female voice yell, "You, with the horse, stop! Wait for me."

When I turned to my right I saw a woman with long blond hair waving and yelling from the crowed doorway of a bar. She was trying to push her way through the crowd as she yelled, "Wait for me!"

From the cart, I heard Patricia sigh, "Now what?"

Traffic was gaining momentum, so I quickened our pace to keep up with it. Behind us the woman continued to yell, but her voice was soon drowned out by the noise of rush hour.

A block farther, traffic was at a standstill again. After I craned my neck to see if I could spot what the holdup was, I turned to look at Della. There was the blonde from the bar beside Della holding onto the bridle, kissing the side of her face. This woman was in her mid-thirties, and while looking nothing like Marilyn Monroe, she had that kind of face and physique, and she was cooing to Della. When I looked back at Patricia in the cart, she was grimacing and shaking her head. I knew what she was thinking. *Who's this flake?*

I turned back to the woman who was grinning at me with lush pink lips that said, "I just love this." Her voice had the vibrato and breath of afternoon cocktails. "Where are you going? Come stay at my place."

Had I been a single man, I might have entertained that invitation–but I wasn't. The car in front of us started to move. I said, "Lady, step back. We've got to go."

"Take me with you. I love this. I love you."

Right then Della stepped forward, and the woman jumped out of the way. But she still had hold of the bridle. I yelled, "Lady, let go!"

I quickened our pace, and she had to jog to keep up. "Please let me go. I love this!"

Suddenly, she stumbled against a parked car and lost her grip on the bridle. We were trekking away as she pleaded, "Take me! I love it! I want to go!"

Walking up Elmwood Avenue, sometimes I felt like we were in a parade. Lots of people yelled and waved at us. Some on the sidewalk clapped as we went by. And we heard plenty of, "Right on, man!" "Awesome, dude!" "God Bless you!"

We had just stopped for a light, and were at the head of the line in that lane, when I heard, "Can I pet? Can I pet?"

She was a brazen, stout, black woman dressed in a flowered Hawaiian shirt, pink sweat-pants, un-laced work boots and a black knit stocking cap. When she marched up to us, it was more like she demanded instead of asked, "Can I pet?"

Her right hand started petting Della as she shouted, "I love to pet! This is nice!"

Lodged in the fingers of her left hand, was an open cigarette paper filled with tobacco ready to be rolled. Not a shred of it fell out as she rubbed Della's nose.

The light turned green. I said, "We've got to get moving."

"Okay."

When she turned to cross Elmwood, I yelled, "Don't get hit!"

"They wouldn't dare."

Then she stepped in front of the car in the lane next to us, aimed her right index finger at the driver and barked, "You wait!"

He lurched to a stop, and so did the other three lanes when she pointed to them on her march across Elmwood Avenue. The whole time, she balanced that unrolled cigarette in her left hand. A block further, we were stopped in traffic again and there she was strolling up the left side of Elmwood. She beamed as her left arm swung back and forth over her head. Clinched in those fingers was a burning cigarette. "I love to pet!"

⋦⧳⧳⧳⧳⧳⧳⧳⧳⧳⧳⧳⧳⧳⧳⧳⧳⧳⧳⧳⧳⧳⧳⧳⧳⧳⧳⋧

And on it went, one urban character after another. But none of them—except the drunk woman—offered us a place for the night.

So with the orange beacon on top of the cart, and flashing red lights on the back, we wandered the dark streets of Buffalo looking for a place to bed down. The lights on the cart, and the sound of Della's steel shoes on the street, brought many faces to front windows. Several people stepped out onto their porches or into their front yards. Some waved, a few said "Good Luck," but no one tried to engage us in conversation. And nobody offered a place to stop for the night.

All we needed was a front yard, a back yard, a vacant lot, or some sort of spot somewhere. Like on the grounds of a huge hospital that we came to. It was in the north part of town and had several grassy acres that begged to be grazed on—but they couldn't find the administrator to give us permission.

In the next hour-and-a-half we made two bad turns that took us in the wrong direction. We had planned to leave north on Delaware Avenue, but somehow ended up headed south back toward downtown on another road. But finally, on a residential street, with our maps, I figured it out.

Patricia was brusque when she said, "So you really know where we're at this time?"

Both of us were grumpy, and by her tone I knew my wife was at the boiling point. I thought I might lower the heat with a bit of humor. "Well, the last time I was here—"

Patricia exploded, "Don't give me that 'The last time you were here.' shit! There's nothing funny about this! Next you'll tell me, 'It's just part of the adventure, baby.' I don't want to hear it!"

She whirled around and tromped back to the cart, climbed in, sat down and started pounding her feet on the floor as she screamed, "This fucking stinks!"

While I walked back to the cart, I expected a porch light to come on at one of the nearby houses—but none did. I was soft, but stern when I said, "Patricia, calm down."

"Don't tell me to calm down!" Although she wasn't screaming, my wife was still loud. "This is serious! We're walking the streets of Buffalo in the middle of the night. We could get shot or mugged. Someone could rob us."

I chuckled, "Rob us? The joke would be on them."

She stamped the cart floor again. "Stop it!"

"No, you stop it! Throwing a fit isn't going to help us at all."

Had anyone been home at the residence we were in front of, surely they would have come to their windows when Patricia let loose with, "I'm venting!"

I grabbed her by the arm, and from deep within me growled the words "Patricia, shut up!" It felt like some monster inside was saying, "I don't want to hear another word out of you! You're going to get us arrested for disturbing the peace. Just sit there and keep your mouth shut!"

My wife was leaned back as far away from me as she could. Her eyes were huge with fear, and when I let go of her arm she scooted to the other side of the cab. I turned around and walked to Della's head feeling very mean. I untied her lead rope from the street sign, looked into her mule face and whispered, "I'm not good at this."

Aside from the clip-clopping of Della's shoes, we continued through Buffalo's nighttime streets in silence. Although Patricia's presence loomed enormous behind me, I felt very much alone right then.

A few blocks later, a police car pulled in front of us and stopped with its blue lights flashing. *Oh God! Someone heard us fighting and called the cops."*

The officer got out with a flashlight, which he shined all over us and the cart as he walked up to me. He was in his early forties, and had concern in his voice. "What are you doing?"

"We walked here from Arkansas and—"

He held up his hand. "I read the paper, I know what you're doing. But why are you out on the street after dark?"

From the cart, Patricia yelled, "We need a place to camp."

I said, "Can you think of some place where we could stop for the night."

The cop stroked his chin. "That's a new one. A campsite for a mule?"

From the radio fastened to his uniform, a female voice babbled a series of numbers. He tipped his head toward his left shoulder and rattled a bunch of numbers back to her. She said something else, which energized him. "Look, I've got to go. I'll try to think of a place for you. But right now, I've got to move."

A couple of blocks farther we came to a large field with a chain-link fence around it. It was a schoolyard, and ahead of us at the end of that block was a monstrous five-story school building. In front of it was a lawn of at least two acres with several towering oaks. A winding drive led from Delaware Avenue to the back of the building. At the entrance to the drive was a sign: Mount Saint Mary's Academy for Girls.

My wife, who went to Catholic schools, was suddenly giddy. "This is perfect."

"If we can get permission."

Although it was well after 8 p.m., there was still lots of activity around the building. A dozen cars passed us as we walked up the driveway and around to the back of the building. There, we found two school buses unloading a triumphant soccer team. So the parking lot was already effervescent. Then we pulled in, and the lot got chaotic.

A coach helped us get permission from the principal to camp on the grounds for the night. They also invited us to use their showers. The coach stood guard in the hall to make sure none of the girls walked in on us.

Unlike the boy's showers I had experienced in public school–where everyone is in one big room–St. Mary's had individual stalls, each with a small private changing area. Hot water had just begun to rain down on me when I had the thought, "This is every boy's dream come true. Taking a shower with your sweetie in the girl's locker room." Then I thought, "Why aren't I in the stall with Patricia?"

I turned off the water, and had just stepped into the changing area, when I recalled the ugliness between us an hour ago. My lust was suddenly overcome by despair. Never before had I grabbed a woman and yelled at her like that. Every fiber of me was racked with guilt as I wrapped a bath towel around me. When I pulled the wooden louvered door to her shower open, my wife jumped and gasped, "What?"

"I'm sorry."

She was in the far corner of the shower stall with her arms crossed to hide her breasts. "Sorry for what?"

I felt like a little boy begging forgiveness. "I'm sorry I got rough with you."

Cowering behind the shower she said, "I've never seen you like that. It scared me."

"I'm sorry. I'll never grab you like that again."

Patricia uncrossed her arms and stepped from behind the shower as she said, "Well, I guess I really had it coming. I was kind of out of control, wasn't I?"

"Even so, you don't deserve to be man-handled like that. I'm sorry."

"Me, too."

I stepped into her changing area, pulled the door shut behind me and said, "Can we kiss and make up?"

It was as if the sun came from behind a cloud as she shuffled toward me. "Sure."

I pulled the towel from around me, laid it on the bench and stepped into the shower as Patricia giggled. "Watch it buster! Looks like you've got more than kissing in mind."

⧼⧽

Although Mount St. Mary's had several acres of schoolyard, they insisted that we camp beside the building near the back door. It's the busiest entrance to the building, and our tent was about twenty feet from it.

The first people to show up in the morning were custodians. The first two arrived just before sunrise. While one of them fumbled with keys, I heard the other say, "What the hell is this all about?"

An hour later, teachers and students began to trickle in. Some students arrived on buses, others were chauffeured by parents. Then there were the lucky girls who drove their own cars to school–none of them clunkers.

Although Saint Mary's was owned by the Catholic Church, it wasn't just for Catholics, and the teachers weren't nuns. That morning the principal told us, "We do have classes on religion, but it's not the emphasis here anymore. Our goal is quality education. We hire the best teachers we can find, regardless their faith."

One of the teachers put it this way: "This is a moneymaker for the Catholic Church. It's not cheap to send your kids here." The same teacher told us about a scholarship program for welfare families. "If a girl really wants to go to school here and she works hard, and if her family is poor enough, she can get in."

So, while the student body at Mount Saint Mary's was all girls, they were from a wide variety of backgrounds. We saw faces of every race coming to school that Thursday morning. They had grades from preschool through high school, so girls of all ages were walking past our camp at the back door. Most of the younger ones were either awestruck or giggled all the way into the building. Many of the older ones just smiled and walked by, and there were some who asked questions. And then there were those who were too cool or self-important to notice. Most of them were the ones who drove themselves to school. They ignored us.

But all of the girls had one thing in common, they dressed alike. Mount Saint Mary's uniform was a green plaid skirt with a white blouse. The hem of the skirt came to just above the knee, and they wore white knee-high socks with black shoes. From first grade up through the twelfth, all of the girls were dressed identically.

Kenneth handed me a Styrofoam coffee cup as he said, "When I taught in the public schools, I used to think uniforms were horrible." He'd been teaching English at Saint Mary's for five years. "I thought uniforms robbed them of their individuality–but I was wrong."

"How's that?"

"In any school, the big thing is who's the coolest, and what they wear is a big part of that–especially with the girls. And a lot of the time that's as far as they go toward creating an identity. But these girls don't have that crutch. They have to dig deeper."

A few minutes after the bell rang for classes to begin, three high school girls came out the back door. One was almost six feet tall, and she said, "Our teacher told us to ask if we could interview you for our school newspaper."

The girl with long blond hair asked the questions, while the shortest one took notes. She had a hard time holding the pad steady, so the tall girl bent over and put her hands on her knees. "Here, I'll be the desk."

After some giggling, the interview continued. At one point, the girl taking notes said, "Do you get tired of answering the same questions all the time?"

I had been asked that so many times, I had a standard reply. "Not really. Because the people asking them are all different, so that makes the questions different."

However, near the end of the interview, one of them did ask me a question I had not heard before–and I wasn't able to answer it.

It was the desk who said, "If you weren't doing this, what would you be doing?"

⌐⌐

New York became the Empire State by way of the Erie Canal. When it was completed in 1825, the three-hundred-sixty-three-mile waterway connected Lake Erie at Buffalo to the Hudson River in Albany. This gave the Great Lakes access to the Atlantic Ocean, and it firmly established New York City as the front door to America.

Farmers and loggers in central and western New York were the first to take advantage of this new access to the world. It was a cheap way to move a lot of goods. And it didn't take the rest of America long to catch on. Ships sailed from as far away as Duluth, Minnesota, to offload products in Buffalo bound for New York City. Traffic was so heavy, that just ten years after it opened, the Erie Canal had to be widened and locks enlarged to accommodate the traffic.

We were near the canal, about five miles west of Lockport on Highway 31, when a man with his five-year-old grandson stopped and asked if he could take our picture. He had seen us on the evening news a week earlier and just had to stop.

During our visit, I said, "People have treated us good here in the Empire State."

The man shook his gray head. "It's the rust state."

"Huh?"

"You just walked through Buffalo, didn't you? What did you see? I'll tell ya. You saw lots of factories, all of them closed and rusting away."

He was right. On our walk through Buffalo and the outlying communities, we saw several abandoned manufacturing plants, and the prevailing color was rust. In varying shades, it was on old water towers, dilapidated chain-link fences, and idle machinery that had been left behind. In some places this industrial decay was surrounded by cornfields, apple trees and other crops.

"Used to be, if you didn't have a job it was because you didn't want one. We had factories all through here. But now they're gone and never coming back. Ain't nothing around here now but farming."

"Why did they shut down?"

"Unions, that's why." He was putting his camera in its case. "And I was a union man all my life."

He'd worked for thirty years at a General Motors plant on the edge of Lockport. "In the old days, unions did lots of good. But now they exist just to keep themselves alive. My last few years on the job, they'd have us strike just to prove we needed them."

After buckling his grandson's seat belt, he slammed the passenger door, turned to me and said, "I had all the benefits I needed, I was making great money, why would I want to go on strike? But every couple years they'd find some reason to hit the picket line."

He slid behind the steering wheel and started the engine. "The American worker has priced himself out of the job market."

⊐⊨

CHAPTER 14

WHERE APPLE TREES SPEAK SPANISH

CHRIS WAS POURING BEER FROM the pitcher into his glass as he said, "It's been a long time since we've had an American picking apples for us. You'll be our token gringo."

A sinister grin grew under his Hitler mustache. "This ought to be real interesting."

Chris, and his wife Karen, owned and operated Watt's Fruit Farm. It was a mile north of the Erie Canal at Albion, New York, and it was not just an orchard. Besides their four-thousand apple trees, the Watts produced cherries, apricots, peaches, raspberries and they had half a dozen pumpkin patches. The farm also had a market with a gift shop, café, huge greenhouse, a straw maze, playground and petting zoo

They also had a train called, "The Orchard Express." It was an old flat-bed truck that had been made to look like a locomotive, and it pulled three wooden passenger cars that could carry one hundred people. On the weekends, they used it to give tours of the farm and take people into the orchard so they could pick their own apples. Through the week, school groups boarded the train for an educational tour that explained not only the workings of the farm but the workings of nature. Under a giant oak, students sat in a circle on logs while a woman in hiking boots explained photosynthesis.

In the green house, a deaf woman–dressed as a bee–did a demonstration on pollination. And because we were camped in the orchard near the oak tree, we were added to the tour.

The Watts had six orchards at different locations around that part of Orleans County. It was October 21st when we arrived at the main farm and apple harvest was in full swing. So Chris had lots of pickers in the trees, and all twenty-nine of them were Mexican.

Most of the pickers stayed at a migrant camp in an orchard nearly ten miles from the main farm. It was a long concrete block building that looked like a dumpy motel. Each room had a door and one window. In the middle of the building was a huge community kitchen with communal bathrooms and showers–like the ones back in high school.

The upper echelon of the migrants–the manager, tractor and truck drivers–stayed in a two story, rambling house at the main farm. Known as the Harding House, the red brick core of it was built in 1834. After many additions, the Harding House now had eleven bedrooms, and for the past ten years had been a migrant house.

"How would you like to stay there for the winter?"

Patricia asked me that question shortly after she and Karen Watt returned from a trip to Walmart in Batavia. Then she said, "Karen told me that usually a few Mexicans stay through the winter, but they're all going home this year. So she asked if we wanted to move into the Harding House and help them take care of the farm."

That night, Chris and Karen took us out for pizza and beer at the bowling alley so we could talk about it. Besides taking care of winter chores, Chris wanted us to cleanup the Harding House. "It isn't going to be easy. Been nothing but Mexicans living in it, and they don't take care of nothing!"

Chris was my age and about my height, but he weighed half-again as much as me. Besides a hefty stomach, his other distinctive feature was the Hitler mustache. "If we get them all out of there for a while, maybe you can make it civil again."

But it was going to be at least a month before they left for Mexico. Until then, the Watts said we could live in the upstairs of their house. Karen and Chris only used the bottom floor. The house was about five miles from the main farm, adjacent to one of their other orchards.

It was after we got that all figured out that I asked Chris about picking apples. He said I could start Monday. So, over the weekend I built a stall for Della in a barn near the Harding House, and put up a paddock for her. Then Monday morning I bicycled the five miles to where I was to rendezvous with the farm manager, Chooey.

We were to meet at seven. I got there a few minutes early, so I leaned my bike against the Harding House and waited. Adjacent to the house was a lane that led to a network of gravel roads into the orchard. While I waited for Chooey, carloads of Mexicans filed past me. I waved at each one, but only a couple of hands waved back—and they were half-hearted. Most of them looked away when they saw me. I was beginning to feel very much out of place. And each passing car made me feel worse.

Suddenly, six jabbering men came bounding out the back door of the house. All of them were laughing as they climbed onto the tractors and into trucks parked in the yard. The morning air was alive with words like, "Arriba!" "Manos a la obra!" "Andando!"

Right then, I was wishing I had learned what Senora Schubach tried to teach me back in high school Spanish. I may have been an American on an American farm, but I felt very much like a stranger in a strange land.

"Sorry I'm late," Chooey said. "I had to stop at one of the other farms."

He spoke the kind of English that can only roll off a Latin tongue. With r's that rippled and j's that were missing in words like Jesus and Juan. He was a dashing, light-complected man who had worked on the Watt farm for half of his thirty years.

"So, you ready to pick apples?"

We met Chooey the day we arrived at the farm, and I liked him right away. He was mature and serious when it came to business of the farm, but under that professional veneer I sensed a mischievous boy. Opening the driver's door of his black late-model pickup truck, he said, "Put your bike in the back."

After he slammed the tailgate, Chooey motioned for me to get in the passenger seat. I barely had the door closed when he put the truck into motion and sped toward the highway. At the edge of the pavement, he stomped on the accelerator, and the back tires screamed as we fish-tailed out onto the highway headed toward town.

"I'll show you where to pick. But I've got to take care of something first."

We stopped at a convenience store and he bought us both a cup of coffee. Then a few minutes later he pulled into an orchard on the east side of Albion where he had a rapid fire Spanish conversation with a man on a tractor.

A few minutes later, as he drove out of the orchard, Chooey turned to me and said, "Habla Espanol?"

"Un poco?"

"A little?" Then he commenced to babble at me in Spanish.

I held up my hand and said, "Whoa! When I say little, I mean very little."

When Chooey laughed, he suddenly had round cheeks that weren't there before. His eyes narrowed to slits and a blush flooded his face. "Oh, okay."

We were on a bridge over the canal, when he turned to me and asked, "Why do you want to pick apples?"

"Well, I've never picked apples before. So I thought it would be a good experience. And we need the money."

"You don't make much money picking apples."

"A little money is better than none."

We both laughed a bit before I said, "I figure if you folks earn enough to make it worth your while to come up here, then I should be able make enough to get me by."

Chooey had sort of a pensive expression on his face as he nodded. "Okay."

"And I'm thinking once I get the hang of picking, I should do pretty damn good. You know, being tall and all."

"Oh?"

When I turned to look at Chooey, the corner of his left eye brow was raised. And I swear, little horns poked up through his hair when he said, "We'll see."

While we rolled along the gravel roads between the rows of trees, I spotted several of the cars that had passed me earlier. Some were parked at the end of the rows, others were in the aisles between the trees. Many had doors open, but none had people in them. They were in the trees.

The main farm was dissected by Oak Orchard Creek, which had been dammed up more than a hundred years ago. Behind the dam was a pretty pond with willows weeping over it and ancient autumn oaks standing tall around it. Several geese and ducks were gliding across the shimmering surface.

After we crossed the dam, Chooey stopped his truck on the east side of the pond beside a row of loaded apple trees. At the end of the row was a small wooden sign that identified them as Jonah Gold. Chooey opened his door, "This is where you start. You pick these three rows."

Apple pickers use a metal bucket that the Mexicans call "buche" (pronounced boo/cha–long "a"). The bucket was concaved on the side against their bellies and hung from their shoulders by a strap that went around the back of their neck. The bottom of the bucket was open with a two foot long canvas tube around it. Stitched across the bottom of the tube was a length of rope with knots on each end. To close the bottom of the bucket, the bottom of the tube was folded up to the top of the bucket and secured by slipping the knotted rope into metal clips on each side of it. When the buche was full, they took it to a wooden bin and released the rope from the clips so the apples could roll out the bottom of the tube into a bin.

"But you have to be careful the apples don't drop out of the buche," Chooey said. "You want them to roll out, because if they drop, it will bruise them."

Then Chooey donned the buche and commenced to pick. His hands and arms moved like they were part of a machine. While he snatched the fruit from the lower branches he said, "You don't want to drop them into the buche. That will bruise them too. Lay them in it and don't use your fingers. Use your whole hand."

He showed me how to caress the apple in the fatty part of the palm. Then with his forefinger and thumb he pinched the stem and twisted it from the branch. "Don't squeeze, that will bruise the apple. You're picking fresh fruit here, and they can't be bruised."

"Isn't it all fresh fruit?"

Chooey laughed. "Yes. But when I say fresh fruit, that means these apples are what you buy in the grocery store. The rest go to processing, for apple juice and sauce."

He had the buche filled in less than five minutes. Then he waddled to the bin about ten yards up the aisle between the trees. After he showed me how to empty it, he put the buche strap around my neck and helped me adjust it. "You got any questions?"

"What about the apples on the ground?"

I was relieved when he said, "They're for processing. We'll get them later."

Thousands were on the ground, and just the thought of being bent over that long made my back hurt. Thank God I didn't have to do that.

"Just try not to step on them."

Then he taught me how to shuffle through the fallen apples. Chooey also showed me how to manipulate the three-legged pointed aluminum ladder in through the branches. "But you want to pick the apples on the bottom branches first."

"Why?"

"So you don't knock them off when you're up in the tree."

After he left, I went to work. I couldn't believe how much fun it was to pluck the golden and red orbs from the tree. Within minutes, my arms were working automatically among the branches. They wove through the limbs to the rhythm of Mexican music from radios of the cars parked among the trees. A base line of tubas in a polka-style beat embellished by trumpets, guitars and Spanish voices. From all directions in the orchard, live voices sang along with the radios. The sun was out, the music upbeat and the voices in the trees were joyous. It was all very festive.

When the buche was full I started toward the bin with the load wobbling on my stomach and thighs. While I waddled between the trees, I wondered, "Is this what it's like to be pregnant? Having to lean back to balance the burden in your belly, and only able to waddle because the weight prohibits you from taking a real step."

With the bottom branches picked, I started up the ladder. Suddenly the fun turned into a struggle. When I tried to climb up through the branches, they snagged my clothes, entangled my legs and grabbed at the buche. Finally situated on the ladder, I began to pick.

Soon my buche was full, so I started down the ladder. When I took the first step I heard something tumble through the branches below me. I looked down just in time to see the last apple fall out the bottom of the bucket.

"Dammit!"

The knotted ropes on the bottom had come out of the clips. I figured the knots weren't big enough. So I put another knot in them and went back to picking. When the buche was full, I started down the ladder again. As I stepped on the bottom rung, I heard tumbling apples. Just the right side had come undone, but it still let all the apples out.

I yelled at the tree, "What am I doing wrong?"

So, it was back up the ladder. This time when I started down, I kept my eyes on the knots. Half way down, a branch snagged the left rope and yanked it out of the clip. When I leaned over to grab the bag, a twig jabbed into my right eye. Instinctively, my lid shut. But that didn't stop the twig from ramming into the socket between the bridge of my nose and my eyeball. I froze as apples bounced off the ladder and down to the ground.

It felt like I had a whole tree in my eye. I was afraid if I moved, it would rip my eye ball out, but I couldn't just stand there. So I slowly backed my head away from the branch. As it came out I could feel the knobbiness of the twig rubbing my eyeball, and I expected to find blood and eye tissue on the twig. Would I be forever blind on my right side?

I wasn't. My vision was blurred for a while and my eye was sore, but otherwise I was all right. Apple picking wasn't so much fun anymore.

Before I went back up the ladder, I tied the ropes into the buche clips so the tree couldn't rob me. By the end of the day I had filled three of the twenty-two bushel bins. At fifty-five cents a bushel that first day netted me $36.10, and a stick in the eye.

⚜

"Why don't you take the day off?" Patricia said.

The next morning when I stood up from our bed, I moaned and quickly sat back down. Every inch of me hurt, especially my shoulders and arms, and my right eye felt like it was three times the size of my left. Patricia rubbed my back as she said, "You aren't used to doing this kind of work. Give your body a day to rest."

"They'll all think I'm a sissy."

When I stood up and walked into the bathroom, my muscles were screaming, "Bud, we *are* sissies! Please don't make us do this!"

After I cooked and ate breakfast, and packed my lunch, I went out in the yard to climb on my bike. I was strapping on my helmet when Chris came out the door and said, "You want a lift to the farm?"

"No thanks, I can ride."

He opened the door to his pickup "How many bins did you get yesterday?"

"Three."

He walked around to the back of his truck. "So how do you feel this morning?"

"Fine."

He opened the tailgate and turned to me. "Who do you think you're kidding? I've picked apples all my life, and even though most of those people in the orchard are half my age, I bet I can still out-pick any of them.

But I also know, if I filled three bins today, I wouldn't be worth a damn for a week."

He motioned me over to the truck. "Put your bike in the back. Let me give you a lift to work, old man."

⁂

On my second day of apple picking, I was the first one in the orchard. It was chilly, but the sun was out. And aside from the geese on the pond, it was peaceful among the apple trees. At first, my body protested when I began to pick, but soon my muscles limbered up and relaxed into the work.

I had just emptied my fourth bucket in a bin, when the first car full of Mexicans pulled into the orchard. Before long the morning quiet was replaced with that south-of-the- border beat, and the apple trees were jabbering in Spanish. The orchard was festive again.

The sky began to turn gray while I ate my lunch. From the north, came a wind with the feel of winter in it. I was up in a tree on my third row of Jonah Golds, when the first bit of ice landed on me. Within moments, it was a full blown sleet storm. Through the sounds of the ice landing on the trees, I heard ladders clang and car doors slam. The Mexican voices didn't have the happy tenor I had grown accustomed to.

After a few minutes, the sleet gave way to snow. It was a Christmas-card kind of snow that quickly turned everything white. I was in awe of how beautiful it was—but it was obvious the Mexicans were not pleased.

I don't know why, but suddenly I started singing. "Oh, the weather outside is frightful, but my dear you're so delightful. . . . Let it snow, Let it snow, Let it snow!"

I sang it at least half a dozen times, butchering the words and getting louder with each rendition. Whether the Mexicans heard, or understood me, I don't know. But when I finished there was not another voice or any music to be heard. The only sounds were those of the snowflakes landing, and the crunching of my foot steps on the way to the apple bin.

It didn't take me long to figure out everyone else had left. No one told me to quit picking if it snowed, so I kept working—but it was a frigid affair. The icy apples were hard to hold and my fingers got numb from handling them. So I put gloves on, but they were soon soaked. So I decided it was better to pick bare handed. The worst part was touching the cold aluminum ladder, which made my fingers feel like they were on fire. But I soon came up with a routine that made it more tolerable. I'd put gloves on to move the ladder, pick bare handed, then warm my hands in my pockets while I walked to the bin.

It had been snowing for almost an hour, when I heard the motor of a vehicle coming toward me. I was climbing down the ladder when Chooey's truck stopped beside me. Through his open window he asked, "What are you doing?"

"Picking apples."

That little-boy grin bloomed on his face. "I thought so. You okay?"

About twenty minutes after he drove off, a parade of Mexican cars and trucks pulled across the dam into the orchard. The snow had slacked to flurries, and before long it stopped. The clouds parted, the sun came out and soon the Mexican music returned.

"Chooey used you today?"

Chris was handing me a platter of roast beef that Patricia had fixed for dinner as I asked, "How's that?"

"After he found you picking apples in the snow, he went to the house and told the Mexicans, 'If Loco Gringo can pick in the snow, you can too.'"

Karen said, "You mean Gringo Loco, don't you?"

Chris pointed his fork at me and said, "No. Him they call 'Loco Gringo!'"

The evening of my third day of apple picking, Chooey stopped by the barn while I was cleaning manure out of Della's stall. He asked, "How's it going?"

"Great! I finished those three rows. Where do you want me to pick next?"

"I'll meet you there in the morning and show you."

The next day when I got to the orchard, I found a stack of empty bins at the end of the rows I had just picked. I was dismounting my bicycle when Juan pulled up on his tractor. He was Chooey's cousin, and one of those who stayed in the Harding House. Next to me, Juan was the oldest one working in the orchard. I met him my first day picking and liked him right off the bat–partly because he spoke some English and was closer to my age, and he was the only one who seemed interested in communicating with me.

Juan had a wife and three children back in Mexico, and he had not been home in three years. His goal was to save enough money to open a small grocery store in his village. So he sent most of each paycheck home for his wife to put away.

"Chooey sent me to show you what to do," Juan said.

"Where are we going?"

He pointed to the apples on the ground. "Here. You pick these up."

My heart sank. My back cringed. I had two broken vertebrae in my lower back. One as the result of a bicycle accident, and the other from when I fell off the roof of my house. Every time I nailed shoes on Della, my back would hurt from being bent over so long. What was this going to do to it?

"I thought they picked the ones off the ground with a machine."

"No, hombre. If you pick the trees, you pick the ground."

Juan grabbed my buche, put the strap around his waist and squatted so the bucket dangled between his thighs. Like a machine he began to rake the apples into it with his hands. In less than two minutes the bucket was full. While he waddled toward the stack of bins he said, "These for jugo. Uh, how you say? Juice."

"So just throw them in?"

"Si. No big deal."

Easy for him to say. Juan was at least a head and a half shorter than me, and he didn't have a broken back. But those were just excuses, and there were apples to be picked up. So with the strap around my waist, I squatted down and tried to do what Juan had done. But I didn't fit under the trees like he did, and my back couldn't take squatting that long. Soon I was on my hands and knees crawling through the fruit, some of which had begun to rot. Within minutes my jeans were soaked with apple juice and coated with pulp. My nostrils were inundated with the sensations of vinegar, and my back was a race track of spasms.

When I crawled out from under the tree, I remembered Chooey's raised eyebrow when I said, "I figure being tall will be to my advantage." No wonder he said, "We'll see."

⸙

Apple picking continued through Thanksgiving and into the first week of December. Weather was always a factor. Some days we couldn't pick because the apples were too cold. Every morning, Chooey and Chris tested them with pressure gauges and thermometers to make sure fingers wouldn't harm them.

They rotated me between three farms. On my bicycle, with the buche on my back, I'd pedal through Albion, or on the tow path along the Erie Canal to the different orchards. The tow path was my favorite. Sometimes I'd go out of my way to take that route.

The only Mexicans that seemed interested in having anything to do with me were Chooey and Juan. All the others would wave and smile when they saw me. Aside from that, they kept their distance, and there was one who acted like he hated me.

"Why do you say that?" Chooey asked as he handed me a Bud Lite. I had just given Della her evening feed, when he walked into the barn with the beer.

"Every time I wave at Alex he turns the other way. And when he delivers bins to me, instead of spreading them down the rows like he does for everybody else, he just drops them beside the road and takes off. I don't get it. What did I do to him?"

"You're picking apples."

"So?"

Chooey swallowed a swig of beer. "He doesn't think it's right that you're picking apples. Alex says it's a Mexican job, not American. You should get an American job and leave the Mexican jobs alone."

If I hadn't had a mouth full of beer, I probably would have yelled, "What are you talking about? This is America! So this is an American job! He's probably illegal anyway."

But I didn't. Instead I swallowed the beer and asked, "What do you think?"

That little boy grin bloomed on his face as Chooey aimed the beer bottle at his lips. "Are you having fun yet?"

❧

You make more money when you pick bigger apples because it takes less of them to fill the bin. How I wish I'd had a chance to pick Courtlands, some were the size of grapefruit. How I hated picking Fuji. It took forever to fill a bin. I was tickled when they sent me to pick Ida Reds. They weren't Courtlands, but they're still a good sized apple.

It was a couple days after Thanksgiving, and apple picking was nearly over. By noon I had filled three and a half bins. I was proud of myself. It would be a banner day for Loco Gringo.

I had just sat down to eat my sandwich, when Juan pulled into the row with his tractor and dropped off a stack of bins at the other end. Less than a minute later, an old white sedan pulled up and stopped by the bins. I had seen this car several times. It always had two men and a woman in it. One of the men was as tall as me. The other was about six inches shorter, and the woman was so short she was almost a midget.

Chooey had told me the tall man and woman were married. The other guy was her brother. They worked as a team and were something to watch. Between the three of them they could strip a tree in a matter of minutes. The woman and her brother worked the bottom branches, while her husband picked the top of the tree. Then, after they picked two or three trees, she would go back and pick the ones off the ground. Scurrying around under the trees, her arms moved so fast they were a blur as she raked apples into the buche.

Chooey said, "They make more money than anybody."

And now they were in my row of trees. My first chance to make some decent money, and here they were. While I ate my sandwich I could hear them rolling the bins down the aisle. They were positioning themselves to strip me of a decent day's wages. It had been cloudy all morning, but now it was downright gloomy. When I stashed the empty sandwich bag in my bike packs, I found myself muttering, "Damn wet-backs! Why don't they go back where they belong."

When I stopped for lunch, I had a bin in the aisle that was half filled. After lunch, by the time I had finished filling it, they had filled five bins and were working on their sixth. And there were only three trees left to be picked.

While I stood surveying the situation, it began to snow. I was so angry the snow must have sizzled when it landed on me. What was I going to do? Start another bin?

I had one empty left, and was rolling it toward the three remaining trees, when I noticed they had no more empties. What did this mean? Should I relinquish my empty to them? No way!

The snow was really coming down when I waddled out from under a tree with my full bucket. When I got to my empty bin I could see theirs was about three quarters full. I paused for a moment and watched the flakes float down into the orchard. What a beautiful sight. The trees, the grass, the bins, me and my fellow workers were being adorned with this soft winter lace. It seems trite to say that the scene was becoming a winter wonderland, but it was. And my anger was tainting it.

Right then, something comfortable inside took control and propelled me past my bin toward theirs. The woman had just emptied her buche, when she looked up and saw me approach. Fear was on her face, and she took a few steps back. While I emptied my load into their bin, she turned and babbled something to the men. Her husband replied "Yo que se?" (How should I know?)

At that moment, I felt downright giddy. This was going to be fun. Astonishment was on the woman's face when I winked at her, and as I turned back toward my tree she began chatter at her husband. Repeatedly the word "dinero" (money) was in her sentences.

When I dumped my apples into their bin the second time, the husband walked up to me and said, "Hombre, we share the work, eh?"

"You mean the money?" I could see the woman anxiously waiting behind her husband for an answer. So I looked at her and said, "Dinero? No amigo. This is all yours."

She tugged on her husband's sweat shirt and simply asked, "Que?"

Before he could reply, I said, "It's getting cold out here. Comprende?"

He nodded his head. "Si."

"Let's get these apples picked so we can go get warm. You keep the money."

Snow was piling up on the hood of his sweat shirt as a big grin spread across his face. "Gracias, hombre."

When I turned toward my tree, she started interrogating him. While I didn't know what was being said, I could tell it didn't make any sense to her. Why would Loco Gringo pick apples for them?

Even if we had spoken the same language, how could I explain myself? Sure, I needed the money as much as they did. But that's not the only reason I was in the orchard. No more than getting to Maine was the only reason we were walking. We were on the road to truly experience America in her own neighborhoods. I was in the orchard to savor the magic of work that hasn't changed in more than a hundred years. I wanted to be one of the champions who brings the fruit in before winter ruins it.

For us, the best part of traveling was when a community included us as if we were part of it. Like the Amish in Holmes County, Ohio. In the orchard, a real bonus for me would have been to be accepted as part of the team that brought in the harvest. Up till now, it had just been me picking for me. I'd been filling bins with my number on it so that come Friday, I got a decent paycheck—but it felt like something was missing. And now, hauling buche after buche to their bins, I found it. Camaraderie. The joy of working <u>with</u> them, rather than beside them. Albeit I forced myself onto their team, I was still part of it, and it felt good.

How could I explain that to this woman? I couldn't. So I just returned her nods and smiles, and kept on picking.

By the time we got to the last tree, the snow had slowed to flurries. So much had fallen that the entire orchard was blanketed in white. The husband and I were on ladders at the top of the tree, when I stopped to gaze around us. I tapped him on the shoulder and said, "Hombre, it's really beautiful, eh?"

He looked around us for a few moments, then turned back to me and said, "Si, es muy hermoso. Muy bonito!"

Suddenly, without thinking, I started singing, "Jingle bells, Jingle bells, Jingle all the way . . . ."

He started laughing, and I could hear the other two laughing below us. When I looked down, the woman was standing next to the bin clapping to the rhythm of my singing. Her husband reached over, patted me on the shoulder and started humming along. Later, as I emptied my last load into the bin, I heard her under the tree humming the melody to, "Dashing through the snow, in a one horse open sleigh . . . ."

When the day's picking was done, we were supposed to take our ladders to the end of the row and lay them under the last tree. The husband and I had just done that, when he turned to me and said, "Hombre, the money. We share work, we share—"

I held up my hand. "You keep the money. Let's go home and get warm."

"Gracias."

The snow had started again, and I was zipping closed the packs on my bicycle, when they drove by me at the end of the row. The woman was leaning out the back window with a pretty smile on her round Mexican face. "Adios amigo. Gracias."

That was my finest day of apple picking.

Bud's last day of apple picking.

CHAPTER 15

WINTER IN THE SNOW BELT

⁂

I Love Snow!

AND NOT JUST ITS BEAUTY, I like the inconvenience. What else can completely disrupt everything–schedules, traffic, life, society–and yet, make the world look prettier than it really is? Nothing harkens adults back to their childhood like snow. It calls them to slopes with skis, sleds or pieces of cardboard. Parents pack it into balls to throw at their children and each other. Mature grownups will lay down in it on their backs then move their arms up and down making snow angels. Then they'll urge their children to do it too. Nothing is so magical as snow!

"I'm glad you like snow so much," Chris grumbled, as he shook some off a Christmas tree I had just cut for the farm market. "Because I've got a feeling we're in for a hell of a lot of it!"

Albion, New York is halfway between Buffalo and Rochester, right in the middle of the snow belt. Chris's forecast was right. We got more than 170 inches that winter–the most ever. And, according to the weather service, it was one of the coldest winters on record. It seemed like the wind was always blowing. Usually it was a westerly, with either a southern or northern tack. They were Canadian winds that blustered across Lake Erie, which was forty miles to our west, or over Lake Ontario–eight miles to the north.

By the end of the first week in December, all of the migrants had gone home to Mexico. The night Patricia and I moved into the Harding House, a storm off Lake Erie and an Arctic blast from Ontario, collided at the Watt Farm.

The sky was gray all day, with a few snow flurries late in the afternoon. But then, about two hours after sunset, the storm windows on the west and north sides of the house suddenly started rattling. The wind wailed around the brick corners and sent the huge pine on the south side to whining. It sounded like a track from a horror film.

We had set up our bed in the old sunroom on the first floor. Those windows gave us a front row seat for the blizzard, which was lit up by a couple of street lights nearby. The trees and street signs were contorted in so many directions it was hard to tell which of the great lakes was sending the prevailing storm. Then, half an hour into it, there was a loud ping on a north window. Then another, and another. Then a barrage of marble sized ice pellets peppered the glass. It sounded like machine guns in a gangster movie.

"My God!" Patricia was sitting on our bed with her back against the wall. "Do you think the glass can hold up to that?"

It probably only lasted a few minutes, but to us it seemed like forever before the ice quit. It was down-right relaxing to have only the howling wind and swirling snow. We both fell asleep to the sounds of the storm.

In the morning the sky was clear and blue, and everything under it was white, or at least had some white on it. The west side of the tree trunks were caked with ice and snow. Dunes of it were humped over every bush and banked up against the buildings. In the open areas, the surface was textured like ripples on water and sparkled like crystals in the morning sun. You had to have sunglasses to look at it very long.

The wind the night before had blown from every direction, but the east. Yet, it was the back door, on the east side of the house, that was snowed shut. It led to the mud room, so it was the busiest door in the house. I had to get it open.

Heeding Chris's advice, I had kept a snow shovel inside. With it, I dug my way out the front door and across the porch. Then I stumbled down the front steps landing face first in thigh-high snow. It hurt.

Under four inches of fluff was a hard layer of ice that was too thin to support me, but thick enough to jar my bones as I fell through it. My face felt like a thousand bees were stinging it when its flesh collided with the white stuff.

Each time I tried to stand, the fluff and crust sent my boots sliding and me crashing back down into the products of last night's storm. I still had the snow shovel in my hand, so I used it as a cane to hoist me up. When I finally got traction, I began to wade my way around the south side of the house. Each step had a crunch before my foot sank down to the bottom with snow above my knees. By the time I got to the back door, I felt like I had just finished a day of apple picking.

After digging the door open, I trudged toward the tractor shed to fire up the snow plow. Halfway between the shed and the livestock barn, a snow spout suddenly whipped up from the rippled surface. Like a tornado, it whirled over me and then down into the orchard, leaving me completely covered with white.

I love snow!

⊰⊱

Chris and Karen Watt said there would be plenty of work for both of us around the farm. At first, it was easier for me because of the apple picking. The work was hard but the time flew by. But it didn't work that way for Patricia.

Her day started with feeding and caring for the animals in the petting zoo. They had Black Bellied Barbados sheep, miniature goats, pot-bellied pigs, all kinds of chickens, peacocks, turkeys and bunnies–lots and lots of bunnies. She fed and watered them, and cleaned out their pens in the morning. The hardest part was the water. Twice a day she had to carry it fifty-yards from the house to the barn in five-gallon buckets.

Most of the time, it only took a couple of hours in the morning to do all of that. Then she would go to the market and wait until there was something else for her to do. Often she would sit around all day waiting for work.

But that changed around Thanksgiving. That's when mail orders for the holidays started coming in. Patricia went to work hand-polishing apples that she packed into gift boxes with jams, cheeses, fudge and other goodies. And there were wreaths to be made, shelves to be restocked, fudge to be cut and on Sundays there was French toast to be cooked. Every Sunday, up until Christmas, the Watt's served brunch in the café. Patricia was the French toast chef. Everybody agreed, hers was the best ever.

In the greenhouse, twenty-one non-profit organizations decorated Christmas trees to be auctioned off a few days before the holiday. The Watts donated the trees, and the proceeds went to the group that decorated them. So through the holiday season there were lots of people in and out of the greenhouse.

With all that traffic, we had to keep the driveways, parking lots and loading pads clear. So we did a lot of snow plowing. It wasn't a typical snow plow on the front of a truck. This was a grader blade on the back of a small, open Kubota tractor. Deep snow had to be pushed while backing up. So, most of the time I was turned in the seat, looking over my shoulder. Plowing snow at the Watt Farm was truly a pain in the neck.

I also kept one road through the orchard slightly plowed so Della could go dashing in a one-mule open-sleigh. When we first got to the farm in October, I found a small cutter sleigh in pieces in a trash pile. I had always wanted to drive a horse, or better yet a mule, in a sleigh. So I rebuilt the little cutter and hooked Della to it. We found some bells, put them on her harness and off we went through the orchard. Originally I fantasized driving it into town. But the state and town were too diligent about keeping the roads cleared. So I kept a snowy path open on the orchard road. Della got excited each time I pulled the little sleigh out of the barn.

We also used the orchard road to cross country ski. Della hated the skis. The day we bought them she watched us with great curiosity as we put them on. Then, as we skied down the road past her barn, she began to race around the inside of her paddock snorting, bucking and farting. When we returned, she angrily pawed the snow. Every time we put the skis on, she did the same thing. Della didn't like the idea of us sliding away with those things on our feet.

We also used that road to get to the pond so we could feed the geese. In past winters, the Mexicans herded them up to the barn and kept them in a stall. Chooey said, "It's nasty! Geese shit on everything. And you've got to haul water for them to swim in."

Everyone agreed, they'd be all right at the pond, as long as it didn't freeze completely over. But they had to be fed. So either Patricia, or I–often it was both of us– would load corn and apples into a back pack then ski or hike to the pond once a day.

When the fourteen geese spotted us coming, it was always a loud affair. They'd honk and shriek as we approached. And there was always one who would run back and forth in front of the crowd with her neck stuck out hissing at us. While we cleared a place in the snow, dropped the apples, stomped on them (so they were easier to eat) and tossed out the feed corn, the hissing goose would continue to get closer. When she got too close, I would stomp my foot and hiss back. Off she'd run flapping her wings and honking.

One afternoon in mid-January, we got to the pond later than usual. It had been a nasty, blowing, frigid day. We put it off thinking the weather might let up. It didn't and nightfall wasn't far away. So we suited up and headed toward the pond. With all the snow that had fallen and blown around that day, I knew the orchard road would be drifted over. So we walked down the town road for a quarter of a mile, then waded in knee deep powder two-hundred yards through the orchard to the pond.

When we found the geese in the rushes at the upper end of the pond, the falling snow had slacked up. As usual, the geese commenced with their boisterous greeting. But this time, after we spread out their dinner and stepped back, they didn't charge the food. Instead, they pranced around it as they continued to honk, shriek and hiss.

I said, "What do you suppose their deal is?"

Right then Patricia grabbed my arm. "There's only thirteen."

We both counted a couple of times, and she was right. One was missing. It was something we feared every time we went to the pond. With fox, coyotes and dogs around, a big fat goose would make a dandy dinner for any of them.

As much trouble, and as obnoxious as they were, we had grown attached to them. So we hiked along the bank in search of the missing goose.

"What's that out there?"

Patricia pointed to a clump of something on the ice. Where the creek flowed through the rushes into the pond was the only place that wasn't iced over. The clump was near there on the ice about thirty yards from the bank. Suddenly, it began to flap and shriek. But it didn't move from that spot.

I said, "It's stuck to the ice."

"What are we going to do?"

"Go get it."

"You don't know if that ice is thick enough." Patricia had hold of my arm. "The last thing we need is for you to fall through."

When she said that, I spotted a long broken limb dangling from a nearby oak. So I trudged through the snow and pulled it down. When I was a kid, I learned you should always hold a long piece of wood in front of you when venturing onto uncertain ice. That way, if you fall through it will catch on the ice and keep you from going completely under.

Patricia said, "Maybe I should do it. I'm lighter than you."

"Yes, but I'm taller."

"What's that got to do with it?"

I didn't answer. Instead, I took a long step out onto the ice and quickly scooted a few feet from the shore. The sound of cracks and snaps filled the air, and it felt like the ice sagged a bit.

"You okay?" Patricia said. "Do you think it'll hold?"

I tried to sound convinced. "It's okay."

Cautiously, I shuffled toward the goose. The closer I got, the more she squawked and flopped. Her left wing was stuck in a ragged ice block that was frozen to the surface of the pond. I stopped about ten feet away and waited for her to settle down. Five minutes later she collapsed and began to pant.

She was so exhausted that she just lay there as I wacked at the block with the limb. My hope was to shatter it so she'd be free. Instead, the block broke loose from the surface of the pond, but it was still attached to her wing.

From behind me, I heard Patricia say, "Do you think the ice will hold both of us?"

I turned around to find my bride ten feet away shuffling toward me, as she said, "I'll grab her. You get the block."

When I lifted the ten pound piece of ice, Patricia swooped up the goose. Then she said, "Now let's stay as far apart as we can, and go back to shore."

She cradled the goose in her arms and held its head with her right hand so it couldn't peck her. I took the chunk, stepped back a couple of feet and unfolded the wing. Patricia winced as she looked up at me. "This is real crazy. Isn't it?"

Right then a snow spout whirled across the pond and plunged us into a white-out. The goose shrieked and fought Patricia's grip. Both of us had to take a couple of steps to stay on our feet as the pond sprang to life with loud cracking.

The white-out lasted only a couple of moments. When I could see my wife again she was covered with a dusting of snow. I said, "This is *real* crazy. You ready?"

With a nervous grin, Patricia nodded. "Easy does it."

While we shuffled toward shore, the ice around us continued to crack. Halfway there it struck me I no longer had my safety limb. This gimp-winged goose would not keep us from going under. Suddenly the cracks and snaps sounded much more dangerous.

I said, "Stop right here."

Patricia turned to me. "What?"

We were three feet from the bank. "The ice on the edge won't hold both of us."

"So what do we do?"

At that point the pond was shallow enough that if we did break through we wouldn't drown, but we would get wet. And there was still a long frigid hike back to the house.

I said, "Think you can jump that far?"

She looked down at the big bird in her arms. Then up at me. "I don't know. Can't say as I've ever jumped with a goose before. But I'll give it a try."

"Okay. On three."

When we landed on the bank, both of us lost our footing and fell down in the snow. She landed on the goose and I on the block. The goose screamed and got its head free. Then it hissed and pecked my wife twice on top of her head.

Patricia screamed. "Quit it!"

I reached over and slapped the goose in the side of its head. When it lunged at me I grabbed it by the neck. The thing sounded like it was gagging as it tried to hiss.

"Bud, you're holding it too tight! Here, I've got it."

I released the neck to my wife, as I said, "Are you alright?"

"Man, did that hurt! I'm sure glad I've got this hood on my head."

She sat up in the snow with the goose in her lap. "Let's get this ice off her wing."

I walked to the grove of oaks to find another limb to smash it. The other geese were under the Jonah Golds I had picked back in October. When we were shuffling across the ice, they all honked and threw a fit. But they got quiet once we were on shore. Then, when I walked past them on the way to the oaks, they all hissed at me.

"Oh, shut-up!"

For several minutes I tried to smash the ice with a short limb but got no where. It was too solid. I said, "The tip of her wing is broken. I think the best thing to do is cut it off. She'll never be able to fly with it anyway."

But we didn't have anything to cut it with. We would have to do it at the house.

So Patricia held the goose, and I carried the frozen block as we waded back out to the road. While we struggled through the powder, it began to snow again. By the time we got to the road the flakes had changed to pellets. When we turned west to hike the quarter mile to the house, we had a sharp headwind that pummeled our faces with ice.

A couple of times the goose got its head loose and tried to bite Patricia. My wife was always able to grab her before she could. Each time it happened there was a flurry of flapping, and once she yanked the ice out of my hands. But I caught it before it fell very far. When we reached the house, both of us felt really beat up and exhausted. My hands were numb from carrying the block. And the goose was too tired to resist anymore.

Inside the back door we laid her and the ice down on a rug in the mud room. Patricia stood up and said, "We're trying to save her life, and all she wants to do is kill us."

With a pair of wire cutters I clipped the wing where it went into the block. She didn't act like it hurt her and there was no blood. The wing was probably too frozen for her to feel it or bleed. Patricia painted iodine on the wound while I fetched a cage from the barn. It was made for hauling chickens. The door was too small for a goose, so I cut the top open and laid her in it on a bed of straw. Then I asked, "Now what?"

Patricia said, "If she's still alive in the morning, we'll decide what to do then."

She made it through the night. And everyone we talked to thought we should keep her in the house until she got her strength back. If we turned her loose now she'd be easy pickings for the coyotes and other critters.

So I fixed a pen for her in the mud room and we named her Lucy. Within a few days she calmed down and quit trying to bite us when we fed her. She still hissed once in a while, but usually she'd just cock her head and look at us with one eye. And every time someone walked in the back door, Lucy would honk. Just what we needed, a watch goose.

⚜

Two weeks after saving Lucy, I was in the barn helping Patricia with evening chores, when I heard her yell frantically, "Bud, help me! Hurry!"

She had gone outside to check the water trough. So I scurried around the barn to find her kneeling in the snow with both hands in the trough cradling a pot belly pig. Patricia had a shiver in her voice. "I found her thrashing around in there. I think she's drowning."

Grabbing the little pig, I threw her onto my shoulder which made her belch water down my back. A coating of ice was forming on her hide, and her body was trembling in my arms.

I turned to Patricia. "Meet you in the house."

I moved as fast as I could, but the lane–all fifty yards of it to the house–was a solid sheet of ice. Each step was a slippery endeavor. Every inch of the way the pig continued to convulse on my shoulder.

When I finally got to the back door and yanked on it, my feet went out from under me. I landed on my butt, which sent the pig flying off my shoulder and out of my grasp. It flopped and slid a dozen feet down the lane, with more water gushing from it.

On hands and knees I crawled across the ice, grabbed her by a rear leg and dragged her to the door. Still on my knees, I went inside and pulled the pig in with me. Then I toted it up the five steps and laid her down on the same floor where we had the goose two weeks earlier.

Lucy's pen was just a few feet away, and she went wild. She honked, shrieked, hissed and flapped her good wing so frantically that I was afraid she'd hurt herself. So I swooped up the shuddering pig, grabbed a couple of towels off the nearby dryer, and took her into the kitchen. There, I laid her down on a throw rug and commenced to rub her with the towels.

"How's she doing?" Patricia asked. She had just come in from the barn. I'd been rubbing the pig for at least ten minutes.

"I've got all the ice off her but I think the convulsions are getting worse. She must be in shock."

Patricia knelt down. "What should we do?"

"I've never dealt with a hypothermic pig before. Have you?"

Patricia called a veterinarian, who told her to fill a tub with lukewarm water and keep rubbing until the pig quit shaking. "If it lives through that, then keep it inside where it's warm, but not hot. A cold corner of the house would be good. Call me in the morning if she's still alive."

When we finally took her out of the tub, three hours and ten minutes had passed. I know, because I timed it. And one of us was rubbing her every moment.

In the northwest corner of the kitchen, I made a corral out of boxes and chairs, and bedded it down with straw. When I put her in it, she was as limp as a live pig could ever be. The only thing she moved were the nostrils on her button-shaped nose. When I laid her down, a faint grunt came out of her. Otherwise, she was completely still.

In the morning she was lethargic, but alive. The vet said, "Keep her out of the cold until she gets strong again. It may take a week or two. When she starts driving you nuts, it'll be time to put her back in the barn."

Then the vet asked Patricia, "Have you named her yet?"

"She's my Little Mermaid."

⊰⊟⊱

My fondest memories of that snowy winter are of Della dashing through it with us in the sleigh. We only did it one time at night. It was mid-February. The sky was cloudless, the moon full and the air crisp. Della's bells jingled in rhythm to the frosty crunches of her steps, as she pranced smartly through the orchard with ears erect.

While we slid by the rows of slumbering apple trees, their moonlit silhouettes looked like they were silently applauding us. The orchard was like a fairyland, and we were the only humans in it. Norman Rockwell could not have conjured a more beautiful scene.

On the hilltop above the pond, I stopped Della so we could gaze at the brilliance all around us. The moon skipped millions of diamonds over the snow, and sent shimmering ribbons across the ice below us. It was splendid!

We sat in silence for a few minutes before my bride said, "I've got to say, that even with all the hassle, and how hard it makes our work, I still like snow."

"Oh yeah? What about your honeymoon? Sometimes it's a hassle and a lot of work. How do you feel about it?"

Patricia snuggled her cheek against my shoulder. When I looked into her eyes, they were sparkling like the moonlit snow.

I love snow!

A one-mule open sleigh.

CHAPTER 16

THE BOYS ARE BACK IN TOWN

❧❦

WE DREADED THE RETURN OF the Mexicans.

When they came back, it would be us two middle-aged gringos with eight young Mexican men—only two of whom spoke English—living in the same house. And the Harding house had only one bathroom and one kitchen. The bathroom lights quit working long ago. So they hung a work light in it—the kind mechanics use under your car. It was attached to a long orange extension cord that ran out the door, down the hall and plugged into Chooey's room. So you couldn't shut the door completely—much less lock it—because of the cord. Plus, there was paint and plaster that hung in festoons from the bathroom ceiling. And when you sat on the toilet it rocked.

The kitchen had no cupboards, shelves or counters. It did have an enamel sink, electric stove, two refrigerators and a Formica-topped kitchen table in the middle of the room. The only light was a hundred-watt bulb dangling over the table, and the only place to set a pan was on the big cast iron radiator next to the stove. Over the years lots of greasy pans had slopped onto it, and obviously the mess wasn't always wiped off. I didn't know there were so many shades of burnt.

Before the Mexicans returned, we fixed ourselves a suite of two rooms upstairs at the back of the house. It had a private stairway that led down to the kitchen, and it was close to the bathroom. (The door now closed and locked. I fixed the lights and the toilet no longer rocked.) Plus our suite had a view of Della's paddock.

We knew when the Mexicans came back, we'd have no privacy. We learned that early one morning our second week in the house when we were still sleeping in the game room. The sun was just below the horizon, but there was enough light that Patricia and I could appreciate what we were seeing as we made love.

"Bud, wait!" Patricia stopped me. "Did you hear that?"

Mexican voices were in the house yelling for a man who had lived there during apple picking. Suddenly a light in the next room came on as our blanket door flung open. Three men stood there staring as we scrambled for covers.

I yelled, "What the hell is going on?"

They just stood there with the blanket pulled back.

I screamed, "Put the damn blanket down!"

The one holding it babbled some Spanish. A bald man behind him grabbed the blanket and dropped it as he said, "Excuse us, Senor. We're looking for Enrique."

⚞⚟

Patricia and I were alone in the Harding House for two and a half months. And at least once a week a stranger would walk in looking for this Mexican or that—no one ever knocked. After a few weeks of that, I started locking the doors at night. Then they would sit in their cars and honk until someone came out.

"It's a Mexican house," said Chooey. He was on the phone from Mexico. "That's how it is. They're always open, and we just walk in."

Two weeks later I forgot to lock the door, and in the middle of the night we woke to voices in the dining room.

I called out, "Who's there?"

A man's voice said something in Spanish. Then a woman asked, "Is Chooey here?"

"He won't be back till the end of the week. Check back then."

After a quick Spanish conversation, she said, "This is Martin. He lives here."

For the past five years Martin had a room downstairs next to the dining room. Florescent stars were on the ceiling and a mirrored ball hung from the middle of it. Velvet paintings of nude women were on the walls with postcards of the Holy Mother and Jesus next to the door. He had black lights, a strobe light and a huge stereo system.

Martin had a wife and children in Mexico. He also had an American girlfriend, one who—sexually—was very vocal. And that night they made up for the time he'd been home.

Two days later, Chooey arrived with his brother Jose and longtime friend Pedro. Chooey had been a legal migrant for years. But his brother and Pedro had to sneak into the country. The people who smuggled them in were called "Coyotes." It cost two thousand dollars apiece. That included the documents necessary to work here.

"They've all got papers." Chris Watt said, "Green card, social security card, the whole bit. You can't tell the fakes from the real ones. Hey, it's a bargain for the Social Security Administration."

I asked, "How's that?"

"We deduct the taxes from their wages and send it in. But they aren't citizens. So there's no beneficiary. That's a pretty sweet deal for Social Security. I'd like to know how much they bring in off bogus accounts every year. I bet it's illegal immigrants that keep Social Security afloat."

⧉

By March 1st, six Mexicans had moved in. Among them was Chooey, his brother Jose and Pedro. We had become fond of Chooey before he left for Mexico, and I guess he must have spoken well of us to Jose and Pedro.

Right away they seemed eager to be our friends. Jose spoke a little English, and Pedro was learning. When Pedro spoke, he was so animated that if I just watched him, I usually got the idea. He was a lanky, comical character.

In Northwest New York, the end of February and early March was pruning time in the orchards. It took lots of hands, chain saws and loppers to prune more than 40,000 apple trees. That's why the boys were back. They were out in the orchard shortly after sunrise, and usually home just before sunset. In the middle of the day, right at noon, they came in for lunch. It was always a big event, with homemade tortillas, rice, beans and some kind of meat with lots of peppers. All washed down with a few bottles of Bud Lite.

During the preparation and consumption of the meal, Martin's sound system would rattle the windows to the tempo of Mexican tubas. It was always a festive affair with lots of chatter, laughter and practical jokes. Often they invited us to join them—sometimes we did.

It was that way in the evening, too. Food, frolic and fun. But not on March 19th.

Upstairs we had a TV attached to an antenna that picked up a few Rochester and Buffalo channels. Downstairs, theirs was connected to a satellite dish tuned to Mexican stations. And from March 19th and the next few days, all of us were glued to our televisions watching America invade Iraq. They saw it on Mexican TV and we, on American.

During those days, the weather was too bad for them to work in the orchard. On those days, meals continued to be made in the kitchen, but without the music or carrying on. And the beer still flowed, but it was all consumed in front of the TV.

"Why are they doing this?"

When Chooey was sober, his English was impeccable. But when he was drunk, like the night of March 20th, he could be hard to understand. I asked, "What do you mean?"

"I don't get it." He was sitting on our floor, leaned against the wall with a Bud Lite in his hand. "Why is Bush doing this? Why is he bombing all those people?"

"Well–"

He interrupted me. "Those Iraqis didn't knock down the buildings in New York. So why does he want to bomb 'em?"

Chooey took a swig from his bottle as I said, "They say it's because Sadam has weapons of mass destruction."

"So what? Bush has got 'em too. Nobody's bombing him."

⧈

Except for taking care of the petting-zoo animals, the boys took over our outside chores. That allowed us to concentrate on fixing the house. The hardest room was the kitchen. We replaced the ceiling, floor, and all but one wall. Patricia used ten cans of oven cleaner to un-crud the radiator. When I scrubbed behind it, the plaster fell down to reveal old red brick. It was part of the exterior wall from the original 1832 house.

I built simple sturdy counters with lots of shelves. We coated the brick behind the radiator with several layers of polyurethane, so it could be washed. On the radiator I built a steel shelf to set pans on. And in the middle of the new ceiling, I replaced the dangling bulb with a suitable kitchen light fixture.

What made the kitchen the hardest room to fix wasn't the amount of work, it was the conditions under which we had to do it. Throughout the renovation, the boys still had to use it. So every day at noon, we'd move the stove and table in from the dining room where they were stored while we worked. After lunch, they'd help me lug them back out. Then at the end of the day, when they came in from the orchard, we'd set it all back in the kitchen for the evening meal. Replacing the kitchen floor was a real challenge.

By the end of March, the kitchen was done, and everyone was happy with it. It was clean and had lots of counter space, so making meals was much easier. We could tell the boys were proud of it by the way they showed it off to visitors.

A couple of weeks later, Patricia and I took the farm van and had a night out on the town with a nice dinner and a couple of toddies at a local lounge. Afterwards, when we pulled into the farm, our headlights shined on a severed deer leg in the yard. My wife said, "Chooey told me they might go hunting in the orchard this evening."

When I opened the van door, I saw half a dozen deer legs beside the back steps. "Looks like they got more than one."

Patricia walked in the house ahead of me. I had just latched the storm door when I heard her gasp. "Damn them!"

She screamed as she stomped toward me. "I could kill all of 'em!"

"What's wrong?"

My wife was in front of me shaking as she pointed toward the kitchen. "Go look."

When I pushed the door open, I found a horrendous scene of carnage. Blood, guts and piles of meat were everywhere. Our pretty white and brown kitchen was awash with red. The boys had done some serious butchering—and serious drinking. Besides the usual plethora of empty Bud Lites, a couple of tequila bottles were laying on the floor.

"I'm not cleaning this up!" Patricia stomped past me into the kitchen. "Can you believe this? After all that work, and now look at it! Where is everybody?"

The TV was on in the living room. I walked in and found two Mexicans I didn't know passed out on the sofa. Everyone else was in their bedrooms with the doors closed.

Patricia said, "It's probably best I don't see them right now." As we started up the stairs to our room she growled, "I'd hate to go to prison for strangling a Mexican."

Usually the boys were up and out in the orchard before we went downstairs in the morning. We couldn't work on the house while they were there, so we waited until they were gone. We had a coffee pot in our room, and I had just turned it on when Patricia said, "I really dread going down there."

"I heard them moving around early this morning. I think they're gone. Want me to go down and check?"

"Would you?" She sat up and swung her legs from under the covers. "I don't want to run into any of them right now. Make sure they're all gone before I go down."

When I stepped into the kitchen, I couldn't believe my eyes. It was spotless. Last night I didn't see how it would ever be clean again. But there it was, in the morning sunlight, just as pretty as the day we completed it.

"So how was your night out on the town?"

Chooey walked in from the dining room holding a cup of coffee. I turned toward him and said, "I can't believe this."

"What?"

"This kitchen. Last night when we came home it was–"

"A real mess, right? We shot two deer yesterday. By the time we got them butchered, we were too tired to clean it up."

"It looks great now."

Chooey poured fresh coffee into his cup. "I told the guys last night we had to clean this up before we do anything else. I don't want Patricia to kill me."

⧉

The boys always treated Patricia with the utmost respect. Besides turning off the Playboy Channel when she walked in the room, if she and one of them were headed for the bathroom at the same time, they always insisted she go first. If one saw her with a bag of trash, they'd take it from her and carry it out. Even when they were drunk, nobody ever got out of line with Patricia.

Beyond respect, the boys really liked my wife. Mainly because she took the time to listen to their personal problems–especially those of romance. Even if they spoke very little English, she always made the effort to communicate with them. Many times she came into our room, flopped down in the easy chair and said, "I'm not sure what that was all about, but I know it's not good."

When they got pictures or video from home, right away they'd bring them upstairs to show us. I was welcome to look, but they *really* wanted my wife to see them. And in May, when four of them decided they wanted to bleach their hair blond, they came to Patricia. "I feel like a fraternity mother."

This fraternity was not easy to get into—it could be a life or death proposition. An example of that was when the Border Patrol found fourteen illegal immigrants suffocated in a trailer in Texas. At the time, our boys were expecting two guys to show up, and they had not been heard from in a week and a half. The Coyotes had them, but what they did with them nobody knew. They weren't just workers, these were family and friends. What if they were in that trailer?

"No! I know it's not them," Chooey said.

He and Jose were on the floor in our room watching the news with us. One of the guys they were expecting was Jose's best friend. They grew up together, and he was wiping tears as the network showed immigration officers opening a cargo trailer with dead Mexicans in it.

Two nights later the call came from the Coyote. "We'll be there tomorrow. Make sure you've got the money!"

They showed up during lunch in a mini-van with Pennsylvania plates and tinted windows. The yard was alive with excitement, and while I didn't understand what was said, I'm sure it was along the lines of "Thank God you're here! We've been worried to death."

"You have no idea what we've gone through!"

"Come have a beer and tell us about it."

⊰⊱

"This country could not survive without Mexicans!"

I heard that from Chooey, Chris Watt and every other farmer we met. Chris said, "I'd hire nothing but Americans if I could. It would be a lot less hassle. But Americans don't want to work. They'll pick for a day or two, then we won't see 'em until payday."

"Nobody thought you'd last a day," Chooey said. "But when I found you picking in the snow storm, well–"

I interrupted. "You thought I was one loco gringo! Right?"

He had that boyish Chooey blush. "I guess so."

"Hey, it was fun! Tough work, lousy conditions and the money stinks. What more could I ask for?"

It was Chris Watt who said, "But you know what? The Mexicans not only make a living doing this work, they all send money back home."

⌐⊨⊨

You'd think our biggest problem living with the boys would have been the bathroom. Even with the toilet solid on the floor, the walls patched and painted, the fact remained: Eight young Mexican men, two middle-aged gringos and just <u>one</u> bathroom.

But the bathroom wasn't the problem. It was the kitchen. Someone was always cooking. Especially after we got it all spiffed up. And with them, it was always Mexican food. Never Italian, or Chinese, or even good ole meat and mashed potatoes. Not that they didn't like those kinds of food. The boys were crazy about Patricia's lasagna, but everything they cooked was Mexican.

When they made tortillas, everybody got in on the act. With two presses, a couple of pans on the stove and a bunch of hands in the mixing bowls, the boys would crank out a mountain of tortillas in an afternoon. Tortilla time called for lots of loud music and plenty of beer.

It was also party-time when they roasted peppers, which always kept the back door to the kitchen busy. Usually it was open because the fumes so overwhelmed the kitchen that you had to go out for fresh air. And when they burnt one, the smoke would even drive us out of our rooms upstairs.

"Hey Butt!" Pedro never did get the "D" on the end of my name. "Have a beer?"

A few times I wondered if they didn't burn some of those peppers on purpose, just to get us to come down and party with them–especially one beautiful mid-May evening. The air inside the house was caustic. Outside the back door they'd set a piece of plywood across two saw horses and it was loaded with tortillas, refried beans, fried rice, all kinds of peppers and fish soup. And of course, a few cases of Bud Lite.

"It's beautiful, eh?" Pedro said.

His head was tipped back so he could see the full moon. It was amazing how much English he'd learned in the past two months. Scarcely a day went by that he didn't ask me or Patricia, "How you say in American?"

"Yes, Pedro, the moon is beautiful."

He laughed, then repeated the word "moon" three times. Each time he stretched the word out longer. We both laughed. Then I said, "You sound like a cow."

"Hey Butt. Why you no talk like other Americans?"

The boys had been roasting peppers since they came in from the orchard, so Pedro was pretty well intoxicated. When the boys drank, seldom were they serious. And even though he was in a festive mode, I sensed something pensive in Pedro's question.

I asked, "What do you mean?"

"You drink with us, but you no yell and want to fight. You laugh and have good time. When I drink with Americans in town, they get mean. They call me 'Wet back.' Tell me go home. They always want fight. You no do that. Why?"

At first, I didn't know how to answer. Patricia and I had really become attached to the boys, some more than others. Pedro was one of my favorites. He was a gangling, funny, lovable character that didn't have a malicious bone in his skinny body. The only thing I could think to say to him was, "Because I love ya, man!"

In the morning, when I went downstairs to feed Della, I found Pedro, Jose and Chooey in the kitchen. The night before, after a couple of beers, I went upstairs to bed. Their pepper party was still going on when I fell asleep. Now, all three sat at the table. Their heads were in their hands, with steaming cups of coffee in front of them.

"What's the matter boys? A little too much fiesta last night?"

Pedro babbled something in Spanish. Chooey looked up at me and said, "Pedro said your stomach pills didn't work for him."

"What stomach pills?"

After Chooey translated, Pedro reached over and picked up a plastic medicine bottle from the middle of the table. When the Watts left town, we took care of their Golden Retriever, Kobe. He was an old arthritic dog. The bottle in Pedro's hand was Kobe's arthritis medicine. I said, "He took some of those?"

Pedro held up three fingers. Chooey said, "He took two before he went to bed. Then another one an hour later. But it didn't do him any good."

"Those are Kobe's pills."

Chooey's face lit up. "What? Dog pills?"

He busted out laughing as he pounded the table. It took him a few moments to compose himself enough to tell the other two what I said. Pedro jumped to his feet and pointed at the bottle. "Kobe?"

I put my arm around his shoulders. "Si, amigo. Dog pills. Chooey, tell him they make Kobe bark."

From then on, every time I saw Pedro, he'd bark at me. My friend, the barking Mexican.

When we traveled, a lot of our meals were prepared in a pressure cooker. A small one with a knob that wobbled on the lid and sounded like a steam engine when it was cooking. On the road, we eat a lot of brown rice and nothing cooks rice faster.

The boys were intrigued with it. The first time Chooey walked in and found the cooker chugging he stopped, then quickly backed out the door. "What is that? A bomb?"

My wife laughed. "It could be."

She explained how it cooked rice, beans, meat and just about anything else faster and healthier. "Want me to show you how to use it?"

"We don't cook like that. That's not Mexican way."

However, nearly every time they heard that knob wobbling, they'd would come in and watch us use it. Jose was particularly impressed with how fast it cooked rice. Patricia said, "Want me to show you how to use it?"

"No. I see how."

A couple of days after Pedro took the dog pills, Patricia and I drove to Batavia to shop, then dine at a great little Chinese buffet. We got home about an hour before sunset, and when we walked into the kitchen it was obvious something big had happened.

Around the table, as if in a daze, stood Chooey, Jose and Pedro. On the table was the pressure cooker, lid off with cooked rice splattered everywhere. All three of them wore sleeveless undershirts, and their faces, shoulders and necks were bright red and shiny. One of Jose's eyes was swelled shut, and each of them had a hang-dog expression.

Patricia exclaimed, "Oh my God!"

None of them said anything as my wife slowly stalked around them saying, "What did you guys do?"

They were like three little boys braced for a lecture from mom. No one said a word as Patricia set her bags down and slowly turned Jose toward her. "Chooey, what happened?"

"We used the pressure cooker." Dread dripped from his voice.

"I see you used the pressure cooker. But what happened?"

It was obvious Chooey had practiced what he would tell her. "We did just like you do. We put one part rice and two parts water in, and then we put on the top and the knob. Five minutes after the knob started moving we took it off the stove, but we couldn't get the lid off. I thought maybe I put it on crooked. So we all grabbed hold and pulled on it. It blew open like a bomb."

"Are you telling me you took it directly off the stove and forced it open? You didn't wait for the pressure to go down?"

Chooey said, "Huh?"

"Holy Jesus, Mary and Joseph, it's amazing one of you didn't get killed!" Patricia turned Jose toward me so I could see his scalded skin and swollen eye. "Honey, they've all got second degree burns. We need to get you guys to the hospital."

"We're okay. We took care of it."

"Chooey, these are bad burns. They're going to blister and may get infected. Look at your brother's eye. That has got to hurt."

Jose piped up. "It's okay. Chooey fix."

"We know in Mexico." Chooey picked a plastic bowl off the table and handed it to Patricia. "Egg. That's the Mexican way."

"Feel good." Pedro said.

They had cracked open half a dozen eggs and separated the yokes. Then they smeared the raw whites on their skin, including Jose's eyelid. When we walked in they were standing still so it could dry.

"If we do it right away, it don't hurt." Chooey said. "Leave it on for two days and it will be okay."

He was right. None of them blistered or peeled, and Jose's swelled eye was nearly normal the next morning. Five days later, none of them even had a red mark. Lends a whole new meaning to the question, "How does it feel to have egg on your face?"

Our plan was to leave the farm a few days after Memorial Day. But the third week of May, I hurt my back when I bent over to pick up a piece of trim. It just went out on me. I have broken my back twice and neither time did it feel as bad as when it went out at the Watt Farm. It took a few trips to the chiropractor and three weeks to get over it.

So it was mid-June before my back was strong enough to get Della's feet ready for the road. On the summer solstice, we moved out of the house and into the cherry orchard down by the pond. We camped there for ten days, which gave us a chance to get used to the new tent, spruce up the cart and finish a few projects around the farm house.

During that time, the Watts had a going away party for us at the market. And a couple of friends had us over for dinner. But we knew the farewell the boys had planned would be the best. It was at our campsite with a bonfire, lots of Mexican food, plenty of beer, some singing and a bit of dancing. It was a grand time.

The next day, we loaded up the cart then hiked up to the barn to get Della. It was a third of a mile from our camp, and by the time we had her cleaned up and got some last minute stuff taken care of, it was past noon. The boys had already eaten lunch and were in the orchard before we walked back to our campsite to hitch up Della.

When we rounded the bend on the orchard road near our camp, in unison Patricia and I said, "Where's the cart?"

For a few fleeting moments, I really was worried, but then I came to my senses. "I'd say the Mexicans stole Loco Gringo's cart."

It was not hard to find. When the eight of them pushed the cart back into the orchard, they left behind a trail in the grass between the cherry and apple groves. When we got close I could hear giggling among the trees. Their trail turned into a row of Empires and there was the cart. Chooey was in it with his feet propped up on the dash, beer in his hand and little boy blush on his face. "You missing something?"

Suddenly, Pedro leaped out from under a tree and dashed toward the cart shafts. Behind him was Jose, swatting him on the butt with an apple switch. Pedro jumped between the shafts and grabbed them like he was going to pull the cart. Chooey yelled, "Hey Gringo! How about I trade you these two ass' for that good looking mule?"

"I never trade down."

They had two ice chests stashed under the trees. "Hey Butt, have a beer?"

"Nope. Got to go."

I didn't know if that hurt Pedro's feelings or not. But while we harnessed Della and said our goodbyes, I noticed he was gone. I said nothing about it, because there was more than enough emotion in that orchard right then. Patricia and Chooey were really a mess. Chooey said, "We say goodbye in the trees. It's best here."

We had just emerged from the cherry grove and stepped onto the orchard road, when I heard from behind me, "Hey Butt!"

I turned around to see Pedro step out from under a tree. He had both thumbs up, a big grin on his face and tears in his eyes. "I see you at my house in Mexico. Okay?"

Then with his right hand, he held up his first two fingers. "Peace, brother!"

⌘

The boys headed for work. Pedro is the tall blond.

CHAPTER 17

WHERE THEY CALLED HER PATTY

⁑

My wife wants to be called "Patricia." Not Pat. Certainly not Patty!

"I grew up with 'Fatty Patty.' I hate it!"

Nope. I give her all three syllables. Patricia!

"Patty? Is that you?"

The "No Patty" rule doesn't apply if you're from her childhood.

"It's Rita!"

Patricia squealed. "I knew it when I saw that smile."

They collided into each other's arms in the middle of the road. Like little girls at summer camp, these two middle-aged women jumped up and down, while they hugged and giggled. My wife stopped, held Rita at arm's length and said, through happy tears, "It may have been forty years, but that smile hasn't changed."

We were on our way into Driving Park, on the outskirts of Avon, New York, when we encountered Rita. Patricia was born in the Bronx, but she grew up in Up-State. When they lived in Avon, her big sister's best friend was Rita King. It'd been four decades since Patricia had seen her.

"Patty, I'd know you anywhere!"

"Give me a break."

"Really! Who else would walk into Avon with a mule and a man?"

Patricia lived in Avon during her first two years as a teenager. Back then, Driving Park was called "Avon Downs." It was a popular track for harness racing, and it was Patty's favorite place–not because of the races–it was the horses that she loved.

Avon Downs was in the Genesee River Valley on the west edge of town. The village, and Patty's house, were up on the hill a couple of miles from the race track. When she could get away, Patty would hike or bike to see the horses.

"It was best when they weren't having races," Patricia said. "Because then I could get closer to the horses. Sometimes, they even let me go in the barns."

My wife told me that as we were setting up camp under a big oak tree in the middle of what used to be Avon Downs. The grandstands were gone, as were the rows of white horse barns and other buildings from back in Patty's day. But the track was still there, and we camped in the middle of it.

Patricia was in the tent pumping up our air bed when I asked, "Did they ever take you for a ride?"

"Are you kidding? I would have passed out if anyone ever asked me. It was a thrill just to touch one." The whoosh of the air pump stopped. A tone of nostalgia was in Patricia's voice. "I remember how I'd wander around the barns and think there was no better place in the world. It wasn't the barns, or the place, it was the horses. I used to think life couldn't get any better than that–living with horses."

For a few moments, in the center of Avon Downs, there was silence. Then my wife stuck her head out the tent door. "And now I get to spend every moment of every day with you and Della. My dream came true. It really doesn't get any better than this."

⁘⧓⁘

The half mile track was still used for training. On the west side of the oval was a long, modern, red barn with forty box-stalls. To the east of the track was a park with baseball diamonds, basketball courts, horseshoe pits, volleyball nets, a playground and places for picnics. And there were restrooms with showers that we were welcome to use.

Morning at the park began around 5:30 a.m. with hoof beats on the track. When I stuck my head out of the tent, the air was silver and thick.

The fog was too heavy to see the horse, driver or sulky (Horse folks call them "bikes"). But I could hear the percussion of trotting hoofs and squeaks from the bikes as they bounced around the track.

Before this journey, my wife was the one who always got up and made the coffee. But once we hit the road, it was I who fixed the morning brew. Probably because before coffee ever got started the mule had to be fed, or there would be no peace in camp. Every morning she would paw the ground until she got her grain. I don't care where we were, or what was happening, Della had best be fed first.

But that morning, in the middle of the track, she ignored me. At first I thought she was sick. So I walked over and put my arm around her neck. "Hey Sis, are you okay? Want some breakfast?"

Right then, Della did something that I don't remember her ever having done before, but now she does it nearly every morning. She bent her head down, leaned her eye against my chest and began to rub. Not a rough rub like she was trying to push me away or scratch some itch. She was gentle and affectionate. It felt like a hug.

While I poured Patricia her first cup of coffee, I told her about the hug from Della. Before she took a sip my wife said, "She sure does love you. I can't blame her. What a great life you have provided for us."

The fog was beginning to lift, and under its fringe you could see the horses, drivers and bikes. For a few minutes, neither of us said anything as we watched them fly around the track. Then I turned toward Patricia and tried to imagine what it was like to be her right then. This had been one of Patty's favorite places in the whole world, and now we were camped in the middle of it.

Right then she looked up me with a smile and tears. "Thanks for bringing me here."

⊰⧉⊱

The village of Avon was up on the ridge above the track and the Genesse Valley. From the town square was a tremendous view of the lush river bottoms. It was in that square that Patty's dad played Santa Claus. Next to the veteran's memorial, the village set up a throne where Bob Myers sat and listened to the wishes of the little kids in town.

When WWII broke out, he enlisted in the Army and was trained to ride with the 101st Cavalry. Bob from the Bronx had never been on a horse in his life, and they gave him a blind one. Patty's dad didn't know it was blind until the horse ran into a brick wall with him on it. Bob never had to ride in combat. The cavalry mechanized before then.

By the end of the war, Bob Myers had been awarded two silver stars, a purple heart and a citation from President Truman. Later he got a letter of appreciation from President Eisenhower. During the latter part of the war he was involved in developing the technology for night vision. Patricia didn't know any of this until after his death. When they lived in Avon, all Patty knew was that her daddy was a traveling salesman.

Across the village square were St. Agnes Catholic Church and school. It was a big complex of old red brick buildings. Patty's family went to mass and she attended the fifth and sixth grades there. I had just taken a picture of Patricia standing in front of the school, when she said, "Did I ever tell you about my dog, 'Chance'?"

"No."

"She was the first thing I ever won, and I won her right in there." Patricia was pointing to one of the buildings. "I was in the fifth grade and they had a festival. For thirty-five cents you could buy a chance for a drawing. The prize was a black and white, six week old puppy–a mutt. I named her Chance."

Patricia laughed. "My mom and dad weren't too happy about it. But that was one of the best things that ever happened to me. I had my own dog. We had family dogs before. But Chance was my *very own* dog."

The population of Avon was almost three thousand, and it had a nice hometown feel to it. Patricia said, "It's been forty years, but I'd have to say the town still looks the same–especially around the square."

Some of the homes and buildings were Victorian. Others would have been modern in the 1920's and 30's. Before the Civil War, Avon was a re-sort destination. Water from a nearby mineral spring was piped into bath-houses and promoted for its healing abilities. Avon no longer has a bathing industry. Cool Whip is made there now.

Patty lived on Lacy Street in a two-story, white clapboard house with a front porch, yard and trees. "What a great house! I loved it. We had wonderful neighbors. There were the O'Brien's. I'll never forget Brian O'Brien. And the Marschkeys, and Quackenbushes. It was such a sad day when we moved away from here. I'll never forget it."

Patricia and I were pushing our bikes along the sidewalk on Lacy, headed for Main Street, when she said, "Dad got transferred to Illinois. None of us wanted to go. That day me, my sister, Rita, my mom and all our friends, the whole neighborhood was crying. We loved it here."

Right then, my wife sniffed back some tears. "But there was nothing we could do about it. So we all got in the car and drove off with everybody crying. Then my dad stopped on Main Street in front of a house. I don't know which one. It wasn't anybody that I knew. Anyway, he turned around to me and said, 'This is as far as Chance goes. We can't take her with us. I gave her to these people.'"

Patricia stopped walking. Her face was red and wet. The tears were about to be sobs. I took her in my arms and she cried. "I think that's the meanest thing anyone ever did to me. He hadn't told me, my mom, nobody. He just took Chance out of my arms and carried her up to the front door. I never saw her again."

Later in camp, as my wife cooked dinner she said, "I don't remember much else about the trip to Illinois. Except that when we unpacked at our new house I couldn't find my rock and fossil collection. I had it in two boxes. When I asked if anybody had seen it, Dad said he left them in the driveway in Avon. He told me I could find more."

Patricia spooned stir-fry onto my plate. "My feelings for Dad were never quite the same after that. I still loved him, but I didn't look up to him like I did before."

The next morning, while we stuffed the tent in its bag, my wife said, "The last time I left Avon a lot of me stayed here. But not this time."

Then Patricia reached over, pulled my face to her and kissed me. "No sir! This time I'm not leaving anything behind."

⇥⇤

Before Patricia's family moved to Avon, they spent two years in Marcellus in New York's finger lakes region. It was a small village about ten miles southwest of Syracuse, and Patty was nine when they moved into the house on Bradley Street.

"That's it right there. Look!"

We were on the west side of town, and Patricia was ecstatic. Just moments earlier she seemed down because she didn't recognize anything. But when we came to Bradley Street, she spotted it right away. Maybe because, besides the typical green residential street sign, at the corner was an eight-foot flower box with BRADLEY ST. on it.

The moment we turned onto the street, Patricia began to recognize things. "Used to be a little grocery store on that corner. When I walked down here with mom I always got a piece of candy."

Now on the corner was a modern concrete block building with a beauty shop in it.

Bradley was a dead-end street that was probably developed in the 1920's. It was a block long, with split level homes of various description on each side. They all sat about thirty feet from the street with lawns, shrubs, trees, paved driveways and sidewalks. It was a sweet old middle-class neighborhood that had the feel of home to it.

Beyond the guardrail, at the end of Bradley, was a steep downhill covered with pines and all sorts of deciduous trees. Impromptu foot trails led down the slope into the heath. "I sure spent a lot of hours playing down there. We built forts and climbed trees."

Patty was a tomboy. "Down there is where Lafayette Jones kept trying to kiss me."

I had heard about Lafayette Jones. He was Patty's first kiss. "But it didn't happen here. I wouldn't let him because my sister or someone might see it."

"Excuse me. Are you folks lost?"

The woman was stepping down from the front porch of the last house on Bradley. "I read about you in the Auburn paper today. Did you make a wrong turn?"

Patricia said, "No. I used to live on this street. In the Ryan house."

"I know the one. I think that is the cutest house. When did you live there?"

"About forty-five years ago."

"Really?"

The woman's name was Kathy. A stocky woman whose parents probably didn't even know each other forty-five years ago. Now she was the athletic director for Marcellus Schools. She asked, "Are you going to stick around for a while?"

After we told her we'd like to spend a couple of days in Marcellus, Kathy said, "You could stay in my back yard."

A camp on Bradley Street seemed too good to be true—and it was. After Patricia went back and checked it out, she said, "Della would have destroyed it before dawn. I told Kathy about the place we heard of by the creek. She knows the spot. It's close to the school, and she thought it would be perfect."

On the east side of town was a road that led to the sewer treatment plant. It paralleled a creek, and fishermen often camped alongside it. So everyone figured we could, too. And a village policeman said, "I don't see anything wrong with that."

Upstream from the sewer plant we found the perfect spot to camp beside that road. It had plenty of shade and nearby was lots of lush tall grass for Della. Although we were camped on the bank above the stream, we couldn't see it because of the dense vegetation— but we could hear falling water.

We parked the cart near a trail that went down through the trees to the creek. After we had Della situated, the tent pitched and camp set up, Patricia and I hiked down. I was ahead of her as we worked our way down to the gravel bar. It was below an old stone dam that was once part of a large mill. Across the creek was the shell of an old three story building. Both the building and dam were dilapidated.

Behind me, I heard Patricia gasp. When I turned around she had both hands clasped on her face. A face that beamed like someone who had just won a prize. "I can't believe it! This is where my daddy taught me how to fish."

On our way to that spot beside the creek, we walked through the heart of the village. When we pulled in front of the church that Patty and her family used to attend, she said, "I'd like to go to mass tomorrow."

But Sunday morning we had so many people stop and visit, that mass was over before we got out of camp. So we just pedaled into town, did some exploring and picked up a few supplies. That afternoon, on the way back to camp, we pulled into the school yard where Patty was in the third and fourth grades. Marcellus didn't have a Catholic school, so she went to public school.

It had several red brick buildings, a gymnasium, ball fields, play grounds and a parking lot. The west wing of the main building was where the elementary kids had their classes. Thirty yards from that side of it was a thick wooded area with all sorts of trees—most were pine.

"This is it," Patricia said. "Here is where I let Lafayette Jones kiss me."

"Right here?"

"Well, not on this spot, but in these woods somewhere. Isn't it pretty?"

Indeed, it was a lovely little forest with a carpet of needles that made for soft walking. I could see where being in such a place might render a young girl vulnerable to seduction.

"Bud, what are you doing?"

I had walked up behind my wife, put my arms around her and began to caress her breasts. I whispered in her ear, "What do you think I'm doing?"

Then I kissed the side of her neck, as she said, "Right here?"

"Not a bad idea, eh?" I slid my hands under her shirt and up into her bra.

Patricia whispered, "What if someone sees us?"

Nibbling her ear lobe I said, "You didn't worry about that with Lafayette?"

She bowed her back so her shapely ass was pressed hard against the bulge in my pants. "No, I didn't worry about it then. And I'm not going to worry about it now."

Patricia turned around and I pulled her to me. Her face was radiant when I said, "Come on Baby. Let's make Lafayette proud."

⚍⚎

"You should be ashamed of yourself!"

The woman had followed us down the lane to our camp in her SUV. When she got out of it, she had a cell phone in her hand, a scowl on her face and demand in her voice. "Is this your horse? This is animal abuse!"

I said, "She's a mule. And how are we abusing her?"

The woman was in her late thirties, wore hiking boots and army green shorts. "You left her here by herself, tied up, with no water."

Earlier that morning, Della kept getting her rope tangled around saplings and brush while she grazed. So I decided to tie her short, in the shade, with a hay bag in front of her. I had offered her water before we left for town, and I offered her some when we returned. She didn't want any either time.

I was setting the bucket down as I asked, "Lady, are you a horse expert?"

"No! But anybody can see this is animal abuse. I'm calling the police and the humane society."

"You're nuts!" Patricia said, as she threw up her arms in disgust, turned around and stomped off. My hackles were up too, but I was restrained. Over the many years I've worked with equines, I have been accosted by many animal rights activists. They did it during my trip across the country in the 1970s. When I ran the mule trolley in Hot Springs, at least once a year someone accused me of animal abuse. And on this journey, we were lambasted for it a few times. It had happened enough that I came up with a routine to deal with it.

"Well lady, maybe that's what you should do. Since you aren't a horse expert, maybe you should get someone down here who is. I'd be happy to talk to them."

She stammered a bit, then said "I will!"

"Good. That way between us we might be able to convince you that I'm not abusing this animal. See, I've been a horse-shoer for about thirty years, and . . . ." I went on to outline my equine experience to the woman. "And I did all that so I would know what I was doing on this trip."

By the time I had finished explaining why Della was tied in that fashion, the woman had completely mellowed out. When Patricia returned to the scene, the confrontation had turned into a conversation. During which, my wife said, "Now, if you want to see animal abuse, I'll tell you where to go."

The day before we got to Marcellus, we stopped at a barn with a lush green paddock alongside the highway. It was obvious no one was using it, so we thought it might be a good place to camp. A woman who lived in the house across the road tried to locate the owner, but never could find him.

While she was trying to track him down on the phone, she told us about a horse that was closed up in the barn. "It belongs to the man who owns this house and that barn. He asked me to feed it for him, but all he left was straw. I asked him about letting it out to graze, but he said no. So all it gets is straw and water. And it stays cooped up in that barn all day. I thought about calling the Humane Society, but I just rent here. I don't want to cause trouble and get kicked out."

After Patricia told the animal rights lady that story, the woman said, "That's horrible! Where is this place?"

While we described where it was, the woman's eyes began to glaze over. Then she said, "You've got to be kidding? I know that place. He's my brother in-law!"

⁂

That woman had just started her car when another one pulled up. In it was Marcellus Mayor Fred Eisenberg with Dena Beratta, who wrote for the *Marcellus Observer*. When the mayor shook Patricia's hand he said, "I heard you grew up here."

"My family lived on Bradley Street for a couple of years when I was a little kid."

"Well, on behalf of the village of Marcellus let me say, 'Welcome home Patty!'"

He gave us a few town mementos and told us a bit of Marcellus history. In 1794 the first settlers set up a grist mill on the creek. The town was named after the Roman General Marcus Claudius Marcellus who lived two hundred years before Christ.

The mayor also told us that during the Civil War, the old mill where Patty's father took her fishing, made material for Union Army Uniforms. He didn't know when it closed down. "It's been that way as long as I can remember."

After Dena completed her interview, they wished us well and got in the Mayor's car to leave. They were turning around, when another car pulled into the lane and came our direction. Patricia leaned over to me and whispered, "Do you suppose this is another visitor?"

It was Kathy from Bradley Street. When she got out of her car she said, "I just stopped for a moment. I wanted to give you this."

She handed Patricia a white envelope. "Everybody in the neighborhood contributed."

Inside the envelope was $62.10 in cash. On the outside was written, "For Patty and Bud. From your neighbors on Bradley Street."

Where Patty's daddy taught her how to fish.

CHAPTER 18

A LIFE WORTH LIVING

⊰⊱

FROM MARCELLUS, WE WOUND UP through Syracuse toward Oneida Lake where we came to R&L Farm Market on Highway 31 between Lake Port and South Bay. It was a large metal building, and adjacent to it was a paddock with llamas. The moment Della spotted them her ears went rigid, she snorted and began to prance.

"Della, whoa!"

Suddenly it was like I didn't exist. Her collar rammed into my shoulder as she turned to go toward the llamas. When I pushed back, her left hoof slammed down on my right foot, and it hurt. "Dammit, Della!"

I jerked hard on her lead rope, but it made no difference. Della was determined to cross the road, and would have trampled me if I hadn't elbowed her in the neck. She winced, grunted and took a step back. I jumped in front of her, grabbed both sides of her bit, yanked and yelled. "Della, whoa!"

She reared her head back and snorted mule snot in my face. It was gross, but I couldn't wipe it off. I didn't dare let go of her.

"It's okay, girly pie," Patricia said. "Mommy's here."

She was stroking Della's neck and she seemed to be calming down. The llamas still had her attention, but she wasn't as intent on going to them. We were both rubbing her as my wife said, "Do you suppose she's thinking about Superman?"

Since her encounter with Superman back in Arkansas, I don't think the Big Sis had seen another llama. When we got moving again, I had control of Della but I didn't have her complete attention. She was still focused on them and was prancing like a show horse as we passed the market. Several people were in the parking lot applauding as we walked by.

Less than a mile past the market, we pulled into a rest area and set up camp. Patricia was in the tent about to pump up our bed, when a pickup truck with a huge man driving stopped next to our camp. I recognized him as one of those applauders back at the market. He said, "Some of my customers said they saw you on TV last night."

Lavern Grant opened the truck door and got out with a big paper bag full of produce in his arms. Celery, carrot tops and romaine lettuce were poking out the top of it and giant grin was across his face as he said, "I didn't see the news last night, so I missed the story."

He handed me the bag. "Here. I figure no matter where you're going you've got to eat. So tell me about it. Where you going?"

After I told him what we were up to, he asked "How do you make money?"

"I'm a poet, and we sell my poetry books."

"Can I see one?"

During our winter at the Watt Farm, I put together a new collection of poems titled, *From This Side of The Road*. While Lavern flipped through it he asked, "How much are they?"

"Ten bucks."

He pulled a twenty out of his wallet. "Give me two. I'm going to my granddaughter's confirmation tomorrow. She likes poetry. I'll take her one"

After I autographed the book for his granddaughter, Lavern said, "I want you to do another one for my friend, Nancy."

He handed me another twenty. "Don't worry about the change. Will you deliver it to her? You'll walk right by her place tomorrow. She's got cancer and isn't going to be around long."

"We'd be happy to."

"She doesn't see very good. So she can't read it."

I said, "I'll read a few poems to her."

An hour after Lavern drove off, another pick up pulled in and stopped. The driver leaned out the window and said, "Could I buy one of your poetry books?"

"Sure."

"Lavern came in Pier 31 with one a little while ago. He had the bartender read a couple of poems. They're good."

I recognized Pier 31 as the name of the restaurant where we were to deliver the book to Nancy. It was a family business, and she lived above it. Before we went to bed that night we sold two more books to people who had heard the reading in the bar.

When we got up in the morning, it looked like we could get rain soon. In the past week and a half it rained on us at least once every day. And it looked like it could happen again soon. The rest area was already a soggy place. More rain would make it worse.

So we broke camp and packed everything away before it could get soaked. Just before we got on the road, Lavern stopped with more produce. "My friend Nancy won't be at Pier 31 when you get there. She went to stay with her sister."

"What do you want me to do with the book?"

"Just leave it at the bar. They'll get it to her."

It was mid-afternoon when we arrived at Pier 31. The building was big and blue with a large parking lot out front. On the back side of the restaurant were huge windows that overlooked the marina, RV sites and Oneida Lake. About half a dozen cars were in the parking lot when we tied Della to the telephone pole. Inside, as soon as we sat down, the barmaid walked over and smiled. "Are you folks directing traffic somewhere?"

We had our orange safety vests on. I said, "No we're traveling with a mule—"

"Oh, you must be the walkers." She slapped the bar. "I heard about you guys. So what can I do for you?"

I laid the book on the bar. "Lavern bought this poetry book for Nancy yesterday and asked me to deliver it to her."

The barmaid's smile drained away and an awkward hush came over the place. The only other customers at the bar were the two men she was talking to when we came in. She glanced over at them, and they just looked down. Then she turned toward us, cleared her throat and said, "Nancy passed away at three this morning."

We never met Nancy, didn't have a clue what she looked like, but in the past eighteen hours she had become a part of our lives. Besides Lavern, the other three people who bought books from us last evening said wonderful things about her. That afternoon in the parking lot at Flo's Diner, we met an older couple who adored her. And now she was gone. I sat on the bar stool and fought tears. Patricia did too.

"I've already signed it for her." I handed it to the barmaid. "You might as well take it."

We ordered ourselves a beer and heard more stories about Nancy. The barmaid Jacque said, "Everybody loved her."

A man down the bar said, "I don't care who you were, she treated you like family."

When we walked into the restaurant, a handmade sign was on the door that said the place would be closed Saturday August 2nd.

"Her granddaughter is getting married then." Jacque said. "Nancy was bound and determined to make it to that wedding. But–."

When Patricia and I walked out into the parking lot to leave, we found a small group of people standing around Della. A couple of them asked if they could take our picture. We were posing for them when a very somber looking man walked up and stood at the back of the crowd. He had passed us going into the restaurant as we were walking out

After the photographers were through, the man walked up, extended his hand to me and introduced himself as John Hadyk. He owned Pier 31 and Nancy had been his step-mother. John shook my hand and thanked me for bringing the book. "Where do you plan to spend the night?"

"Somewhere down the road."

"How about here? Let me show you where."

I got in his car and he drove me down to the lake front where the marina and RV spots were. "Any open spot is yours. The mule can graze where-ever she wants."

After we climbed back into the car, I said, "With Nancy's funeral Tuesday, and your daughter's wedding Saturday, you've got a heck of a week ahead of you."

John started the car, then turned to me. "I would really appreciate it if you'd spend the night here. My family could use the distraction."

That evening we met many of Nancy's family and friends, and we heard lots of stories about her. And each story, be it funny or otherwise, illustrated a woman of unconditional compassion and generosity.

The next day, in the resort town of Sylvan Beach, we stopped at the Beachy Clean Laundromat so Patricia could wash some clothes. Della and I were outside when a middle aged man stopped on the sidewalk and asked about our trip. "So where do you stay at night? Where were you last night?"

"We camped behind Pier 31 Restaurant."

A big smile sprang to his face. "Oh yeah? A friend of mine lives there. Nancy. She's one of the finest people I know."

It began to sprinkle as I carefully said, "You know she died yesterday."

A look of horror dashed the smile away as he exclaimed, "What? No!"

He was a tall man and his whole body shook as his face got red. "Excuse me."

Then he whirled around and quickly walked away as the sprinkles gave way to a shower worthy of my rain coat. Several minutes later, it had slowed to a drizzle when the man returned with red eyes and said, "I'm sorry about running off like that." He choked back tears. "I didn't know Nancy had died. Do you know when the funeral is?"

I told him Tuesday, then said, "We sure have met a lot of folks who knew her. She must have been a really special lady."

The man was petting Della's neck as he fought tears. "When somebody dies, everyone has something nice to say about them. You just naturally do that. But with Nancy, there really is nothing else to say about her."

When we walked away from Onieda Lake, Patricia and I felt like we were in mourning. Nancy was a great woman. We missed her. I wish we could have met her

⚜

"So, you're just wasting your life."

This boy was probably twelve or thirteen, and had a face full of pimples. He rode one of those small bikes that kids do stunts on. With him was another boy on a scooter. On our way into Rome, New York, Patricia spotted a Big Lots store and went in to pick up a few things. Della and I were waiting under a shade tree across the street when the boys stopped to talk.

I asked the kid on the bike, "What do you mean?"

"Well, you're just walking your life away. You ought to do something worthwhile."

"Like what?"

"Get a job! That's what I'm going to do when I grow up. People around here, that's what they do. They stay here, get a job and have a family."

In reality, fewer people were doing that in Rome. According to the 2000 census, the city lost nearly ten thousand people over the past decade. This city of 34,334 used to be a manufacturing center for steel and copper products, but many of those companies were gone. When we walked into town we passed lots of boarded-up buildings.

I said, "So that's your idea of a worthwhile life? Stay in Rome, get a job and be a slave to the system?"

"I won't be a slave," he snapped. "They'll pay me. I'll have a house. I'll have a car. I'll have a family. I'll have a life!"

He paused, then pointed at me and snarled, "It's better than just walking around doing nothing!"

Then he turned around in the direction they had come from, motioned for his friend to follow and peddled away.

While I watched them roll down the sidewalk, I couldn't help but wonder, *Is he right? Am I just walking around doing nothing? He may be just a pimple-faced kid on a bike, but he could have a point. Just like the customer in the restaurant back in Indiana who told his everyday waitress, "In other words, they don't really have a life!"*

Under that shade tree across from the Big Lots store I wondered, *Are they right?*

❦

Near the heart of Rome we stopped at an Eckert Drug Store to get a roll of film developed at their one-hour photo. We were waiting under a tree in a nearby parking lot, when a woman in her mid-forties approached us pushing a wheelchair. Strapped into it was a tall lean man with jet black hair. He looked to be in his late teens or early twenties. His head bobbed slowly from side to side as his arms and hands kept moving spastically.

After the woman introduced herself, she said, "This is my son Shawn. He has Cerebral Palsy." She had a wide grin on her face and a note of pride in her voice she added, "But he doesn't let it get him down. Do you honey?"

He blurted out, "Nope, not me!"

His speech was a bit halted, but he was easy to understand. A contorted smile lit up his handsome face as he stammered through, "I just graduated from high school."

While it was painful to watch him try to contain the erratic movement of his body, there was a confident aura about Shawn that made him irresistible. His brown eyes had a sparkle that beckoned you to engage him.

I said, "So what are you going to do now that you've graduated?"

"I'm not sure. Maybe I could go around the world with you guys." He laughed.

"I guess we could hook your chair up to the back of the cart."

"Naw, I'll just have Mom push it."

She said, "In your dreams."

After we all laughed, Shawn stuttered, "There's lots of things I'd like to do. I just haven't decided what yet. Maybe go to college. Who knows?"

His mother chimed in, "He has his whole life ahead of him. Whatever he does, I know he'll be great at it!"

He raised his trembling right arm and tried to point at me as he asked, "What did you do before you started walking?"

"Oh, I've done a lot of different things in my life. I've been a disc jockey, a tour guide, a salesman and I ran a coffee house for a few years. For a short time I was an emcee at a strip club."

Suddenly both of his arms shot up in the air and flailed above his head as Shawn sputtered and shouted, "Whoa, baby! That's the job for me!"

His mother grabbed both arms and gently pushed them down onto the arm rests of the chair as she laughed. "I don't think so honey."

Fun was in his voice as Shawn whined, "Aw, come on mom. Working with naked girls all the time, what a cool job!"

Truthfully I said, "I thought so too, but it was one of the worst jobs I ever had. Never in my life have I been around so many miserable people. I'd never do it again."

Shawn had a serious tone as he said, "So what's the favorite thing you've done?"

"What I'm doing right now—walking across the country."

For a moment Shawn's body was still as he asked, "What's the best part?"

"Meeting people like you."

A few minutes after they left, a motorized wheel chair rolled into the parking lot and headed toward us. The man driving it had shoulder-length light brown hair with a few silver strands in it. His beard was the same color and had a big grin beaming from it.

I was sitting on Della's water bucket in front of her when he stopped the chair a dozen feet away and said, "I don't want to get too close and spook your horse."

"She's a mule, and she's okay if you go up to her slowly."

The chair whined softly as it moved him closer. "So what are you doing?"

Every time someone in a wheel chair asked me that question and I answered "Walking to Maine," I always felt a bit of guilt when the word "walking" came out. Each time it happened I expected one of them to look up at me and say something like, "Well, aren't you special!" But it never happened. Like this man, they always responded in the positive with some version of, "That's really cool!"

After I answered Bob's questions, he slapped the left arm rest with his hand. "This is my new ride. Only had it out a couple of times. Gets forty miles to a charge."

Like Shawn, this wheelchair rider had an air of confidence about him that made it comfortable to ask, "So, how did you come to be in that thing?"

"I fell through the roof of a burning house."

What else could I say? "Wow!"

Bob sounded like a news man on the radio when he said, "It happened a little over three years ago. I used to be a fireman and I knew the roof could cave in. But we heard there were children inside. We couldn't get in the house because of the smoke and flames. So someone had to chop a hole in the roof to vent the fire. We had to get those kids out."

He went on to tell me that after the roof fell in, he was able to crawl out of the burning house to safety. But he hadn't walked since then. "Turned out no one was inside. They got the kids out before we arrived. Nobody told us."

Bob paused and grimaced a bit before he said, "That hurt. I didn't have to be on that roof, and I got bad bitter about it. The first year was really tough."

The fireman laughed and stroked his beard as he said, "Yes sir, had myself a damn good pity-party and everyone was invited." Bob shook his head. "I wore everybody out."

He leaned back in the chair with his head against the rest. "But it's better now. One day I was rolling through town in my old chair all hunched over when something out the corner of my eye caught my attention. It wasn't anything special. I think it was one of the trees in this parking lot. Maybe this one. But whatever it was it made me sit up and look around. Suddenly I saw things in my own neighborhood I had never seen before."

Like a master of ceremonies presenting a stage full of pageant beauties, Bob gestured to his right and left as he said, "Finally I had the time to look at where I was."

Bob smacked his forehead with the palm of his right hand. "Then it hit me, 'I've got it made!' I mean, I don't have to work another day in my life. I can do anything I want as long as I don't have to be on my feet."

He slapped both hands down on their corresponding knees and said, "I get around and see more these days than I did when I could walk. It's really not bad—especially now that I've got this new super ride."

And Bob had a dream. "I want to ride this chair from here down to Daytona, Florida. Always wanted to go there. Wouldn't that be a great ride?"

"It sure would!"

Then, for the next half hour we talked about the possibilities. Maybe he could get the company that made his chair sponsor the trip. Maybe he could rig it up with solar panels to keep the thing charged. He said, "Wow, wouldn't that be something?"

So there we were, two middle-aged guys in a parking lot in Rome, New York, kicking around ideas on how to make a dream come true. Does life get any better than that?

Watching him roll away, I started thinking about the pimple faced kid on the bike. He had his health, he could walk and had his whole life was ahead of him. It's too bad he was so crippled with tunnel vision.

CHAPTER 19

THE ADIRONDACKS

❦

WE TOOK HIGHWAY 28 NORTH into the Adirondack Mountains. Above Woodgate, the roundness of the foothills turned into steep slopes with huge boulders and rugged crags. All around us were monumental rock formations interspersed with the green of towering pines and tamaracks. It was as if all of nature aspired to soar there. The scenery was majestic. The traffic non-stop.

Adirondack Park was established in 1892, making it one of the oldest parks in America. Yellowstone and Yosemite are older, but at six million acres, Adirondack Park is bigger than the two of them–plus Glacier and Grand Canyon National Parks <u>combined</u>. At 5,433 feet, Mount Marcy is the highest in the Adirondacks. The park has forty-five other peaks that are over 4,000 feet.

The first white men to exploit the Adirondacks were trappers and loggers. In those days, hemlock bark was used to tan leather, and the forest was full of it. Around 1810, tanneries began to spring up throughout the mountains. In just eighty years, so much hemlock had been stripped from the forest that the tanning industry collapsed.

The headwaters for five major rivers–including the Hudson–are in the Adirondacks. With more than 30,000 miles of streams and rivers, getting timber out of the mountains to markets in the east was no problem. Furniture factories opened all over the Adirondacks. At one time, Ethan Allen had a dozen factories in the area. Now there's only the one in Boonville.

"And it's barely running."

He was a retired logger who had worked in the woods all his life. As a young man, he skidded logs with mules—he had to stop and see Della. While he was petting her with a hand that was missing the last two fingers, he said, "The problem with the furniture industry ain't that there's no wood." He toddled a bit when he turned around and gestured toward the tree-covered slope behind me. "Just look around you, there's timber everywhere! What the factories around here ain't got, is workers. Everybody around here has priced themselves out of a job."

In the 1830's, a famous geologist by the name of Ebenezer Emmons explored the area and wrote extensively about the beauty of the mountains. His published stories sparked the beginning of the Adirondacks tourist industry. In the 1850s, so many people were visiting the mountains that railroads were built to bring them. Luxurious hotels and resorts sprang up everywhere. People like the Vanderbilts, Morgans and Carnegies bought vast tracks of wilderness and built palatial vacation homes called "Great Camps."

By the 1870s, exploitation of the Adirondacks was so out of control that conservationists, journalists and politicians began to lobby the state to save them. In 1892 the New York State Legislature created Adirondack Park.

Even so, when we were there, more than half of the six million acres in the park was private property. So you can't set up camp just anywhere. As we got further into the park, we were astounded by the increase of "No Trespassing" signs. At one point, Patricia said, "I think it was easier to find a place to camp in Buffalo than it is here."

One of the major tourist destinations in the park was the hamlet of Old Forge. It's on the west end of First Lake in the Fulton Chain of Lakes. Tuesday, when we arrived, the lake was covered with boats, and the town jammed with tourists.

Tourism was a year-round industry. Some winters, Old Forge gets over 300 inches of snow. Nearby McCauley Mountain had twenty-one ski trails on it, but the big winter draw were the hundreds of miles of snowmobile trails. Old Forge touts itself as "The Snowmobile Capital of the East".

The biggest tourist season of the year, however, was summer. Besides all the lakes and streams, Old Forge also had the largest water theme park in New York. "Enchanted Forest Water Safari" had over fifty rides, and averaged 3,000 visitors a day. And Old Forge had lots of shopping. Five miles of Highway 28 was lined with restaurants, hotels and shops. Most of the shops were in old houses whose locations were too valuable to be lived in. They sold everything a tourist would want. The more stately homes, those with verandas and bay windows, were mostly high-end antique shops. While the smaller houses had whirly-gigs spinning in their front yards, with racks of tee-shirts on their porches.

When we got to Old Forge, Officer Brombacher arranged for us to camp in a town park adjacent to the soccer fields. On our way to the park, we were amazed at all of the deer roaming the residential areas. People in Old Forge didn't have dogs laying in their front yards. It was all deer.

While we walked through Old Forge, Della was on constant deer-alert. She didn't freak out or try to go to them, like she did the llamas. For her, deer were a bother. The Big Sis didn't like having them around. If they were too close, she'd snort. By the time we got to the town park, my right arm was covered with mule snot.

We stayed for two nights. Our camp was on the side of a mountain that had been terraced to make way for athletic fields. We set up the tent and staked out Della on the second terrace. Because of all the grass on the mountainside, and down on the playing fields, it was a popular destination for hungry deer. The second sundown we were there, I watched a herd of thirty graze and poop on the soccer field below us. Earlier that afternoon it had been mowed and lined for games the next day. I tried to imagine what it would be like for some preppy-goalie diving for a save and landing in a pile of deer dung.

Della may not have cared for the deer, but they were fascinated with her. Most checked her out from a distance and then went on about their business. But there was a group of four who had to know more. They came twice during the two days we were there. We could tell it was the same group, because one of them had a limp. She was the first to approach Della.

While the other three waited below, the doe slowly made her way up onto the first terrace. Della's ears were rigid as she stared at it. When the doe got halfway up the hill to the second terrace, Della let loose with a fierce snort, stomped her right foot and shook her head angrily.

Immediately, the doe whirled around and in gimpy leaps charged down the hill to her companions. They all ran across the soccer field where they stopped, turned and looked back at Della. Within a few minutes they were back on our side of the park, and another one made its way toward our girl. She chased that one off too—only to have them return for another try. This went on for a couple of hours before they wandered off. But the next morning I woke to Della snorting at them again.

"Yeah, the deer can be a pain, but it's the bears you've got to watch out for," said the old guy at the other end of the bar.

It was Wednesday afternoon and we had stopped at the Tow Bar Inn for a beer after doing our laundry. I had just finished telling the bartender about the deer and Della, when the man down the bar started in with bear stories.

"This morning I had to rebuild the back wall of my garage. One clawed right through it last night to get to my garbage can. Tore up the siding and broke a couple of studs just so it could get in my goddam trash."

The bartender said, "Didn't one tear up your garage door last spring?"

"Sure did." The man slammed his beer mug down on the bar. "Ripped the boards right off it. So I replaced it with a steel door. Now what does he do? Son-of-a-bitch plows right through the damn wall."

From that point on, it was bear-story-time in the Tow Bar Inn. Nearly everyone in the place had one to tell. Tales of porches demolished, kitchen doors ripped off their hinges and camps ransacked by bears on the prowl for people food.

That evening in the tent, Patricia said, "What do you think Della's going to do if a bear comes into our camp?"

"I don't know. These bears are vegetarians, so I don't think we have to worry about one attacking her—especially as big as she is."

"Maybe," my wife said. "But what are *we* going to do if one comes to our camp?"

"Get out of its way."

⁂

Rain had become a daily affair. They weren't horrendous storms with vicious wind, lightning and thunder–just off-and-on showers. It seemed like every time I turned around I was wringing something out. Our morning departures were dictated by how long it took to get the tent dry enough to pack it. After several days of that, we just started packing it wet.

When showers popped up, we'd stop and put on rain gear. Then a quarter of a mile down the road we'd have to stop and take it off because the sun came out. We both tried just leaving it on, but it was like walking in a sauna-suit. The sweat made us as wet as the rain did. A couple of times I didn't put it on and walked in the rain. But then my socks got soggy and made my boots feel like they were filled with slime. And the breeze created by the traffic that passed us chilled me. So I had to put the rain coat on, and took it off, and put it back on–on and off and on it went.

"It must rain like this around here all the time," Patricia said.

We were on Highway 28, beside a swamp, somewhere between Inlet and Raquette Lake. It was Friday afternoon. The rain was light and the traffic heavy. Most of it was motor homes. We had only gone ten miles that day, but both of us were worn out. Walking in the rain was a lot of work, and we were ready to call it quits for the day. But we hadn't seen a dry spot that wasn't posted. Even some of the wetlands had no trespassing signs.

The hamlet of Raquette Lake was about a mile off the highway. But we figured if the place had buildings, there had to be some dry land. The swamps, bogs and marshes were beautiful. All the ferns, rushes, and larch looked exotic in the silver fog that the afternoon showers had created. It was all lovely, but what we needed was a dry spot to pitch our tent and stake out Della for the night.

277

"How about across the street," said Jimmy. "You could camp on the common."

He owned Raquette Lake Supply Company. It was in a large two story brick and stucco building that housed a general store, grocery, hotel, café, liquor store, the Tap Room and a laundry. Jimmy was also the unofficial mayor.

Of the 2,800 lakes and ponds in the Adirondacks, Raquette Lake was one of the largest. Its shoreline and islands were dotted with permanent camps. Places that, in many cases, had been a family retreat for generations. The only access to most of them was by boat or sea plane. So the hamlet of Raquette Lake had a business called, "Camps Services Company." They maintained camps, ferried families out to them and brought them supplies while they were there. The only other business in town was a tour boat.

Jimmy asked, "How is your mule with bears?"

We had just pitched the tent on the Raquette Lake common, when Jimmy pulled up in his car. I told him, "I don't know. We haven't seen one yet."

"Well, you're about to. When I said you could camp here, I didn't think about the bear. We have one that comes through every afternoon on his way to my dumpster. I just saw it up on the mountain headed this way. Thought I'd better warn you."

When Jimmy drove off, Patricia said, "What are we going to do?"

"Wait and see. What else can we do?"

I did have a plan. Every night, since we left home, I kept the ax next to my bed. If a bear, or anything else, tried to harm Della, I would defend her, and us, with it. I figured a whack or two would probably do the trick. I'm a big guy. It was a big ax.

I leaned it against the front tire of the cart. If this bear messed with Della, I wanted it handy. Then we pulled out our chairs, sat down and waited for it. We could hear dogs barking up the mountain and at one point, a dog nearby went crazy for a few minutes. But we never saw the bear.

Around sundown, we decided it wasn't coming. So I got the stove out and Patricia fixed rice and vegetables. After dinner, we decided to go across the street to the Tap Room for a night cap. My wife said, "I'll throw our trash in Jimmy's dumpster."

When we walked behind the building, two waitresses were at the kitchen door smoking cigarettes. One of them said, "You aren't going to throw that bag in the dumpster, are you?"

Patricia said, "Jimmy told us we could."

"You might not want to right now. The bear is in it. He comes every night."

The next morning Jimmy said, "That bear always walks right through where you were camped. He must have detoured to avoid your mule."

All across the Adirondacks, it seemed like every local person we met had a bear story. We heard horrendous tales of the sides of barns clawed open, sheds destroyed, and it seemed like back porches were the bear's favorite targets.

"And it's getting worse," said a woman who'd lived in the Adirondacks all her life. "It's because the tourists feed them."

When I told Ken in Blue Mountain Lake what she said, he laughed. "You mean the tourons? That's what we call tourists in this neck of the woods. Well, I think that's one you can't blame on tourons. The problem is, they closed all the landfills around here. Used to be if you wanted to see a bear, you went to the dump. For generations, that's where they ate. Then they closed all the dumps and filled them in. So now they come to town to eat."

Ken and his wife Nancy had invited us to stay at their place on the edge of the village of Blue Mountain Lake. They had an apartment above their garage and we were welcome to use it. Nancy had four horses, a barn, a paddock and a huge back yard that needed mowing. Della was welcome to graze on it.

We were on the highway walking up a hill toward their place, when Patricia grabbed my left arm and squealed, "Did you see that?"

A black bear had just crossed the highway about 100 feet in front of us, and he did it in three leaps. Then he disappeared into the woods.

My wife's voice shrilled with excitement. "Bud, that was a bear! Did Della see it?"

When I realized it was a bear, I looked at Della. Although she was intently watching it, she didn't react to it much at all. That is, until we got to the place where the bear had crossed the road. Then she started snorting as she looked in the direction it'd disappeared. She shivered a bit, then stepped up her pace.

Patricia said, "She sure doesn't like the smell of bear!"

"I never heard of a horse that did," Nancy said. "Mine hate it."

In her late thirties, Nancy was petite and wiry. Above her barn door was a sign that read "Pig Headed Blond Woman's Farm." Earlier that year she had an encounter with a 150 pound black bear in her barn.

"Three nights in a row he got in the barn and trashed it. Threw saddles down, scattered hay and feed everywhere, and he got into the horses meds. The second night he ate a bunch of Icy Hot. You'd think a mouth full of that would have kept him away."

Nancy shook her head. "But no, he came back. I didn't see him in the barn until I started for the door. He was just inside, and I don't think he'd been there very long, because it wasn't trashed yet. But the horses were going nuts in the corral. I was afraid they'd try to go through the fence. So I picked up some rocks and threw them at the bear to chase him off. But he turned around and started toward me.

"So I ran back to the house and got my brother's 30/30. I'm not a hunter. I like animals too much to kill them, but this bear scared me. So I shot him. Hit him in the shoulder. He turned, ran and then collapsed on my property line. Then he began to bawl. It broke my heart. He was suffering. So I shot him again to put him out of his misery."

Nancy paused for a moment and wiped a tear from the corner of her eye. "Everyone around here thinks I'm a hard ass. But it really tore me up. I had never killed anything before. Then my neighbor started yelling at me—called me a murderer. He saw me shoot the bear the second time and said he was going to call the law. So I went in and called the state troopers and told them what I did. I figured I'd probably go to jail."

A judge eventually ruled the killing as justified because Nancy was protecting herself and the livestock.

"My neighbor is still pissed about it."

⬥⬥⬥

The Mercedes was new, and the driver was in his mid-fifties. While the car idled, he stared silently at our flyer that my wife had just handed him through the window. After a few moments, without looking up, he said, "I don't know about you camping here."

He owned a piece of land east of Long Lake on the south side of Blue Ridge Road. It had a pond and enough un-mowed grass to feed a twenty mule team for a week. We were standing beside the highway eyeballing it when he pulled into the drive and stopped.

"Who's going to be liable?" Through the window of the Mercedes, he handed the flyer back to Patricia. "I don't want to take that chance."

Right then, from across the road, Doug yelled, "Hey, come over here."

He looked to be in his early sixties and was standing at the base of his driveway waving for us to cross the highway. The driveway was gravel and led up through a stand of pines to a small cabin. "I ain't got all that greenery, but it's a place to get off the road."

No traffic was coming, so I turned Della left to cross the pavement. When the cart pivoted I heard a loud crack directly behind her right leg. She bolted and there was a clang followed by what sounded like something dragging.

Patricia was walking behind me. So I yelled back to her, "What was that?"

"Oh my God," she exclaimed. "The cart's going to hit her!"

Then, in what looked like a choreographed move, my wife leaped up into the cab and stomped on the brake. With a thud, everything lunged to a stop at the foot of Doug's driveway. I turned around to see the back end of the right shaft on the ground. It had broken loose from the cart.

I looked into Della's face and said, "Your mama just saved your ass, girl."

Between Della, Patricia, me and Doug, we got the busted cart up into his yard. Then with Doug's phone we found George the welder. He would fix it in the morning.

After a steak dinner and conversation around a bonfire in Doug's front yard, we went to bed. When I crawled under the covers, my wife said, "I'm glad the cart didn't break in that guy's pasture across the road. He might have been liable."

⚍⚎

We took Blue Ridge Highway because we heard it was less traveled, and we'd see the mountains better from it. The traffic *was* less and the scenery amazing. Those Adirondack vistas will forever linger in my mind. From that ridge road, we could see some of the park's highest peaks jutting up from a forest that seemed to go on forever. And so did the no trespassing signs. In one place, for at least half a mile, they were on every fence post and nearly all of trees alongside the road.

Patricia said, "They sure know how to ugly-up a forest around here."

It was around 7:30 p.m. when we got to Newcomb. Dark would be upon us in an hour, and we needed to find a place to camp. So far, every place we spotted that might have worked was posted. The Newcomb House Bar & Grill was the first open business we came to. So we went in to see if anybody knew of a place where we could stop for the night.

"Over at the trail-head to Santanoni." The man was getting up from the bar to leave as he said, "I know you can camp there. And it's got plenty of grass for your mule."

"Where's it at?"

"Across the highway and back in about a mile or so on the dirt road."

It was almost dark when we got there, and by the time I got Della situated I had to use a flash light to find my way around. The air was so laden with moisture it looked like mist in the light's beams. Even before we got it pitched, the tent was soaked.

"I'm sick of this," Patricia said as I handed her our bedding bag.

"Traveling?"

"No. I love traveling. It's dealing with this wet tent and damp bedding all the time. And I'm sick of the no trespassing signs." The sound of a slap came from the tent. "And I've had it with all these stinking mosquitos! I can't wait to get out of the Adirondacks."

In the morning, when Patricia handed him a cup of coffee, Chris said, "You really shouldn't give up on the Adirondacks, yet."

We were camped at the beginning of a trail that led five miles back into the woods to Camp Santanoni—a Great Camp built in 1893 on Newcomb Lake. Abandoned by its owners in the early 1970's, it was now owned by the state. Chris had a summer job doing maintenance there, and he was a tour guide. The rest of the year he was a college student studying historic preservation.

My wife told him how frustrated we were with all the posted signs. She told him, "It was easier to find a place to camp outside the park."

Chris said, "This trail leads into a 12,900 acre preserve and it's all open to the public. Five miles back in on this road you can camp on the lake near the main lodge. I've got a canoe back there that you're welcome to use. And there's a spot with lots of grass for your mule."

While Chris drank his coffee and talked about the campsite, I began to warm to the idea of taking the side trip. Four other people who visited our camp earlier that morning had expounded on the beauty of Santanoni. All of them said, "You have to go see it!"

After they left, I said to Patricia, "Maybe we should check it out."

"Look, since we've been in these mountains we've taken two side trips to what were supposed to be great spots for us. Each time it was a bust. And this one is five miles. If we get there and have to turn around and come back out, we'll have blown a whole day."

"Well, it just seems to me—"

Her volume was up and her cheeks turning read. "All I want to do is get out of these fucking mountains!"

I threw my hands up in surrender, "Okay, okay."

Grabbing Della's water bucket, I stomped off toward the creek grumbling to myself, "Why does she have to be such a bitch about it?"

The road to the Santanoni trail-head crossed the creek on a wood and stone bridge. I was next to it mumbling my way down to the water, when two gray draft-horses trotted onto the bridge pulling a covered wagon. The driver was a stout man with gray hair and a beard. About half way across the bridge he urged the horses into a gallop.

When he passed me, I yelled, "Watch out for the mule up there."

He turned around and yelled something back. I didn't hear what it was, but from the expression on his face I could tell it wasn't friendly. So I turned around and continued on down toward the water. Just as I got to the edge of the creek, from the top of the hill I heard a frantic, "Whoa! Dammit, whoa!"

That was followed by lots of clanging up by our camp. But after several more "whoas," the racket stopped.

We had been expecting the wagon. Some of the people who visited our camp told us that Doug was going to haul them and their stuff back into Santanoni with his horses. With full buckets, I was walking up to the wagon when Doug turned toward me with a sheepish grin on his face. "Sorry I was so ugly back there. I thought you were being a wise guy. Thanks for trying to warn me about the mule."

Doug Alitz owned High Peaks Stables, and with his wife Maggie, ran Aunt Polly's B&B. We passed it on the west edge of Newcomb. Doug said, "I saw you go by yesterday and wanted to invite you in. But I was tied up with customers and couldn't get away."

While his passengers loaded their gear and canoes into the wagon, Doug asked us about our trip. Then he said, "You're going to Santanoni, right?"

Patricia said, "I'm afraid we won't find a place for Della."

"There's a perfect spot for you guys a little ways before you get to the main lodge. It's got lots of grass, and it's beside the lake. I know it's open. When you come back out, bring Della and come spend the night with us.

I've got a nice bedded stall for her and for you two we have a private room with a bath."

When Doug drove off with his wagon load of campers, I was ready to hike back into Camp Santanoni. But Patricia said, "Well I'm not!" A rumble was in her voice. "By the time we go in and come out of there that'll be ten miles and we won't be any further down the road. I want to get out of the Adirondacks!" Her fists were clinched to her sides as both the tempo and the pitch of her voice crescendoed. "I am sick of the traffic, the damp, the bugs, the swamp, the fucking no trespassing signs, the snooty people—"

I said, "Wait a minute. We've met a lot of nice folks in the Adirondacks."

"Okay, okay." Patricia had both hands in the air like someone surrendering to a cop. "We have. But you've got to admit, we've run into some real ass-holes in these hills."

In a bad attempt at a Brooklyn accent, I said, "Hey, this is New York! So's, what did you's expect, eh?"

That got a chuckle out of her. "Yeah, well, a night at the B&B sounds good, but I don't know about going to this Santanoni place."

Without forethought I said, "Okay. You stay at the B&B, and I'll hike back in and camp a night or two."

I was both shocked and exhilarated when those words came out of my mouth. Suddenly my mind buzzed with, *Wow, an adventure without the bitching!*

Patricia's eyes looked like those of a deer in headlights when she said, "What? You would go back in there without me?"

My flame of excitement fizzled into a vision of me swimming naked in a moonlit lagoon by myself, wishing Patricia was there. At that moment, I felt incredibly lonely. I had to change the subject. "Look, people come from all over the world to vacation in these mountains and here we are trying to run through them. Maybe the problem is us."

"What?"

"Maybe we've been so hell-bent on getting down the road we haven't really paid attention to where we are. We need to set up camp somewhere for a few days and relax. And this Santanoni sounds like the perfect place."

"I don't know—"

"Patricia, just look at this weather. This is the prettiest day we've had since we've been in the Adirondacks. Let's go and kick back in the woods by that lake. You get in the cart and ride. Let Della and me take you back in."

The only motor vehicles allowed on the road to Santanoni were for maintenance and to haul in the handicapped. Otherwise you had to walk, bicycle, ride a horse or take a horse-drawn wagon back in. That Wednesday the trail was busy with all of those modes of transportation. It was wonderful to be on such a road. The farther we got back into the forest, the more relaxed I felt. It was as if a weight was gradually melting off me. Like an apple tree being picked, I could feel my branches begin to lift.

A mile in we came to the farm complex for the Great Camp. At one time Camp Santanoni had more than forty-five buildings, most built from stone and wood harvested on site. Twenty of the buildings were part of the farm, which included two massive stone and wood barns—one with a milking parlor, three large farmhouses, several cottages for workers, a stone creamery, smoke house, huge chicken house and various other out-buildings.

Camp Santanoni was built for Robert and Anna Pruyn. He was a banker and business man in Albany. The farm supplied meat, produce and dairy for the family year round. The farm buildings were scattered up the side of a mountain, with the houses being the highest on the slope. They all had a panoramic view of the Adirondack High Peaks. As far as I could see it was mountain after mountain with dark pinnacles soaring up into a baby blue sky. Gazing at all of that, I thought, *I could handle being Mr. Pruyn's farm hand.*

After we got past the farm, and deeper into the woods, I could tell Patricia was starting to unwind. She perked up and started noticing things along the trail. "Did you see that bunch of flowers? Stop this thing. Let me out. I want to get a better look."

Patricia was walking beside me when, through a gap in the trees, we got our first glimpse of Newcomb Lake. Reflected on the shimmering surface was the rocky peak of Mount Santanoni. The blue water was surrounded by the various greens of firs, ferns and fauna. My wife gasped, "Oh my God! Is that beautiful, or what?"

The poet in me could only muster, "Wow!"

Patricia grabbed my left arm and pulled my biceps into her cleavage. "Thank you for bringing me back here." She reached up and kissed me on the cheek. "You were right. We need to spend a few days in a place like this."

Our camp at Santanoni was about a third of a mile from the main lodge. On the lake side of the road was a long wide grassy area. We pulled the cart into one end of it, then staked out Della on the other end. When I did, she was calmer than she had been in more than a week. It seemed like every night since we entered the Adirondacks, she got increasingly restless. The night before, when we were camped at the trailhead, Della threw a fit at the end of the rope. She bucked, reared up and pawed the ground so much, I had to tie her short to a post. But that afternoon at Camp Santanoni when I let her loose, she rolled and rolled, then just laid there and basked in the sun.

Below the grassy area was a flat spot in the woods beside the lake. We pitched our tent there and I made a fire pit down by the water. A little after the sun set, the moon came up fat and golden. As it climbed up into the sky, it sent white and silver trails across the water. And somewhere in that cove were a pair of loons who kept calling to each other. Behind us, in the woods, two owls hooted back and forth. And a couple of times we heard coyotes yipping in the distance.

"This is just perfect." My wife sighed as she took my hand and held it in her lap. "A perfect place. A perfect night. A perfect moon."

I kissed the back of her hand. "I think this moon is just right for making honey."

⊣⊨⊢

The camp was named after the mountain across the lake. Mount Santanoni was 4,361 feet high. When French explorers came through the Adirondacks they named the mountain "Saint Antoine." But when the local Indians said the name, it came out "Santa-known-ee". So the name stuck. Santanoni.

Robert Pruyn, who was head of Chase Manhattan Bank, found the property while on a hunting trip. It took 1,500 red spruce trees to build the main lodge, which was actually six separate log buildings under one roof. It had a main living and dining lodge, seven bedrooms, a kitchen, a service area and seven staff bedrooms situated in the separate buildings. All of it was under one roof connected by a system of porches. Many of the architectural features had a Japanese flair about them. Pruyn's father served as minister to Japan under President Lincoln.

Among the guests who stayed at the getaway was Teddy Roosevelt. He spent a lot of time in the Adirondacks hiking, hunting and fishing. When President McKinley died, Vice President Roosevelt was vacationing in the mountains. He took the presidential oath in a stagecoach as it passed through Newcomb.

Back in those days—as with the other Great Camps—when people came to Santanoni they dressed up for the visit. Ties and suit coats for men, and women wore long dresses. In the letters that I read from people who visited the camp, it was often mentioned how relaxed the atmosphere was at Santanoni compared to the other Great Camps. Practical jokes were encouraged and celebrated at Santanoni. While she was looking at photos from those days, Patricia said, "Do you notice anything different about these pictures?"

"What?"

"The people all have smiles—some are even laughing. Whenever you see photographs from this era, everyone looks so serious. But these folks were having fun."

In 1953, Pruyn's heirs sold the camp to the Melvins of Syracuse. While at Santanoni on holiday in 1971, Melvin's eight-year-old grandson disappeared in the forest. Despite a massive search, he was never found. The family left and never returned.

The place sat empty for two decades. Then, in the 1990s, a consortium of organizations got together with the state and worked out a plan to save the Great Camp. Friends of Camp Santanoni organized as a non-profit to help the state restore and maintain the camp. It was certainly a place worth saving.

⊰⊱

Tentatively I pushed the store door open and asked, "Are you closed?"

It was Thursday August 14th and I had just bicycled six miles out from Santanoni into Newcomb to get ice and a few other supplies. All the lights were off at the North Woods Store, but I could see people moving around in the building. A man's voice from the back of the store called out, "We're open. Come on in."

"With the lights off, I thought maybe you were closed."

A flashlight was bobbing toward me as the man said, "Nope. The electric is off."

"Someone hit a light pole or something?"

"Haven't you heard? The whole eastern half of the country is dark from Ottawa down through Baltimore. And as far west as Detroit, nobody's got power."

"Terrorists?"

"Nope. Some sort of fire at a switching station in New York City. It's been off all day. They don't know when it will be back on."

Before I biked back to camp, I stopped at the Bar and Grill for a beer. Of course, all the talk was about the black out. If the electricity wasn't on by sundown, the place was going to close. When the barmaid handed me the beer she said, "I guess it doesn't bother you."

"Nope. We've got plenty of power."

The guy next to me laughed. "What, a Coleman lantern?"

"No. We have electric lights. They're powered by a solar panel and a generator that runs off the tire." I handed him one of our flyers. "Here. I printed this about an hour ago."

After finishing my beer, I climbed on my bike and headed back to camp. Then I turned on the computer and printed a dozen poetry books just so I could say I did. I figured I was probably the only publisher in New York printing anything that day..

⊰⊱

Sunday afternoon when we walked out of Camp Santanoni, all three of us were different than when we trekked in five days earlier. The weather was beautiful every one of those days we were there. We took the camp tour twice. Swam in the lake countless times. Paddled Chris' canoe on it and did some fishing. (As usual, my wife caught the most.) We both rode Della all over the place, and I wrote. We ate well. And the moonlight loving was wonderful. We were all much more relaxed. Everyone had a better attitude.

That morning as we were breaking camp, Doug brought a wagon full of folks back into Santanoni. He reined the horses to a stop and said, "You're going to let us treat you to a night at Aunt Polly's B&B, aren't you?"

Patricia said, "Quit twisting my arm. We'll do it."

It's a superb inn. The main house was a long two story structure built in 1845 as a stagecoach stop. Aunt Polly Bissell ran the place back then, and in those days you got a night's lodging, dinner and breakfast for forty cents. When we were there, lodging for two, and a gourmet breakfast, was sixty bucks. The accommodations were beautiful and Maggie made us an exquisite meal in the morning.

That night at Aunt Polly's was the first time it rained since we walked back into Santanoni. It was a fierce thunderstorm. But Della was safe in a stall in the barn, and we were in a beautiful dry bedroom. Let it rain!

From there on, our trek through the mountains was completely different. It didn't rain much and campsites were easier to find. One was at the headwaters of the Hudson River. The rest of our Adirondack experience was delightful!

⊰⊱

He yelled at me from the cab of a log truck, "You stupid bastard, get the hell off the road! Someone needs to beat some sense into you!"

We were on Highway 74 between Paradox and Chilson at Eagle Lake on the east side of the Adirondacks. When I heard the diesel engine babble up behind, we were in a blind curve, with two cars behind us. But instead of taking his place behind them, the driver blew his air horn, pulled into the oncoming lane, roared up beside us, stopped and started cursing at me.

Calmly, I said, "You're on the wrong side of the road."

"What did you say?" He pulled the nose of the truck over to the right so it was directly in front of us. We had nowhere to go. The brakes hissed a blast of air as the driver's door flew open. He sprang out of it and up onto the hood. On his hands and knees on the hood, with his long flaxen hair and beard, he looked like a lion about to leap onto prey. He shook his left index finger at me and roared, "What the fuck did you say?"

Right then, a car in the oncoming lane skidded to a stop less than fifty feet from the truck. I said, "You need to move your truck. You're going to cause a wreck."

A car behind the truck blew its horn and so did the one stopped in the other lane. The trucker quickly looked both ways, shook his finger again and yelled, "You ain't seen the last of me!"

He clambered back into the cab, ground a few gears, then with black smoke spewing up out both exhaust pipes, the truck roared away. I never saw him again.

That night, after we crawled into the tent, Patricia said "That trucker scared me. I really thought he was going to try to hurt you. Were you scared?"

"Not really. I just figured he was having a bad day. What he needs to do is slow down and take a few days off at Santanoni. He'd feel a lot better."

Down for the night.

CHAPTER 20

INTO NEW ENGLAND

⊰⧉⊱

WE CROSSED LAKE CHAMPLAIN INTO New England on the Ticonderoga Ferry. It's been in operation since 1759 – making it one of America's oldest businesses. Captain Larry told us, "Della's the first mule we've ever toted across."

Like the ferry we crossed the Mississippi on, this one also was a barge powered by a tugboat attached to the side of it. Larry and his family had been running the "Ti-ferry" for fifteen years, so maybe it was the first time *they* took a mule across. But in the past 244 years, other operators must have hauled a bunch of them. And like the captain of the Hickman Ferry on the Mississippi, Captain Larry refused to take our fare.

But unlike our ride across the Mississippi, we were not the only ones on this boat. The Ti-ferry had fifteen parking spaces and they were all full. And unlike the previous ferry, Della didn't slip on the ramp or the deck of this one. She just strolled on board like she did it every day.

At first, I'm not sure Della knew we were on a boat. She probably thought we were just stuck in traffic–like back in Buffalo or Cincinnati. But when the tug revved up, and the barge began to move, *that* got her attention. Her ears went rigid, and she almost knocked me over with her head when it turned toward the tow boat. She didn't seem scared, just concerned.

I don't think Della realized what was going on, until we got out into the lake. As she watched a pleasure boat go by, it was like she got it. "I'm on a boat." She relaxed and seemed to enjoy the rest of the ride. Especially when two passengers brought her apples.

The moment our feet touched Vermont, everything seemed different. It felt softer. Things were not so abrupt as back in New York. Instead of rising up into peaks, like the Adirondacks, the Green Mountains were round in the sky. Vermont felt soft and supple.

"Excuse me. Could I pet your mule?"

She was the first person to walk up and say something to us in New England. We had just disembarked the ferry at Larabees Point. A dairy farm was nearby, and she walked out of one of the barns dressed in tight blue jeans and knee-high rubber work-boots. In her mid-teens, she had delicate features and light red hair pulled back in a bun. She exuded the kind of wholesomeness you would expect from a milkmaid in Vermont.

However, the best part was her accent. I had heard the Vermont accent before–but to have it come from her, there on the shore of Lake Champlain, was truly sweet. Vowels were rounder in Vermont. They involved more of the mouth, not spit from the tip of the tongue. Words rolled about the palate before they were spoken. Yes, we really were in New England.

<hr/>

Highway 74 took us up out of the Champlain Valley, past dairy farms with fields of alfalfa and corn. Some hillsides were covered with apple trees in well-kept orchards with neat stacks of bins ready for the harvest. It was on that road that I first saw a farm with the barns attached to the house. Enclosed walkways connected them, so in the winter farmers didn't have to wade through the snow. We saw this all across New England.

That route took us through the hamlets of Shoreham and West Cornwall. Quiet little places with tall church steeples and tidy white Victorian homes, most of which had either black wrought-iron or white picket fences around them.

Then we came to Middlebury, which was chartered in 1761. It was a beautiful bustling little city with steep streets and quaint old stone and brick buildings that housed charming shops, eateries and inns. In the center of Middlebury, Otter Creek flowed over a waterfall. And as we walked across the stone bridge above it, a man wearing waders was down in the rapids fly fishing. Downtown also had a park with a wooden bandstand where people lounged under ancient oaks and maples in the middle of Monday afternoon. While we walked through Middlebury, I felt like we had arrived at the heart of New England.

"Yeah, but it ain't got no soul." His voice had a smoker's rattle to it. He wore farmer's overalls, a dingy red cap and sat on a stool halfway down the bar. "Middlebury used to be a real town. But not no more."

We had stopped at Two Brother's Tavern for an afternoon beer. They had fifteen different brands on tap, most of which I'd never heard of. We got one of the local brews.

I asked, "What do you mean, it's not a real town?"

He motioned toward the front windows. "Look out there. See all those people?"

Right then the windows framed a constant flow of humanity. They were people of all ages. Some with camera's slung around their neck and dipper-bags on their shoulders. Others wore day packs on their backs and hiking boots on their feet.

He blurted, "None of them live here! I've been here all my life, and I don't know a one of them. They're all tourists. Strangers. They come here to see 'Quaint New England.' Well, guess what, they're ruining it!"

Patricia said, "A pretty place just naturally attracts tourists."

Slamming his mug down, beer erupted from its top and splashed down onto the bar as he declared, "Well, they've ruined this town!"

He grabbed a fist full of bar napkins and began to sop up the mess, as he grumbled, "Used to be, you could walk up this street and buy a pair of work jeans. But not no more. Now, if you want a three dollar postcard, by God, they've all got 'em." He grunted as he lifted his mug. "That's not a real town. That's a tourist trap!"

⇥⇤

Patricia gasped for air before she yelled, "I don't think she can do it."

We were on the side of Sand Hill in the Green Mountains below Ripton, and all of us were breathing hard. Della's sides heaved and her legs quaked as she leaned uphill. Patricia had just put the wood blocks behind the back wheels so Della didn't have to hold the weight of the cart as she rested.

During the past two days we'd heard how steep Sand Hill was. But it was the only way to get up the mountain to Robert Frost's cabin. The hill was less than a mile from our camp in East Middlebury. So I biked to the base to see how steep it was. It didn't look like anything the Big Sis couldn't handle. And she did get up that part just fine. It was the next turn that stopped her. The pitch of the turn, the sudden grade change, it was too much. I could feel it in my legs too.

This was our second attempt. The first time we backed down to a wide level spot beside the road. After a few minutes rest, Della leaped into the pull. She charged up the hill but stopped in the same place. So rather than back down, Patricia put the blocks behind the wheels so we all could rest.

Between breaths, I said, "This is what we'll do. Leave the blocks where they are. You take off the brake and we'll start from here."

"What if she still can't do it, then what?"

The night before, we had camped behind the East Middlebury Library. Most of the neighbors paid us a visit, and all of them said if we needed help, to let them know. So we had those alternatives available.

I said, "Then, we'll turn around, go back down and get help."

While we stood on the slope resting, the Middlebury River roared through the gorge below us. At that spot the river fell in turbulent white water down through huge boulders. It was such a dramatic falls that I can't imagine anyone trying to kayak it. The sound was so intense I had to yell to Patricia so she could hear. "Get ready!"

My voice echoed off the rocks. "Come up, Big Sis! That's my girl! That's my girl! You can do it, Della! I know you can!"

She lunged up the hill. The cart's front wheels came off the road and it lurched forward about a dozen feet. Then Della began to slip. She struggled for traction as sparks flew out from under her shoes. The cart began to pull her back down the hill. Then the left rear tire rolled into one of the wooden blocks. That made the cart jackknife out into the middle of the road.

Patricia screamed, "No!"

Both of the right tires were off the pavement and the cart looked like it was about to tip over. While Della continued to skid backwards, the cart teetered further toward disaster.

I yanked Della's head to the right. "This way, girl!"

When she hopped that direction, the momentum brought the wheels back down onto the highway. Now both she and the cart were perpendicular to the slope. That stopped the cart from rolling over, but it had us across both lanes of traffic. We already had two cars stopped—one in each direction. Something had to give.

I yelled, "Patricia, get in the cart and run the brake! We're going back down."

At the bottom, in the parking lot at East Middlebury Library, Patricia climbed out of the cab and asked, "Now what?"

One of the people we met in our camp last night was Jack the toy-maker. His company made wooden toys in a small factory just a few blocks from the library. We unloaded the cart and put all of our stuff in his pickup and he drove it up to Ripton. Jack's friend, Dick, owned the Ripton Store, and he let me put our stuff in his garage. Then we hooked up Della and she pulled the empty cart to the top with no problem.

Dick arranged for us to camp on some mountain property owned by Middlebury College. It was a wide grassy area down a dirt road across from the South Branch of the Middlebury River. Robert Frost Wayside and his cabin were about three miles up the highway. We were welcome to stay a few days and explore.

Before we loaded our things back on the cart at the Ripton Store, Dick drove me to the campsite. Then he took me up to Middleberry Gap where the highway crested the Green Mountains. Dick said, "That way you know what it's like. If you think you'll need help getting over it, we can load your stuff in my truck and take it to the top."

The Gap crossed at 2,144 feet. That's about a 2,000 foot climb from the town of Middlebury. Without a doubt, the worst part of it was Sand Hill. The rest of it would be a long steady climb, but Della had pulled much worse.

On our way back to his place, Dick told me a few horror stories about brakes going out and other catastrophes on Sand Hill. "I've owned the place twenty seven years. And every year there's some major event on that piece of road."

A few days later, I met a bicyclist on a cross-country tour of the northern states. His trip had been planned by a bicycle club. Sand Hill was rated the worse incline on that route.

I have never been a big Robert Frost fan. That's not to say I don't like his poetry. A couple of his are among my favorites–particularly "The Pasture." But I can't say he has inspired me as much as Lewis Carroll, Dylan Thomas or Robert W. Service. Still, I admire his work. After all he won the Pulitzer Prize four times. When he recited his poem "A Gift Outright" at President Kennedy's inaugural, it was the first time a poet ever read at a US inauguration. Among poets, Frost is a hero. Of course I wanted to explore his old stomping grounds.

Thursday we packed a lunch, Patricia saddled Della, I rode my bike and we headed for Robert Frost's cabin. It was farther up into the mountains. On the way, we came to the Robert Frost Interpretive Trail. A network of boardwalks across wet lands and foot trails that led back into the woods. Posted along the way were signs with some of his poems on them. The first was "The Pasture." The end lines were appropriate for the beginning of the trail. "I shan't be gone long.–You come too."

Horseback riding wasn't allowed on the trail. So Patricia got off and walked Della, who graciously helped to trim it. All through the walk, we'd turn to find her with a vine or tree limb in her mouth. I think Frost would have loved it.

Alongside the highway there is no sign with, "Robert Frost Cabin This Way" on it. A person would have to put some effort into finding it. Not far from the trail of poems was Robert Frost Wayside. It's a roadside park that was dedicated to him by the National Forest Service the year after he died. In it was a sign with a map of highlights of the area. It made reference to his cabin with no specifics as how to get there. Fortunately, some of the local folks had already told us how to find it.

Three quarters of a mile from the highway, at the end of an unmarked dirt road with pine, oak and maples beside it, we came to a large white farm house. It was mid-afternoon, and in the front yard were half a dozen young men standing around a bonfire drinking beer.

I asked, "You guys live here?"

With a green beer bottle in his hand, one of them walked toward me. "Naw, we're with the men's choir from Middlebury College. We're just spending the night. We're going to sing for the alumni at Bread Loaf tonight."

I asked, "Do you know where Robert Frost's cabin is?"

"Robert Frost's cabin?" He was a preppie looking boy, with perfect teeth and every black hair in place. After a swig of beer he said, "Is that around here?"

"Supposed to be."

He turned around and called to the other men in the yard. "Anybody know where Robert Frost's cabin is?"

One of them yelled back, "Robert Frost has a cabin around here?"

A man walking down the porch steps with a green beer case in his hands, nodded up the hill as he yelled, "Dude, there's a log cabin up at the top of the field behind the house. Maybe that's it."

It was tucked into the edge of the forest, with a steep sloping meadow in front of it. A small log cabin, on a stone foundation with a screened-in porch on the front. The place was locked, but through the windows we could see where the bard wrote every summer from 1939 to 1962. It had a stone fireplace with a brick hearth and generous windows that flooded the main room with sunlight. The inside walls were made of wide, unpainted, vertical planks. On the floor was a plain blue/gray carpet, with a large straw tatami mat in the middle. Furniture was minimal. A beige lounge chair with matching ottoman—the style would have been popular in the late 1950's. Frost also had a wood and rattan rocker, two straight back chairs and a couple of small tables. The one next to the fireplace was probably his writing table.

But, the most impressive thing about the place was the view. It faced southwest, toward a not too distant mountain. In the front yard was a large flat rock that had obviously been brought in from somewhere else and propped up on a small stack of stones so it was level. It was granite and must have been placed there so Frost could sit on it and gaze at the panorama. Over the years, the grass in front of it had been worn down into a dusty depression by the feet of those who had sat on the rock before me. Frost must have been a boney-ass poet, too. The indentations on top of the rock fit mine perfectly.

⚜

The next morning when we got up, the sky was clear. But while we broke camp, clouds began to drift in. By the time we got to the Bread Loaf Campus it was completely overcast. Rain was on the way.

Every year Bread Loaf was the site of the oldest and most prestigious writer's conference in America. Frost was one of the founders. We got there a week after it was over. Even so, the place was busy. Every summer, alumni flock there for a few days of play in the mountains. Classes were offered on topics that weren't in pursuit of a degree. A group of people we met on campus had just come from a course on terrorism.

The campus was in a huge meadow surrounded by the Green Mountain National Forest. Most of the twenty or so wooden buildings looked like they'd been built in the 1920's and 30's. They were all tan and green with lots of porches and wicker furniture. The place fit in well with the environment.

A couple of miles from Bread Loaf we came to a wide paved area on the left side of the road. From there it would be a steady climb up to Middlebury Gap. So I tied Della to a small tree and we had lunch.

The whole time we were there, she kept trying to get to some nearby saplings. It didn't take her long to munch all the tender limbs near her. Now Della wanted the rest of it. She stretched her lead rope tight and began to paw the ground.

I yelled, "Della, quit! You've done nothing but graze for the past two days. You don't need those stinking little trees."

It didn't make any difference, she kept it up. I decided to ignore her and she eventually quit pawing the ground. But when I untied her to hit the road, she tried to go toward the saplings, and we got into a tug of war. She was determined to get to those little trees, and I was determined not to let her have her way. She kept trying to pull away, so I slapped her on the side of the neck.

Della recoiled, grunted and then lunged at me with her mouth open. I reared my hand back. "You'd better not!"

She recoiled again as I said, "Now settle down. Let's go."

Reluctantly she followed me out onto the highway and we started up the hill. We had scarcely gone a third of a mile when Della stopped.

I tugged on her lead rope. "Come on, Sis, let's go."

It was steep but nothing like Sand Hill. She had pulled many slopes much steeper back down the road. But she wouldn't move, and we had cars stopped behind us. I motioned for them to go around as Patricia asked, "What's with her?"

"I don't know."

"This isn't that steep."

"I think this is an attitude thing."

My wife said, "What?"

"I think Della learned a bad lesson back on Sand Hill."

"Now Bud, I really do think that was too steep for her to pull."

"I agree. But I think she figured out that if she just quits we'll lighten the load."

Patricia leaned against the cart. "What are we going to do?"

"Teach her it doesn't work that way. Get the riding crop."

Della was a great mule to ride. She had the most comfortable trot I've ever experienced. But sometimes she'd get it in her head that she wanted to go a different direction than the rider. So we always took a riding crop with us. It's a length of fiberglass rod with a handle on one end and a doubled over piece of leather on the other. A couple of whacks with that on her butt usually inspired Della to cooperate.

I told Patricia, "When I tell her to get up, let her have it."

And she did. Patricia hit her twice on the left haunch. Della lunged forward a few feet and stopped. I yelled, "Hit her again. Come up Sis!"

This time she didn't even move. I motioned for the cars coming up behind us to go on by, as my wife said, "It's like I'm not even back here. I can't stand here and beat her. We've got to get out of the road."

I had heard many times that if a mule learns how to get its way, she's ruined. You will never be able to depend on her again. Della had always been so big of heart. She always gave it her best. Had she learned that if she balks, I will give in to her?

If we turned around and walked back down the hill, we would be doing just that– giving into her. But my wife was right. We couldn't stay where we were. So Della won. Patricia got in the cart, ran the brake and we went down to the spot where we had lunch.

My heart was heavy–not because I lost–because if she was not going to pull for us anymore, what would we do? We couldn't stop at every steep hill and find someone to pull the cart up.

"Are you having a problem?"

We had met Carol on the Bread Loaf Campus an hour and a half ago. While we were telling her about our dilemma, a man who passed us earlier on a bicycle, stopped. Bruce was also staying at Bread Loaf and wondered if we needed help. We told them we had to unload the cart and get the contents up to the top of the gap. Bruce said, "I have a Subaru station wagon back at the campus. We can haul some of your stuff up in it."

We still needed another car. Carol's was too small to hold much, but she knew someone with another station wagon. Within an hour we had both Bill and Bruce's cars full. Off they went to the top of the mountain.

I grabbed Della's lead rope, and turned toward the highway. She yanked back on it, then stepped toward the saplings she had tried to get to earlier.

"Della!"

I jerked hard on her rope. She grunted and reared her head back which pulled the rope out of my hand. Immediately she started shuffling toward the saplings.

"Oh, no, you don't!"

I sprinted for her, grabbed the side of her bridle and yanked her face toward me as I hollered, "Whoa!"

With her ears laid back, she tried to shake loose from my grip, but I held on. "Della, I said Whoa!"

She stopped and stood still.

"What is with her?" Patricia said.

"All she can think about is eating those little trees."

"Well, hell!" My wife threw her hands up. "Let her have them."

"No. Because that's giving in to her. If we give into her this time, she'll do this from now on. Let's go!"

Out onto the highway and up the hill we went. Then, at nearly the same spot, Della stopped. Even with the cart empty, she refused to go any further. We tried the riding crop again. She would not move.

A green pickup with blue flashing lights on top pulled up beside us with two game wardens inside. The one in the passenger's seat said through the open window, "You folks are causing a traffic hazard here."

I nodded at Della, "She won't go any farther. I guess we'll have to go back down."

The warden said, "We'll drive up a bit and stop traffic so you can turn around."

At the bottom of the hill, they pulled into the parking area behind us with their lights still flashing. The wardens were opening their doors, when a state trooper drove up and said, "What's up?"

"They had traffic stopped on the mountain. Their mule doesn't want to go up."

The trooper was in his mid-twenties, and wore a Smokey The Bear style hat. He turned to me and asked, "Where you from?"

"We walked here from Arkansas. We're headed for the coast of Maine."

The trooper pointed west. "So you already came up Sand Hill?"

"A couple of days ago."

One of the wardens said, "If she pulled Sand Hill, this should be no problem."

"We had to unload the cart and have everything hauled up to Ripton before she could do it," Patricia said.

The two station wagons with our stuff pulled in as the trooper said, "So should we do that here?"

"We already did," Patricia said. "That's what's in those cars."

One of the wardens asked, "Now what?"

Bruce got his cell phone out of the glove compartment of his station wagon, and called Howard Kelton in East Middlebury. He had a one ton pickup, and would be happy to pull the cart up to the top. With his wife Linda, he arrived half an hour later and hooked the cart to their truck with a chain. Patricia rode with them as they pulled the cart followed by Bill's station wagon with our stuff and the trooper with his lights flashing. Bruce was going to follow Della and me up the mountain with his four-way flashers on.

While I was untying Della from a metal sign post, I felt like I was on the verge of tears. I couldn't believe she was quitting on us. After I undid the knot, I turned to lead her out of parking area. Suddenly, she reared back and yanked her rope out of my hands. Then she spun around and started for the saplings.

Immediately my hurt feelings flared into anger. I leaped for her rope, grabbed it, yanked her head toward me and roared, "You Bitch! Who the hell do you think you are? You want one of those little trees?"

I stomped toward the saplings with her in tow. "Okay, by God, I'll give you one!"

Pumped up with adrenaline, I jerked a small one out by the roots. Whirling around, I shook the little tree in Della's face. "Here's one to go! Now go!" Then I yanked her head to the left and tried to hit her on the ass with it. But I couldn't do that and lead her too. We went round and round in circles.

Bruce was leaned against the car with his arms crossed watching us. I stopped, turned to him and held out the sapling. "I hate to ask this, but—"

He held his hand out. "Give me that thing."

When he popped her on the butt it sounded like a firecracker. She literally leaped out of the parking area and onto the highway. From behind us, Bruce yelled, "You'd better keep going, Della! I'm back here with this stick!" With that he smacked the pavement three times with it.

Bruce made a believer out of Della. That was the fastest mile and a half she and I had ever walked. It was also the saddest. How I hated that we had to hit her like that.

"Well, she is a mule," Bruce said at the top. We were unloading our stuff from his station wagon. "I don't know a whole lot about them. But I always heard that the one with the strongest will is the one who wins."

Della never again balked like that.

⊰⊱

Up on Middlebury Gap, we almost had all of our stuff loaded back onto the cart when it began to rain. It had sprinkled off and on all day. But this was a downpour. We crammed in stuff wherever we could. Then with our rain gear on, we started down the other side of the mountain.

About half a mile down, we came to a maintenance access for one of the slopes at Snow Bowl Ski Area. The ditches were gushing and dark wasn't far off. So we pulled in for the night.

After I tied Della out and fed her, Patricia and I climbed in the cart to wait for the rain to let up. The seat in the cab was a tight fit for Patricia and me with just regular clothes on. In rain gear we had to squeeze in. Our baloney sandwiches that evening were soggy and fell apart in our hands.

"This isn't fun," Patricia said. "I'm real tired of it."

I knew what she meant. We were both sick of the rain. Here we were, on the evening of one of the most heartbreaking days of this journey, and we couldn't put the tent up. We were in the middle of a deluge, on the side of a mountain, with lightning and thunder all around us.

It was not a good situation to pitch a tent, but we had no choice. As the storm raged we bucked the wind, waded through ankle deep water and eventually got the thing up. By the time we got the bed made, everything was soaked. The only saving grace was that it was not cold.

You have read about many wet nights in this book. So I'm going to spare you this one. Other than to say, of all of them so far, it was the most miserable.

Besides everything getting soaked, and our spirits being low, one of the things that made that night difficult were the intrusions. Each time I fell asleep, Patricia would shake me and say, "There it is again. I'm telling you something is clomping around out there."

My first thought was that Della had gotten loose. So I poked my head out into the storm with the flashlight and pointed it toward her. Each time, I found her still tied. Usually the first thing I'd see was the shine of her eyes. Then I'd scan around our camp. I never saw a thing. And sometimes I heard clomping too. So I'd get up, go out and look around. The results were always the same. Della was where she was supposed to be and I found nothing else around. Neither of us got much sleep that night.

The rain stopped just a bit before sunrise. When I climbed out of the tent, we were totally engulfed with fog. It was so thick I couldn't see Della from the tent. However, I did see what the commotion in the night had been. All around the tent and the cart were moose tracks and droppings. I could see where they had ventured toward Della, but then turned back. Why I didn't see the moose, I'll never know.

At the bottom of the hill, on the White River, was the village of Hancock. What we needed more than anything, besides a full night's sleep, was a washer and dryer. But Hancock didn't have a laundry. So we turned south on Highway 100 headed for Rochester.

About a mile down the road we came to a farm, with the house on the left side of the highway and barns on the other. On one barn was a sign that read "Cobble Hill Stable." We were about to walk past it, when a pickup truck pulled into the barnyard and a woman in her late thirties go out. She was packed into tight blue jeans and wore high top riding boots.

She strolled toward us as she said, "My, what a beautiful mule! What are you folks doing?"

After we told her, Leslie asked, "Do you need a place to camp for the night?"

She bred, raised and trained Welsh Cob horses and ponies. Leslie, and her husband, also had an organic beef operation. Less than a quarter of a mile further down the highway was one of their farms. On it was an old house that recently had been renovated so they could rent it to vacationers.

"No one is there now," Leslie said. "You're welcome to use it. And if you need to do some laundry, it has a new washer and dryer."

Who says there is no God?

Doing a poetry show in the heart of Rochester, Vermont.

CHAPTER 21

NEW HAMPSHIRE AND KNOWING WHY

⊰⧓⊱

WHITE SETTLERS MOVED INTO NEW Hampshire a hundred years before they ventured into Vermont. Most came up to the Granite State from Massachusetts and Connecticut because they'd been given land patents by the King of England. John Hancock got one fifteen years before he signed the Declaration of Independence. New Hampshire was the first to declare its independence from Great Britain. The state motto is "Live free or die!"

Walking across New Hampshire, we passed many open pits where long ago men with picks, spades and steam shovels plundered the hills and valleys, leaving mounds of spoil behind. Near some of those diggings, and often in the middle of open fields, there were the brick shells of old factories. Long two and three story buildings whose roofs had collapsed and rotted inside those walls decades ago. A few times we saw a tall smoke stack standing by itself in the middle of a pasture. And in many places, the huge pieces of rusted machinery had been there so long, they'd become a permeant part of the landscape.

Still, New Hampshire was beautiful. It's the second most forested state in the nation – Maine is first. Unlike Vermont, we didn't see many dairy farms or orchards because most of the time we were walking through woodlands. Like Vermonters, when people in the Granite State stopped to visit us along the road, they seemed more relaxed than folks in New York. And one of the things that really impressed us about New Englanders was how complimentary they were about each other's state. "You think Vermont's pretty, wait till you see New Hampshire."

And all across the Granite State it was, "Weren't the Green Mountains wonderful?"

In both states, everyone said, "Just wait until you see Maine!"

We took Highway 25 through Meredith and Central Harbor on Lake Winnipesaukee. A large natural scintillating body of blue with the slopes of the White Mountains rising up all around it. Forested slopes, many of which were capped with ragged granite peaks.

It's a popular tourist area year round. The summer attractions were the lakes, streams and hiking in the mountains. What brought them in the winter were the ski areas, and the White Mountains had plenty. It was mid-September when we were there, so the big draw then was the leaves. Autumn was beginning to bloom.

One of the things we had looked forward to since the onset of this journey, was walking through New England in the fall—and we were not disappointed. No photograph, painting or film could do justice to how beautiful New Hampshire was right then. Through those mediums you can appreciate how radiant the trees were with their myriad shades of red, orange, yellow and purple. But you have to be there, completely surrounded by it, to truly appreciate a New England autumn. While we walked down the road, it was like we were in a kaleidoscope that changed in hues, shades and shapes with every step. Then there were those moments when we'd come around a bend and ahead would be a maple or hickory whose brilliance upstaged every tree around it. A color so vibrant, that one of us couldn't help but exclaim, "Wow, look at that!"

And then there's the smell of the season—a pleasing, pungent aroma that had a hint of cinnamon and nutmeg to it. Right then, in some places, New Hampshire smelled like pumpkin pie. You can't get that from a picture or a movie. Nor can you get it riding in a car, even if the windows are open. To really experience a New England autumn, you have to get out and let yourself be inundated.

But driving was how most folks were experiencing that autumn. Sometimes the highway was bumper to bumper with motor homes, motorcycles, and automobiles of every description. Often it was like a parade was passing us on the left.

"Leaf peepers!" snarled an old man in Meredith. "Gets worse every year."

We met him when we stopped to give Della a drink in a parking area adjacent to Lake Winnipesaukee. He was a head shorter than me and wore baggy new blue jeans that were too long for him. The legs were rolled up into high cuffs so they wouldn't drag on the ground.

He coughed up some phlegm and spit it on the asphalt before he said, "Lived here all my life and seen it happen. When I was growing up, the roads were narrow and steep. It could be pretty rough going around here in those days. Especially in the winter. Back then, we didn't have all these damn tourists. It was too hard getting in and out of here. But they fixed the roads and built the stinking interstate. Now they can hop on it and zip up here from Boston in no time."

In his voice was a wheeze. "It's a dirty shame. Back in those days there were lots of places you and your mule could have camped right next to the lake. But not now. Too many goddam houses!"

Suddenly he was seized with a spasm of coughing that made the veins across his bald head swell. I feared one was going to burst. When the coughing stopped, he spit on the pavement again.

He said, "Ain't nobody from around here can afford houses like that. It's all them city folks from down south. Came here to get away from the city, but they brought the damn city with 'em."

A few minutes after he walked off, a younger man told us, "Problem is, all these big expensive houses have jacked up the property values to where our taxes have gone out the roof. People who've lived here all their lives can't afford it anymore."

Meredith was conspicuously up scale. The homes, the shops, the cars, the clothes, the whole style of the Lakes Region was chic—but all of that was tempered by the natural beauty around us. The mountains and the forest got more awesome by the mile.

During the two days it took us to walk around that part of the lake, the weather was perfect. The sky was blue with occasional puffy white clouds and the temperatures were ideal for traveling. Warm in the day, but not enough to make you sweat. At night it was cool enough for a blanket and sweet cuddling. But it wasn't going to last long.

Hurricane Isabelle was tormenting the Carolinas and was about to send storms up over New England. The forecast called for the hurricane to go out to sea, gain strength and possibly come back on land in the northeast. In 1938, New Hampshire was devastated by a hurricane, and Isabelle was behaving exactly like that one.

"Bud, what would we do if a hurricane came through here?" Patricia asked that question as we were setting up camp adjacent to Fuller's Store and Station west of Moulton Falls on Highway 25. "Have you thought about that? Do you have a plan?"

"Find high ground and hold on."

Isabelle didn't come to New Hampshire, but she sent us a lot of rain. Off and on for two days it came down, always as a deluge. We kept our dirty laundry in a plastic bag on the roof of the cart. By the time we got to South Tamworth it was a huge black shiny ball full of soggy clothes and bedding.

"Let me take it to my house and do it for you."

This was the second time we met Dot. The first was at the South Tamworth Store a mile or so back down the road. We were at a pull-off near the junction of Highway 113 and 25. Dot was a stout woman, in her late fifties with short, salt and pepper hair. She had brought her grand-daughters to meet us. One of them had just finished reading us some of her poetry, when Dot offered to do our laundry.

Patricia said, "I can't let you do that."

"Why not? I doubt you've got anything I haven't seen before."

"It's not that. I just—"

Dot pointed her finger at me. "Get that bag off your roof and put it in my car!"

I had just pulled it down when a Tamworth Police car pulled up next to the cart. We had also met Chief Dan Poirier back at the store. In his mid-forties, Dan had the looks and presence that befitted a TV personality. He was a horseman and had initially invited us to his place for the night, but he lived too far off the road. Then he offered to get us a couple bales of hay. So when he stopped beside me and the laundry bag, I said, "You don't have hay in that cruiser do you?"

"No. I'll get that later. There's been a change of plans."

Before we met Dan, we had planned to take Highway 5 to 16 on up to Conway. But he convinced us to take Highway 113 up through the village of Tamworth. "You'll miss a lot of traffic and it's a prettier route."

I asked, "So, what's the plan now?"

"The town would like to treat you to a night at the Tamworth Inn."

Dot gasped. "Oh, how wonderful! You will just love it!"

Dan said, "That includes dinner for two and breakfast in the morning."

"That's awesome," the poet granddaughter said. "I love to eat there. It is so cool!"

"And . . ." Dan was beginning to sound like a game show host. "if you're up for it, after dinner we have two tickets for the show tonight at the Barnstormers Theater."

Dot yanked open the back hatch of her car and motioned for me to bring the laundry bag over. "They've got you set up. I'll bring your clothes to the Tamworth Inn."

It was a three mile hike to Tamworth. The sun was out and the trees were full of fall. Both our steps and spirits were lighter than they had been in several days. We were about a mile from the village when Patricia ran up beside me and took my hand. "I can't believe this. I am so excited! A room in an old historic inn. A night out on the town. It's almost too good to be true!"

When we traveled, not often did my wife and I get to walk holding hands. Usually she was right behind me, holding onto a strap attached to the cart shaft. Hand-in-hand would put her out in the driving-lane too far. But we did walk that way in a few places where we felt safe to do so. And our walk to Tamworth was on one of those kinds of roads. And like every other time we did it, Della finagled her head up between us. Patricia thought she did it because Della was jealous of her. I think she did it be-cause she wanted to be sure she was the center of attention. It's always all about Della.

Tamworth was a tiny village on the Swift River. It had two churches with tall pointed steeples, a few white clap-board stores, a library, post of-fice, the inn and the Barnstormers Theater—the oldest professional summer theater company in America. It began in 1931 in the barn of the Tamworth Inn, which opened a hundred years earlier as a hotel on a stage line.

When we walked into the village, I said, "Isn't this sweet?"

Besides the quaintness of the buildings and setting, there was the view of the White Mountains and Mt. Chocorua, which was truly something to behold. At 3,475 feet, it had a rugged granite peak with a skirt of ev-ergreens and broadleaf trees in their autumn finery. The mountain was named after a Pequawket Chief who was killed on the summit by a white settler.

Over the years, Tamworth has wooed many notables. A number of authors went there to write, including John Greenleaf Whittier and Henry David Thoreau. President Grover Cleveland owned a summer home in Tamworth, and his son Francis started Barnstormers Theater.

When we turned onto Main Street, at least a dozen people—mostly women and children—were sitting on the curb. They looked like they were waiting for a parade. Then, as we walked down the short street they stood up and began to applaud and cheer.

While we waved back, Patricia said, "Were they waiting for us?"

We were both immediately enchanted by the Tamworth Inn. It's *the* quintessential New England country inn. A gray wood building with tan trim and red shutters. It had three floors, a pitched roof and dor-mer windows. The view from the front rooms was Mt. Chocorua. The back ones looked out over the gardens and lawn that led down to crys-tal clear Swift River. I can't imagine anyone not being charmed by the Tamworth Inn.

Across the street was a park with a small parking lot that we pulled into. Chief Dan said it was all right to tie Della out in the park to graze.

The Schraders, who owned the Tamworth, gave us a second floor room that overlooked the cart, Della and the mountain.

Our whole experience in Tamworth was delightful. Both meals were tremendous. It was easy to see why famous food critics, like Boston's Phantom Gourmet, raved about the place. Any room out of the weather, with a hot shower, would have been great. That one was tremendous.

Sunday morning, when Margo Mallur interviewed us for the *Carroll County Independent*, I told her how kind everyone in Tamworth had been. "And when we walked into town yesterday, it was like people were waiting to welcome us."

"They probably were," Margo said. "With all the controversy around here lately, Tamworth needs something positive."

When we walked into the area we saw signs that read "No Zoning." Chief Dan was the first to explain, "A group of investors want to put a Grand Prix type race track on one of the mountains nearby. A lot of folks don't want it. So we're going to vote on a zoning issue."

Margo said, "Most people don't want the track, but they don't want zoning either. New Hampshire people take the state motto to heart. Live Free Or Die!"

⊰⊱

In North Conway we did something we had not done on this journey. We rented a room at the Yankee Clipper Motel. The rain was torrential, and the forecast called for it to continue through the next day. It was my birthday, and when Patricia asked me what I wanted, I said "To be dry!"

⊰⊱

KNOWING WHY

Yes, there are moments when I wonder, "Why are we doing this?"

Like when it's raining – and I don't mean your average soft sweet shower.

But more like it's being poured from an endless bucket, and it's cold, and it's been that way all day.

And that New Hampshire highway has no shoulder.

And everything is leaking from the rain coming down and the traffic splashing up.

And your boots are like wading pools and your body is worn out from lugging them along.

And you curse every driver who comes a little bit too close, which means you're cursing everyone who splashes you by.

Yes there are moments when I want to cry, "Why in the hell are we doing this?"

"Hi, do you remember me?"

She was pretty. Her name was Mary. She wrote for a local paper. We met her yesterday.

It was dry, way back then. And the rain was not so heavy just now.

"Can I talk to you guys for a moment? It's kind of important."

It was a place where we could get off the road. So we did.

Then all of us, in our rain gear, got closer together so we could hear through the rain and the traffic on the road.

"Do you remember me telling you about my brother?"

I did. She had said he was dead.

And as a poet she hadn't been able to write in the months since it happened.

"But what I didn't tell you was that he dreamed of doing something like you're doing.

"He wanted to see the world slowly, softly, sweetly, close up and personal.

"But he didn't get to do that."

The showers intensified as she pulled her hand from under her slicker.

When she extended her clenched fist toward us she said,

"If you tell me no, I will understand."

Right then she opened her fist to reveal a silver locket in her palm.

"In this locket are some of my brother's ashes.

"Would you take them with you so he can live his dream, too?"

Yes, there have been times when I've cried in the rain.

But never have I cried so sweetly as I did right then.

Yes, there are moments when I wonder, "Why are we doing this?"

But not there, not then, in that rain.

Right there, right then, I knew why.

⧯⧮

CHAPTER 22

MAINE

❧

"So tell me Bud, why the coast of Maine?"

The first time we met John Littlefield was in the Adirondacks—a few days after our retreat at Camp Santanoni. Back then, I heard his voice before seeing his face—a video camera was in the way. Now, in the parking lot of the Yankee Clipper Motel in New Hampshire, John was behind the camera again.

"I've never been there before, and I'd like to live by the Atlantic Ocean for a while."

John said, "But it gets real cold in Maine. And winter isn't that far off."

He was short, had brown hair streaked with silver that was combed back from his face. John had the presence of a real-estate salesman, but he was a retired airline pilot who produced documentary films. His company, Logan Productions, was based in Montgomery, Texas. He was working on another project in the Adirondacks when we first met him.

A week before we got to Tamworth, when I checked my email, I had one from John, and he wanted to do a film about us. In the email he asked, "Could I walk a day or two with you?"

John and his assistant arrived early on September 25th. The air was fresh from the rinsing it got the past couple days, and it was the first morning in over a week that the sky was cloudless. It was crisp enough to begin the day with long sleeves and a sweater, but all of us had shorts on. You could tell that it was going to get that warm. It would be a great day for walking and perfect for filming.

Moving around me, with the camera to his face, John squatted, stooped and stretched to get different shots, as he said, "Just be yourself. Act like I'm not here."

–Just *try* being natural as someone with a camera is scurrying around you.–

"So this is a big day for you, eh Bud? Today you walk into Maine. Right?"

Strapping the harness onto Della, I looked into the camera and said, "Yes it is."

John pulled the camera from his face. "I'm a Mainer. I grew up on the coast."

He was the first person to tell us about the history of Maine. "The first white settlements were on the islands off the coast. Inland, the woods were too wild."

Back in the 1970s, before I walked across the country with the pack pony, I considered exploring northwestern Maine on foot. It astounded me that in New England there was such a vast area with no towns, no paved roads and only a few dirt ones. On the map, it looked like just mountains, rivers and lakes–the kind of place I'd like to see.

I read everything I could find about the area and soon figured out why it was so desolate. In the winter it gets thirty below with snow roof-top-high in some places. Then, in the spring, biting black flies and huge mosquitoes rule the forest. Mosquitoes lay their eggs in still water, and black flies lay them in running water. So they've got you standing or flowing. Sometimes, black flies will swarm a moose to where it goes crazy and runs itself to death. People who venture into the woods have to cover themselves with netting to keep from getting bit up.

Then there were the bears. Black bears can be found all over New England, but their population was densest in Maine. I read a story about the state sending a team of sharpshooters in to thin them out. The bears ravaged their camp and sent the hunters fleeing for their lives.

I wanted to have an adventure–but not that kind. So in the 1970s I played it safe and just walked across the continent and half way back, with a pack pony and a dog.

Thirty years later, I was finally walking into Maine with a cameraman in my face who said, "And you're going to let me walk with you—right?"

"Yes. You'll be the first person to spend a day walking with us."

"Great! Let's do it!"

John gave the camera to his assistant, Joyce, with instructions on what kind of shots he wanted. Then, after she drove off in his Lexus, we four hit the road. It was an eleven mile day, and John walked nine of them. He was in the cart when we got to the state line.

It had no billboard, monument or fancy welcome center. Just a simple blue sign with white letters that read, "State Line Maine."

⊰⊱

The second town we came to in Maine was Bridgton—population 2,500. Bridgton was about twenty miles into the state. It's situated between two natural lakes with several streams running through the heart of town. We spent Saturday and Sunday nights in a small park at Highland Lake on the northwest side of Bridgton. Sunday afternoon we had lots of folks stop to visit. Around 3 p.m. eight people were in our camp when a man in his late forties walked up and stood silently behind the group.

A couple of the people had just bought some of my poetry books, and one of them asked if I would read them a poem. After I finished "Fantasy to Reality," the man behind the crowd applauded with the rest. And like some of the others, he too had tears. But somehow I got the feeling his weren't generated by the poem.

The hair on both his head and face was curly and sandy brown. His beard framed a smile, but I sensed sadness when he shook my hand and introduced himself as Bruce Gehly. "I live in Ossipee, New Hampshire, and read about you in the paper.

While the others walked away, he shoved his hands into his pockets and said, "Actually, I've been looking for you for the past two days."

"Really?"

"After I read the story, I had to find you." He pulled a gray book, the size of my poetry book, out of his back pocket and handed it to me. "You're living my dream."

Ride The Gypsy Moon was the title. On the cover was a pencil drawing of a man on the front of a gypsy wagon driving a pair of horses. In the bottom right corner were the words, "A poetic journey by Bruce Gehly." When I looked back up at him, the smile didn't seem quite so sad. I asked, "Is this your poetry?"

"I used to sell those when I was on the road."

Patricia yanked the book out of my hands as she said, "No kidding?"

"In 1996 I hitched a pair of Shire horses to a gypsy wagon that I built, then took off to travel around the country selling those poetry books." His hands were in his pockets again, and he was rocking back on his heels. "Like I said, you're living my dream. I had to find you."

I was astounded. "Where did you go?"

"I started in the fall, and headed south. Figured I'd spend the winter wandering around Florida. But I started hitting snow before I even got to the Hudson River. So I stopped and had everything trucked to Jacksonville, Florida. Figured I'd follow the coast down to the Keys."

Bruce stopped rocking on his heels, and turned his face toward Highland Lake as he said, "Five miles out of Jacksonville, a woman rammed into the back of the wagon."

Patricia gasped. "Oh, no!"

He turned toward my wife, and in a matter-of-fact tone said, "The wagon was destroyed and both horses got hurt. Eventually I had to put one of them down. I got banged up some, but not too bad."

Obviously he had told this story many times, and it was as if telling it again was emboldening him. Bruce folded his arms across his chest and said, "The woman was drunk, had no license and no insurance."

In unison, Patricia and I both said, "No!"

My wife had put on a pot of coffee just before Bruce showed up. He accepted her offer of a cup, and sat on Della's water bucket as he explained some of the details. Tears were in his eyes when he concluded with, "But the worst part was what it did to my soul. It's like something inside me died."

Bruce pulled a bandana out of his pocket, and wiped his eyes. "Sorry. It still hurts."

Right then Patricia and I were both fighting tears. For several moments none of us said anything. He was the one who broke the silence. "That's why I had to come find you. I thought being around someone living my dream might help me heal."

That night in the tent, Patricia said, "It really makes you think. Doesn't it?"

"What's that?"

"The thing with Bruce and his horses. Something like that could happen to us."

We had talked many times about the possibility of someone running into us. The discussion always ended with me saying, "I could get run over just walking down the street back home. We've all got to die sometime. I'd rather do it living my dream."

⋈

A couple miles east of Lewiston, we set up camp in a large open field. Dark was descending on us as we staked down the tent. We had just finished erecting it when dusk let loose with a deluge. The rain was too heavy to get out the stove for a cooked meal, so we had cheese and crackers for dinner that night.

"Do you hear that?" Patricia was shaking me out of slumber

Yawning I said, "Hear what?"

"On the tent. Listen."

I snuggled deeper into my bed. "It's raining."

"No it's not. That's ice! Listen."

She was right. It wasn't raining. I grabbed the flashlight, opened the tent door and shined it at the cart. Everything was covered with sleet, and it was steadily coming down.

"Bud, this is not good. It's the fourth of October, and already it's sleeting."

"So?"

"We're in Maine. Winter could happen at any time."

"What do you want me to do about it?"

"I don't want to still be on the road in the winter!" Panic was in my wife's voice. "Can you imagine what this tent would be like during a blizzard?"

"Patricia, you're getting yourself worked up over nothing. I don't want to be on the road in the winter any more than you do. Yes, this tent would be a disaster in the snow. It's not much in the rain."

When she spoke, each word was more frantic than the one before it. "That's for sure! And I'm telling you—"

"Patricia, stop right there! That's enough!" I paused and lowered my voice. "Baby, I am on your side. Remember? When we get to Belfast, we'll start looking for a place to stop. You still want to go to the coast, don't you?"

Her voice was soft. "Yes."

"Good. Now I have faith that when we get to the coast we're going to find the right situation. But we have to get there first. Give me a kiss, and let's go back to sleep."

⚜

About twenty-five miles from Belfast, Pam and Don invited us to spend Saturday night indoors at their farm near Palermo. Pam was a veterinarian who specialized in animal acupuncture and holistic medicine. Her clinic, "Healing Haven," was in the barn. Don, who was a carpenter, made bio-diesel for their vehicles out of discarded vegetable oil from local restaurants. Sunday morning they invited me to use their computer to check my email.

When we first walked into Maine, we were interviewed by Maine Public Radio. During the interview, I mentioned that we hoped to find a place to put down for a couple of years on the coast around Belfast.

On my email account at Yahoo, there were four messages from people who'd heard the story. One was from Penny Altman. It read:

"Dear Bud, Pat and Della. We heard about you on Maine Public Radio and understand you are heading toward the Camden/Belfast area for the winter. We are in Prospect Harbor on the Schoodic Peninsula, about an hour and a half away (not by mule) and would like to make our house available to you for as long as you would like to stay. We have a B&B that we just got going this year. We are still renovating, but have plenty of viable room. The property consists of a farmhouse built in 1847 and three attached barns. The barns are not heated, but I'm sure we could do what would be necessary to accommodate Della. We have 31 acres with a 1/4 mile of shore on the shallow side of the harbor here. I am an artist and a writer (no reputation to speak of) and my husband, Michael, is a carpenter. We have an Old English Sheepdog and two cats. We'd love to meet you, and if you are not already set up, see whether you would enjoy staying in our house. I think we would enjoy it. Hope to hear from you. Penny Altman / Mermaid's Purse Farm / Prospect Harbor, Maine."

I called The Mermaid's Purse Farm and got an answering machine. So I left a message that we were near Belfast and were interested in their proposal. Then I said to Patricia, "She sent that email two weeks ago. A lot of things can happen in that amount of time. We can't count on this until we get a verbal yes."

So Sunday when we left Healing Haven, we were still in search of a home.

⌐⌐⌐

I said, "There it is Patricia, welcome to the Atlantic Ocean."

It was Tuesday afternoon, and we were at the crest of Park Hill on Highway 3 on the outskirts of Belfast. Overhead was a clear sky and shimmering below was Belfast Bay. It was the bluest blue I had ever seen.

"Can you believe it," Patricia said. "We're really here!"

When we walked down into Belfast I had a mixture of emotions. The excitement of getting to the coast was tempered with uncertainty. We hadn't talked to Penny or Michael in Prospect Harbor–so we still didn't know if we had a place to live. And even if they said yes, how could we know if it would work for us? On the map it looked so tiny and remote. Could we find employment there?

Originally, we picked Belfast as a place for our home on the coast. On the map it looked like it had commerce–hence, jobs. Plus, like with Madison, Indiana, we heard over and over what a great place it was. A progressive community with a thriving arts scene in a picturesque seaside setting. Downtown was mostly nineteenth century brick and stone buildings with elaborate cornices, decorative iron work and slate roofs. It looked like our kind of place.

And, like when we walked into Madison, we were more and more charmed the further we got into town. Main Street in Belfast was a steep grade that led down to the waterfront. Out in the bay, lots of colorful boats were moored to buoys. Most were for pleasure, but the bay held work boats too. Lobster boats that in the wee hours of morning would chug their way out into the ocean to bring back the catch. This was what I had always pictured a town on the Maine Coast to look like.

"Welcome to Belfast," Mayor Michael Hurley said. He, and a reporter from the *Bangor Daily News,* had walked down to the waterfront to meet us. "I heard you folks are thinking about spending the winter here."

"If we find a suitable place."

The mayor said, "Let me know if I can help."

An instructor at the Audubon Expedition Institute invited us to camp behind their office building on a ridge above downtown. It was a rough parking lot with a couple of school buses and half a dozen cars. Tall grass and weeds were growing around it, and the view of the bay was terrific.

After we set up camp, Patricia and I hiked back down into town to have dinner. Several folks told us Rollies Tavern was popular with the locals. So we went in and had lobster quesadillas with a pitcher of beer.

Two topics dominated the discussions in the tavern that evening. One was that night's play-off game between the Boston Red Sox and the New York Yankees. With the exception of one woman, everyone in the place was rooting for the Sox. They lost four to two.

The other topic was the weather. A nor'easter was in Maine's forecast for the next day– heavy rain with near hurricane force winds. When we set up the tent, I battened it down like I never had before. Besides the stakes, I used rocks, saplings and old shipping pallets to anchor it. I had no idea how the tent would fare in seventy-mile winds.

Around six the next morning, Patricia said, "I think it's here."

Neither the rain nor the wind started gradually. It came with a vengeance. First the rain. It was like someone in heaven opened a fire hydrant. A few minutes later the wind began to pop and flutter the rain fly on the tent, and the poles on the leeward side bowed in. But everything held and the tent stayed dry.

Around seven, Patricia and I put on our rain gear and walked downtown to Dudley's Diner for breakfast. The wind made it hard to walk–especially down Main Street, where it was a headwind blowing rain into our faces. Twice I saw women blown over as they tried to make their way along the sidewalk.

Dudley's Diner was packed because electricity was out in many spots around town. While we waited for our meal, the café lost power for several minutes too.

The storm was even more intense when we got back to camp. It was like we had pitched our tent in the middle of a lake. When we opened it, we found that the lake had made its way inside, and our air-bed was floating. The rain was no longer falling down. It came at us sideways and the cart was rocking in the wind.

Patricia had just crawled inside the tent when a hefty gust ravaged it. With a loud crack, the tent collapsed on my wife as she screamed, "No!"

"Are you okay?"

I pulled the door open as she said, "I'm alright. But one of the poles broke."

While I helped her out of the tent, my wife had to yell to be heard above the storm. "No sense going back in there until this blows over."

Right then a gust ravaged the trees around us. Some bent all the way to the ground then popped back up and shuttered violently in the gale. Sideways, from the northeast, the rain slammed into us in torrents. The wind was so loud it nearly drowned out the thunder. Right then our world was total chaos.

Della frantically pranced at the end of her rope as the trees near her whipped and wound around in the storm. She was trying to break loose from the rope and run away from it all, but there was nowhere to go—for her or us.

I was leaning to my right, into the storm, when I felt a tug on my left arm and turned to see Patricia yelling something I could not hear. But, when she nodded toward Della and started trudging toward her, I got the gist of it and followed. When the Big Sis saw us coming, she started to calm down and seemed to welcome our arms around her neck. Patricia was on her right side and I was on the left—all three of us with our backs to the storm. It went on for two more hours.

Around noon the wind settled down, the rain stopped and it looked like the clouds might let the sun break through. That's when Patricia said, "I have got to get our stuff to a laundry. Everything is soaked. I'll call Lynn and see if she can help us."

We met Lynn Karlin a week earlier at the boat ramp on Three Mile Pond. She had been testing out her new kayak. Lynn was a professional garden photographer who lived in Belfast. She was going to try to find us a place to live around there. Four times as we walked toward Belfast she drove out to check on us. Patricia called her from the offices of the Audubon Institute, and within an hour Lynn had our wet clothes and my wife in her car headed for the laundry.

For the past week we had been experiencing an Indian summer, but the storm brought it to an end. The next morning when we got up, the sun was out but there was a bite in the wind. The nor'easter had stripped much of autumn off the trees, and the forecast was for more rough weather in the days ahead.

Thursday afternoon we were visited by Lynn and two other ladies who wanted to help us find a place around Belfast. We had a couple of options, but none of them seemed to fit us. That evening I called the Mermaid's Purse Farm again. This time Michael answered the phone and told me they had been out of the state for the past week. Then he said, "We were excited when we got your message. When do you think you'll get here?"

"So you still want us to come?"

"We sure do. If you want, I'll find a horse trailer and come get you."

"No thanks. We'll walk up."

Michael told me they had only lived on the farm for a year and a half. "When we bought the place it was a real mess. We're turning it into a bed and breakfast. So we've been working hard to make it presentable. In May I got my foot caught in a bush hog. I didn't lose it, but it got wacked up pretty bad. That slowed things down around here. We still have lots of work to do."

I said, "I'm a pretty fair hand with a hammer. Maybe I can help."

"Sounds great. Come on up."

It was sixty miles to Prospect Harbor, so we had nearly a week's worth of walking ahead of us. Sunday morning when we left Belfast, a frigid drizzle was falling and the weatherman said it was going to get colder with a chance for snow.

Monday night in LuAnn Wasson's barn, Patricia said, "Are you sure you don't want Michael to haul us up there?"

LuAnn Wasson boarded and trained horses on her farm east of Bucksport, and had two empty stalls in her barn. Della was in one and we set our bed up in the stall next to her. She was peacefully chewing hay as the wind wailed around the corners of the barn. Sometimes it sounded like the blizzards we had experienced on the New York apple farm. I was crawling into my sleeping bag when I said, "Is that what you want to do? Have Michael haul us up there?"

"It sounds like the weather is really going to turn to shit."

We had just finished watching the forecast with LuAnn's father and it called for sleet and snow over the next few days. I told my wife, "But we know we have a dry home ahead of us."

Patricia snuggled deeper into her sleeping bag. "Hell of a lot of good that does us now."

"Well, personally, I wouldn't feel right about him hauling us up there. I walked this far, I want to walk all of it. But if you want to call Michael and have him come get you—"

Patricia popped up in her bag and snapped, "Stop right there, Bud Kenny!"

She yanked her right arm out and shook that index finger at me. "We are in this together! You're not going to walk up there without me!"

Without saying another word she snuggled back down into her sleeping bag.

While winter whipped around outside the barn, I felt this huge warm glow well up inside of me. I leaned over and kissed the only thing showing out of Patricia's sleeping bag—the top of her head. "That's my girl."

The gray and silver head tipped back, and when her face appeared, Patricia was beaming. She winked at me and said, "It's all just part of the adventure."

❧❦

In the morning the weather was lousy and got worse as the day wore on. It started out as rain, which turned to sleet, then snow and back to rain again. We wore rain gear all day. That Tuesday we didn't walk, we trudged along Highway 1.

Patricia had arthritis. Before we started this trip she was concerned it would keep her from walking very much. It's one of the reasons I built the seat in the cart. But once we hit the road, she found the more she walked the better she felt. But that Tuesday my wife ached too badly to walk, and she spent most of the day in the cart.

328

That night, we camped at radio station WERU. It's a non-commercial community station that was started by Paul Stookie of the folk group Peter, Paul and Mary. Their studios were along Highway 1 halfway between Bucksport and Ellsworth, and as we walked out of Belfast we met two of the volunteer announcers who asked us to stop in for an interview. Freezing rain mixed with snow was coming down when we got there. So when they invited us to camp in their basement for the night, we were quick to take them up on their offer.

The next morning it was overcast and cold, but at least there was no precipitation – until a little after noon. First it rained, then it turned into a heavy wet snow that began to accumulate on the ground. That night on the edge of Ellsworth was the second time that we rented a motel room. It was at the Twilite, and there was a sheltered place behind the motel to tie Della. After we checked in, the owners, Linda and Marv Snow, invited us to have dinner with them. (Yes, their last name really was Snow.)

"It doesn't feel like we're traveling anymore," Patricia said, as she sat on the bed drying her hair with a bath towel.

"What do you mean?"

"We're not exploring, just putting on miles."

"Seems to me we need to get settled before winter *really* clobbers us."

"I know." Patricia sighed. "It's just that I miss ambling along like we usually do."

The weather the next day was the same—intermittent rain and snow. Other than stopping for lunch, a TV interview and two newspaper reporters, we just breezed through Ellsworth. I liked the feel of the town, but the Mermaid's Purse Farm was only twenty-five miles away. We could come back and explore on a nicer day.

Eight miles east of Ellsworth a short man with a round belly, white scraggily beard and hair marched out to the edge of Highway 1 and yelled across the road "What in the world is going on here?"

His hair stuck out from under an orange stocking cap that made him look like he had a pointed head. The belly portion of his red sweat shirt was stained with grease, and with the jolly grin on his beaming face he looked like an unkempt Santa Claus.

I yelled across the highway. "We walked here from Arkansas."

"Really? Well come on over and visit."

"We need to find a place to camp for the night."

"You can camp here. I've got plenty of room."

Raye, also known as the "Wild Mountain Man," was a chainsaw artist. He had life sized wooden statues of bears, an eagle and an angel lined up across the front of the property. A show room of his work was in a two story wooden building, on front of which was a sign that listed Raye's accomplishments. He claimed to be the world's first chainsaw artist. His first piece was done in 1953 at age eleven. Since then he had sawn over 50,000 pieces and was listed in *Ripley's Believe It or Not* seven times. In 2000 they filmed him sawing ten numbers on a toothpick. When I shook his hand I couldn't help but notice that Raye was missing half of two fingers.

We spent that night in his wood shed. When he opened the door to show it to us Raye said, "An artist lived in here for two years a while back. He was from Arkansas too. Think I'll start calling this 'The Arkansas Suite'"

⚜

Around midnight Patricia shook me awake and said, "I think Della got loose. I heard something stomping around outside the door."

My wife got up with the flashlight and threw open the door. Della was right there in the doorway with her ears turning back and forth. "What are you doing, girly pie?"

While I scrambled for my boots and jeans, Patricia stepped out and grabbed hold of Della's halter. "It looks like the rope came untied from the snap on her foot strap."

She stroked Della's nose. "What a good girl. You came to find mom and dad, didn't you?"

I had staked Della out in a grassy area not far from the woodshed, and she watched us tote our bedding into it. So she knew where we were.

The night before, at the motel, I had cut off the end of her rope that was tied to the snap because it was beginning to rot. I was afraid it might break in the middle of the night and she'd get loose. Obviously, I did a lousy job when I tied the new knot. With her lead rope, I tied Della short to a nearby post and hung a hay bag for her.

When we crawled back into bed Patricia said, "That's scary. What if she'd gone out onto the highway? The way traffic flies past here, if she was out there in the dark—"

My wife paused and shuddered. "Thank God she came to us instead."

⋈

I turned to Patricia and said, "I think I know who this is."

We were walking alongside Highway 1 in the town of Hancock when a Ford pickup stopped across the highway from us. After the driver got out and slammed the door, an Old English sheep dog stuck its head out the window. The driver limped as he made his way across the pavement. There was no doubt in my mind that this had to be Michael from Mermaid's Purse Farm. I extended my hand to him. "Hey, Michael. How's it going?"

His gray bearded face beamed. "You figured that out pretty quick. You guys are making good time."

"We should be there tomorrow afternoon."

⋈

Along the Atlantic seaboard, when you say you're going up the coast, it's natural to think north. But in Maine it means east. From Ellsworth on up, the coast is known as "Down East."

When you look at a map of the state, the coast line looks like it has fringe dangling down into the ocean. Going up the coast Highway 1 in Maine is 278 miles long. But if Highway 1 followed the actual shore line it would be 3,478 miles. All of those peninsulas, reaches and spits of land created hundreds of bays and harbors. While we continued up the coast a few of those inlets came right up to the pavement. But we couldn't see open ocean because of the mountains and ridges on the land masses that made up the fringe of Down East Maine.

From Highway 1 we took Route 195 out onto the Schoodic Peninsula to Prospect Harbor. It was five miles of ups and downs and when we got to the village, all we found were a few homes, a deli, a post office and a tiny library.

Mermaid's Purse Farm was on Light House Point Road. And when we got to the junction of it and Highway 195, Michael and the sheep dog, Pye, were waiting for us. "I hope you don't mind if we walk with you to the house."

It was a narrow lane with homes and trees on both sides. But when we got to the farm all of that disappeared. Ahead of us was the open Atlantic. It was a brilliant blue with frothy white waves breaking over ledges out at the mouth of the harbor. On the left side of the road was the house. A white two story wooden structure with several dormers and bay windows. It almost looked like a castle. Attached to the back of it were three barns. On the right, across the road, was a large open field that bordered the harbor. Moored out in the harbor were several brightly colored lobster boats. On the opposite shore was a sardine cannery. We truly would be living in a New England fishing village.

⌘

The farm had no paddocks, fenced in pastures or even a stall for Della. I would have to build all that. For now I'd have to stake Della out like we did on the road. After I did that, Michael gave us a tour of the place. Two of the barns had been made into workshops and storage. The largest of the three barns was empty, except for some stacks of lumber.

We talked it over and decided I could build a stall in that barn for Della. I had told Michael on the phone that I wanted to build a new wagon. One we could sleep in. He said. "You can build it in this barn."

On the house tour, Michael showed us our room, which was upstairs with a king-size bed and two windows that faced the Atlantic. After lugging some clothes up to the room, we joined Michael in the kitchen where he fixed cocktails. Lifting his glass he said, "Welcome home."

CHAPTER 23

IS THIS REALLY
THE END?

I KNEW THIS WAS HOW Maine would be. Sweet sand beaches lapped with gentle surf under perfect blue sky. Romping barefoot through the soft sand around Prospect Harbor, I stumbled over a rock. Scurrying for traction on slimy seaweed, my feet slid out from under me and I tumbled down toward ocean boulders.

Suddenly, something shook me. "Wake up Bud! Wake up!"

Crawling out of sleep, I recognized the voice was that of my bride. We were in the bed, in our new bedroom at Mermaid's Purse Farm. Thank God I didn't fall down on those boulders.

"Someone is knocking on the door downstairs."

I could hear it. They were pounding hard. Dawn had just begun, so there was just enough light to see when I went to the window. First I looked out to where I had tied Della for the night–she was not there. I looked in every direction. She was gone. Then I looked down and saw a pickup truck with a camper. Something told me this was all connected–Della missing and someone knocking at sunrise.

I scrambled around for pants, boots and a shirt while I sputtered to Patricia what I had just seen. When I grabbed the bedroom door knob, she wailed "Oh no!"

Downstairs, I flung the front door open to find a middle-aged man wearing a black ball cap and dark down vest. "Are you the guy walking across the country with a mule?"

After I answered him, he pulled back the left side of his vest so I could see his badge. "I'm with the Gouldsboro Police, and we've got your mule up on Highway 1 about ten miles from here."

Right then the police radio in the pick-up began to babble. The officer reached in the truck and pulled out the microphone. "I found him at the farm on Lighthouse Point Road."

When the radio babbled back, I heard ". . . got hit by a semi-truck!"

My knees began to buckle from under me. My spine turned into jelly, and suddenly I had vertigo. Going down, I grabbed the officer's arm and whined, "She got hit by a semi-truck?"

⬩⧓⬩

Driving down Highway 1 in Maine, in the dark hours of morning, always made him edgy. Those hours are when the big animals were most active. In all his years of driving eighteen wheelers, he never hit one, but he had seen plenty. And he'd heard the horror stories of drivers who slammed into deer or moose on a night-time highway. Moose were the worst. Their dark color made them harder to see, and their eyes don't shine in headlights like deer eyes do.

Plus, they're enormous. When you're barreling down the highway at sixty miles an hour if you hit an 1,800 pound animal with antlers, there's going to be damage. One driver was killed a couple of years ago when he hit one. The impact threw the moose up through the windshield– antlers first. The thought of moose antlers crushing the driver's skull sent a shiver down his spine.

Up ahead, lights came on at Young's Market. Suddenly, something big darted out of their driveway onto the highway. He didn't know what it was, but it was huge. Simultaneously he laid on the horn and stomped on the brake pedal. The big rig skidded toward the animal whose eyes shined in the head lights. It had stopped on the highway directly in the path of the semi-truck. The driver struggled to control the skid. "Move Dammit! Move!"

⊰⊱

"No! He said she *almost* got hit by a semi-truck. She's okay." The officer said. "We've got her tied to a tree up by the highway. Come on, I'll take you to her."

Officer Jim Malloy had just climbed out of bed, when he got the call that they needed him to track us down. Because of the two stories that had been on local TV, and the picture with the story in the *Bangor Daily News,* everyone knew who Della was and what we were doing. Plus, for the past few days, we'd been very conspicuous as we walked along Highway 1. But no one knew where we were. After more than an hour of trying to find us, the police got a call from someone with a scanner. They had seen us pull into the yard at Mermaid's Purse Farm.

"We need to find a way to get your mule back here."

"I can walk her back."

Jim said, "I'm sure you can. But after what you've been through, don't you think a ride in a truck and trailer would be nice?"

In case they didn't find us that ride, I threw our saddle and bridle in the back of his truck. Then Patricia and I climbed in the cab, and off we went to retrieve Della. While we backtracked the route we had taken the afternoon before, Jim asked us about the trip. Then he said, "I heard you're writing a book."

"Yes. I call it *Footloose In America - Dixie to New England.*"

"So the end of the book is when you got here?"

"Right."

Jim laughed, then said, "So, I guess Della just wrote you a whole new chapter. Eh?"

⊰⊱

336

The knot at Della's end of the rope had come undone again. When I got the saddle and bridle off the cart, I saw her tracks all around it. I could also see where she'd circled the barns and farm house several times. The Big Sis had been looking for us.

When she saw me get out of the truck, Della began to paw the ground and call to me. When I got to her she immediately started rubbing her forehead on my shoulder. Officer Malloy said, "I'd say she's glad to see you."

A community effort got our little vagabond family back together. First there was Lisa at Young's Market. Around 5 a.m. she saw Della dart out in front of the truck and called the police. She also called Anne, who lived nearby and had horses. In the dark, Anne Osborne brought a bucket of grain with which she caught Della and tied her up. The police found us with the help of the couple with the scanner. Then the police called Suzie who had a horse trailer. She owned Chase's Restaurant in Winter Harbor and was supposed to cook that Sunday morning. But she got someone to cover for her while she toted us back to the farm. No one would take payment for anything. They were just glad to help.

After we were all back at our new home, I hung a hay bag in a tree and tied Della so she could eat from it. Then I fixed her rope so it could not come untied–ever! Tomorrow I would start building a fence for her.

After a cup of coffee, Patricia and I walked down to the beach in front of the farm. In reality, a sand beach on the Maine coast was a rare thing. It's mostly rocks and boulders, like the shore around Prospect Harbor. The tide was on its way out, so lots of seaweed laid exposed on the rugged beach.

Patricia walked in front of me as we picked our way across the boulders toward the water's edge. She was shuffling across a seaweed bed when suddenly she slipped and both of her feet went out from under her. Horror raged through me as I watched my wife's back slam down on one boulder and her head bounce on another.

Frantically, I slipped across the seaweed toward her yelling, "Patricia! Are you okay?"

When I slid down to her side on my knees, a smile slowly spread across my wife's face as she raised up on her elbows. "I think so. This stinking seaweed is so thick here it gave me something soft to land on."

Tears welled in my eyes as I swept my bride into my arms and clutched her to my chest. I crowned her head with kisses, then looked to the sky and said, "Thank you!"

-The End-
October 26, 2003

Mermaid's Purse Farm
Prospect Harbor, Maine

AFTERWARD

❧⟡❧

BUD, PATRICIA AND DELLA REMAINED at Mermaid's Purse Farm until the fall of 2006. When they hit the road again, Della was pulling a new plastic and aluminum wagon that the Kenny's were able to sleep in. Initially they planned to tour New England for another year before shipping everything to Europe for more wandering. However, circumstances arose that required them to return home to Hot Springs, Arkansas in 2008.

More photos and information at www.usonfoot.com. To contact Bud, go to www.budkennybooks.com

ACKNOWLEDGMENTS

THE HARDEST PART OF WRITING about this trek was deciding which stories to leave out. This book could easily have been more than a hundred pages longer.

What makes doing the acknowledgments difficult is that so many people helped us. Just a list of their names would fill a chapter. You met a few of those folks in the book. I hope their inclusion will serve as my "Thank You!" To those of you who were not included, please know your kindness along the way was greatly appreciated. I wish I had room to thank all of you individually.

But here are some people I must say a special thank you to: Mike Arnold for the great cover of this book. Peter Gelfan and the staff at The Editorial Department, as well as Susan Setteducato, Dr. John Crawford, Pat Laster, Bill White, and Patricia Kenny for their help with the writing of this book.

The following folks helped in lots of different ways: John Cooksey, The Oeders of Ohio, Jack Hill, Holly Anderson, Dr Jess Clement, Diane Ellaborn, Jim Grant, Val & Kevin Karikomi, Howard Lee Kilby, Lenore Person, Bob & Susan Weiss, Peter Hersey, Maggie Meyer & Whistlewood Farm, Chuck & Laurie Morgan, Clinton Reed & Francis Cross, Roy & Gloria Haller, Gordon & Madeline Hamersley.

Thank You America!
Bud Kenny

Made in the USA
Columbia, SC
29 June 2018